"Carolyn Whitzman is one of Canada's leadi.... ... . shows. She provides a wide suite of tools to address housing issues and covers issues from supply to zoning to speculation. This is a fantastic and impactful book!"

— BRIAN DOUCET, associate professor, School of Urban Planning, University of Waterloo

"*Home Truths* delivers exactly what the title promises: a clear and accessible narrative of how we got into the housing crisis and real solutions for getting out of it. The depth and breadth of Carolyn Whitzman's housing policy knowledge are on full display, but you don't need to be a policy expert to dig in. Most importantly, she weaves through an intersectional feminist analysis, ensuring no one is left behind. This is an indispensable resource!"

— LEILA SARANGI, national director of Campaign 2000: End Child and Family Poverty

"The recent debate over Canada's housing crisis – and in particular, calls for more supply – has obscured the precise nature of the crisis, which is that we've failed to find ways to add truly affordable housing for those in greatest need. Carolyn Whitzman's work pushes back against the dominant narrative with much needed data and analysis that should provide policy makers with an effective roadmap for reform."

— JOHN LORINC, senior editor at *Spacing Magazine*

"*Home Truths* provides a practical reframing of housing programs and policies in Canada, drawing on our own history and innovations from international contexts. Whitzman hammers home the evidence that we need to build affordable, sustainable housing, providing inspiring examples of supportive housing, taxation to raise funds for affordable housing, and development approaches based on collaboration across the public, private, and nonprofit sectors."

— REN THOMAS, associate professor, School of Planning, Dalhousie University

"*Home Truths* is the definitive book on the Canadian housing crisis. Carolyn Whitzman explains what went wrong, why, and the extent of the damage, and then draws from examples in Europe and Asia to identify viable solutions that will scale."

— KAREN CHAPPLE, director, School of Cities, University of Toronto

"*Home Truths* is a must read. Whitzman brings the complexity of our current 'wicked problem' – a devastating global housing crisis – to a succinct and pointed truth: the solution lies on our shoulders, all of our shoulders. I love Whitzman's ability to interlace cold, hard data with best (and worst) practices from around the world and shots of humour, humility, and hard truths. She tells a compelling story of how we got here, pulling no punches when it comes to blame – and there is plenty to go around – while embedding the possible solutions in evidence-based strategies that promise hope for our future.

– MARGARET PFOH, thirty-year housing and Indigenous rights advocate, CEO of the Aboriginal Housing Management Association

HOME TRUTHS

Carolyn Whitzman

Home Truths

Fixing Canada's Housing Crisis

a UBC Press imprint
Vancouver

UBC Press is a Benetech Global Certified Accessible™ publisher. The epub version of this book meets stringent accessibility standards, ensuring it is available to people with diverse needs.

Printed in Canada on FSC-certified ancient-forest-free paper (100% postconsumer recycled) that is processed chlorine- and acid-free, with vegetable-based inks.

Library and Archives Canada Cataloguing in Publication

Title: Home truths : fixing Canada's housing crisis / Carolyn Whitzman.
Names: Whitzman, Carolyn, author.
Description: Includes bibliographical references and index.
Identifiers: Canadiana (print) 20240371445 | Canadiana (ebook) 20240371461 | ISBN 9780774890700 (softcover) | ISBN 9780774890724 (EPUB) | ISBN 9780774890717 (PDF)
Subjects: LCSH: Housing—Canada.
Classification: LCC HD7305.A3 W45 2024 | DDC 363.50971—dc23

UBC Press gratefully acknowledges the financial support for our publishing program of the Government of Canada, the Canada Council for the Arts, and the British Columbia Arts Council.

UBC Press is situated on the traditional, ancestral, and unceded territory of the xʷməθkʷəy̓əm (Musqueam) people. This land has always been a place of learning for the xʷməθkʷəy̓əm, who have passed on their culture, history, and traditions for millennia, from one generation to the next.

On Point Press, an imprint of UBC Press
The University of British Columbia
www.ubcpress.ca

Contents

HOME TRUTHS

Introduction

Whenever I talk about housing with a journalist, policy-maker, developer, advocate, or interested friend, two things tend to happen. They say, "Housing's so complicated!" Especially if they're under forty, they tell me a horrific story about their housing situation.

This book is for them – and for anyone who's concerned about or wants to help fix Canada's housing crisis.

Some people criticize the term "housing crisis" because it suggests a phenomenon that's new or short-term. In *The Tenant Class*, Ricardo Tranjan defines "crisis" as "an event or series of events that represents a critical threat to the health, safety, security or well-being of a community or other large group of people, usually over a wider area." He argues that the housing crisis is not one event or a series of events but rather capitalism working as intended: to the benefit of those with more wealth (homeowners and landlords) and the detriment of those with less wealth (tenants).

I have a slightly different perspective. Like the climate crisis, the housing crisis resulted from a series of political decisions that built up over time to pose a critical threat to all Canadians. Other capitalist countries made better decisions, with better results. Canada made better decisions in the past. In some cases, we need to return to those good ideas – modified for new realities.

Like Ricardo Tranjan, I'm concerned about the people with the fewest resources. Canada's housing crisis harms renters, homeowners, and – most of all – those without homes:

- According to the latest federal government figures, there are 40,000 very-low-income people without shelter or sleeping in emergency shelters, and the number of people without shelter doubled during COVID-19. This number is based on a head count of only seventy-two communities on a single night over two years. It grossly underestimates homelessness.
- Between 2016 and 2021 in British Columbia, one in ten renter households were evicted. In the rest of the country, one in sixteen households were forced to move. One-third of all households, those who rent, are under greater stress than ever before. Low-income renters living on minimum wage can afford a one-bedroom apartment in only four small Canadian cities, all in Quebec, and Quebec has lost the most affordable rentals in the past ten years.
- People seeking to own rather than rent are increasingly locked out of the market. Between 2015 and 2021, the **average** house price doubled, but wages increased by only 7 percent. In other words, the average house price increased at over fourteen times the rate of the average wage.
- The cost of a home, which was 2.5 times the **median** household income in 1980, was 8.8 times the median household income in 2021. In Vancouver, high-income households who earn 250 percent of local median income can't afford a first home. Across Canada, house prices would need to be less than a third of what they are now be affordable to moderate-income households. In Vancouver, they'd need to be a fifth of what they are now.

Canada's housing crisis isn't about tenants versus owners. An entire generation has been locked out of home ownership.

Incomes: Very Low, Low, Moderate, Median, and Higher

Canada needs one clear definition of affordability that answers the question, Affordable to whom?

I use household income categories developed by and listed on the Housing Assessment Resource Tools website. These categories, in turn,

Average versus median: Quick anecdote. I failed Grade 10 math, twice. I loved history and geography and didn't see the point of math. But to get my geography degree, I had to take statistics, and I got hooked on numbers that tell a story. Warning: there are numbers in this book.

"Average" and "median" indicate "middle" values. To calculate an average, add up all the individual things and divide the total by the number of things counted (this is also called the "mean"). To calculate the median, take the "middle" value, the value for which half the things are larger and half are smaller. When we talk about income or housing costs, there are extreme values (very rich or expensive; very poor or inexpensive). In these cases, the median is usually the better measure to use. But the average is sometimes the only number available.

are based on percentage of median income for metropolitan or regional areas, as used by the US Department of Housing and Urban Development, rather than on household-income quintiles (lowest 20 percent = low income), which are used by the Canada Mortgage and Housing Corporation. The former method considers differences in income between, say, rural New Brunswick and Victoria, British Columbia, which has a big impact on median housing costs. I use "household" instead of "family" because there are infinite variations of people who want to live together, and many don't fall into the traditional definition of family (one or two parents living with children under the age of eighteen):

- **very low income** (0 to 20% of median income, 1st quintile): mostly fixed-income, social assistance or pension
- **low income** (21 to 50%, 1st quintile): reliant on minimum wage
- **moderate income** (51 to 80%, 2nd quintile): key workers such as teachers, nurses, care providers, and construction workers
- **median income** (81 to 120%, 3rd quintile): middle-class households
- **higher income** (121+%, 4th and 5th quintile): upper-middle-class and wealthy households.

Why does this matter to most Canadians, you might ask? After all, two-thirds of Canadian households own their homes, and almost half have paid off their mortgages. The home-ownership rate has decreased slightly, from close to 70 percent in 2011 to nearly 66 percent in 2021, but most people will benefit from rising housing prices.

Looking at the problem this way is like looking out the window during the summer of 2023 and saying, "My community isn't on fire! Everything's fine!" Look a little closer, and you'll see wisps of smoke:

- The only age group in which the home-ownership rate has increased in the past ten years is heads of households over eighty-five.
- Baby boomers such as me, born between 1946 and 1965, account for the largest cohort of homeowners – over four in ten own homes.
- Millennials such as my son, born between 1981 and 1996, are the largest group of renters – over a third.

Canada houses a stark intergenerational wealth divide. People in their late fifties to mid-seventies who have been homeowners for over twenty years saw their net worth increase from $323,700 in 1999 to $685,400 in 2019 (cost adjusted for 2019 dollars). In the same period, renters' net worth only rose from $14,600 to $24,000. Over the next few decades, these young people will be the majority, and my generation will be looking for affordable seniors' care options, which are in short supply. Canada's housing system doesn't work for anyone.

Homeownership still seems like an easy way to gain wealth. So perhaps everyone in their mid-twenties to early forties should just save enough for a down payment. Maybe they should stop eating avocado toast, as an Australian multimillionaire property developer once suggested. Back in the halcyon days of 2017, it would take 17,451 avocado toasts to save up for a down payment in Vancouver. Maybe tax-exempt home-savings accounts or first-time home buyer grants are the magic bullet?

Not so fast. Over half of mortgage holders, and an even higher proportion of renters, have trouble paying their bills, and the problem only gets worse with high interest rates. Almost two in five mortgage carriers and almost half of renters borrow to meet daily expenses. Seventeen percent of mortgage carriers and 22 percent of renters have used a payday loan or online lender. Both groups are in severe financial straits. It's hard to save up money if you're already underwater financially. And buying a house is a huge risk in an era of increasing interest rates and uncertain jobs, especially if that house isn't affordable. Canadians like to think of their nation as prosperous and fair, a place where each succeeding generation will have a better life. Growing inequalities threaten the foundations of this belief.

And this isn't a temporary COVID-related blip. Canada has had one of the highest levels of household debt in the world for over a decade, a source of concern to almost every national and international economic organization. In nearly every financial system review, the Bank of Canada warns about the high debt load of households and elevated house prices. In 2017, the World Economic Forum warned of the risk of a "housing price bubble" in Canada like the one in the United States before multiple mortgage insolvencies sparked the Global Financial Crisis. The Organisation for Economic Co-operation and Development, in its 2023 economic outlook for Canada, stressed that high and increasing household debt levels and the crushing cost of housing were having a significant impact on the nation's overall productivity.

That's a lot of scary numbers, some of which might represent you or someone you know. What do these numbers tell us in terms of the past, present, and future of housing in Canada?

To understand the larger history of Canadian housing policy, I often ask people to tell me about their housing histories. Let me tell you my own.

I've been fascinated by housing since I was a child in Cornwall, Ontario, a small city of forty thousand people. I was born in 1963, long after my brothers. My first four years were spent in a detached house, three blocks from the store owned by my grandmother and managed by my parents. Cornwall is near the border between anglophone Ontario and francophone Quebec, a few kilometres away from the US border, and right on the border between settler society and Indigenous land. Cornwall is next to the Akwesasne First Nation, a member of the Haudenosaunee Confederacy, the people of the Long House. My first conscious memories have to do with my front lawn (which I considered huge) and the neighbourhood kids, who were being told to stay off the lawn by my parents. Even as a kid, I thought that didn't seem fair.

When I was four, my parents separated, and I moved with my mother to the big city of Montreal. We lived in a succession of rented duplex flats, and my mother became a real estate agent. On the weekends, she took me, the only child still at home, to open houses. "Tell me what price this house is going for," she'd say. "If you guess within ten thousand dollars, I'll get you an ice cream." I ate a lot of ice cream (hint: location, location, location). But I felt like an interloper on someone else's lawn: the kids at my Jewish school told me I was living in the "wrong" neighbourhood and "poor." When I moved to a public high school, I hung out with the other poor kids. Many of these kids slept on a sofa in the living room. I had my own bedroom. I realized I was middle-class.

In Canada in the early 1980s, it was easy to move away from home as a university student, even if you went to a university in the same city. Two friends and I moved into a triplex flat in 1984, in what was then called Montreal's "student ghetto." I worked as a part-time waitress and then as a research assistant. I had no problem paying rent. When I moved in with the man who would become my husband, we had no student loans and a bursary that covered our rent. I got involved in a group called Les Voisin(e)s de Devonshire. We fought for funding for a new housing cooperative instead of a proposed condominium. We won that fight, leaving me with the mistaken impression that getting better housing for low-income people was easy.

We moved to Toronto in 1986. Our rage at being physically assaulted by a landlord in a dispute over a 42 percent rent increase after the previous tenant was harassed out of our apartment transformed into engagement with the Parkdale Tenants Association and a lifelong interest in the right to housing. In the 1990s, my interest in feminist urban planning led to a career developing urban policy for gender-based violence prevention for the City of Toronto, where it seemed obvious that the lack of affordable housing trapped women in violent relationships. We lived for eight years in a housing co-op downtown. When we moved back to Parkdale, we bought a fixer-upper that carried a mortgage for the same cost as rent. We didn't fix it up, and yet the purchase still put us on the path to wealth.

As undergraduate students, we lived in one of the sixteen
apartments in this small single-stair apartment building.
Montreal's tradition of triplexes and small apartment
buildings, and strong renter rights, helped create
a renters' paradise for many decades.

My PhD focused on 125 years of neighbourhood policy in Parkdale,
where every level of government seemed better at closing off affordable-
housing options than creating them. By the early 2000s, I was teaching
urban planning in Melbourne, Australia, where three-storey apartment
buildings were being called "blockbusting high-rises" by NIMBY (not in

my backyard) residents' associations. I led collaborative research with governments, private and nonmarket developers, and advocates, on affordable, accessible, sustainable, family-friendly housing for the future. I talked to children growing up in apartments and homeless people squatting in buildings slated for demolition. Meanwhile, with two young children, we traded up to a larger, better renovated house that, like our previous homes, was a short distance to work via bike or public transit.

We returned to Canada in 2019 and paid cash for a house in Ottawa. So far, we sound like the poster children for boomer affluence, and we were. We had good health, the good fortune of a long-lasting relationship, and the privilege borne of having white skin, speaking the majority language, and being cisgender and heterosexual. As a household, we'd moved from being renters to homeowners and traded up three times. I knew, through speaking with housing advocates, developers, financiers, planners, and politicians all over the world – from Nairobi to Santiago, Portland to Paris, and Singapore to Sydney – that we were wealthier than most.

But when COVID-19 hit, our family felt the effects of the fraying social safety net. My mother, who bought a house after years of saving, saw her money vanish when she moved to high-priced assisted living. When she was diagnosed with dementia, we tried to find a decent nursing home. She ended up as one of three in a long-term-care bedroom, not a dignified end to her life. Meanwhile, my son and his wife struggled with social isolation in a one-bedroom apartment with a big dog in downtown Ottawa. Their only options for a more affordable, bigger place were outside Ottawa's public transit system. We didn't want to end up like my mother, and we wanted to be close to our children.

At the time, I was Zoom teaching an undergraduate course in housing policy at the University of Toronto's Innis College. I started by telling my housing story and asking students for theirs. Most of my students, mostly in their early twenties, had lived in residence until COVID. Many moved in with their parents in the outer suburbs because they couldn't afford rentals near the university. One moved back to China, another to Turkey. Both joined my classes in the middle of the night. When I asked students where they thought they'd be living in ten years, none said Toronto.

For the past two generations, under Liberal and Conservative leadership, Canada has failed a basic moral test. Are we ensuring that the society we leave behind is better for the next generation?

For many lucky people like me, housing was a "them" issue for a long time. It's now become an "us" issue for everyone. Like health care, education, and climate change, we've neglected problems for so long that they've become crises that can't be ignored by anyone anymore. I have a family member who came close to homelessness. Most people know someone who lost their home.

For the past three years, I've worked with a project called Housing Assessment Resource Tools (HART), based at the University of British Columbia. (Due to the wonders of Zoom, I live in Ottawa, teach in Toronto, and work in Vancouver!) We analyze census housing data to answer one question: Who needs what kind of housing, where, and at what cost? Working with fifteen municipalities, including Canada's six most populous cities, we've mapped well-located government land that could be used for affordable housing. Talking with nonmarket and market developers, provincial and federal governments, and advocates, we've created a best-practice guide for acquiring **market housing** at risk of losing affordability. I've examined housing policy from an international perspective, based on countless conversations with "housers," people trying to create affordable housing.

What I've learned is this: Canada's housing crisis is fixable. If enough people knew about what worked in the past and what's working right now, in Canada and other places, we could collectively and successfully advocate for a housing system that allows everyone to achieve the basic right to a home. It won't take the overthrow of capitalism, although it will take a political shift toward investing in the collective good.

In this book, I explore what people mean when they talk about a home, how we got into this mess and who's responsible, and what kinds of homes are needed, at what prices, and where. Then I look at what can be done – to end homelessness, to scale up **nonmarket housing** (which so many Canadians need), to support well-located and secure rental housing, and to make home ownership affordable again.

Throughout, I refer to nine countries that got some things right (and a lot of other things wrong):

- **Germany, Austria, and Switzerland:** three rich countries where living in rental housing doesn't make you a second-class citizen
- **Singapore, Japan, and Sweden:** three countries that built a lot of housing quickly and cheaply
- **France, Denmark, and Finland:** three countries with innovative affordable-housing strategies.

I purposely leave out the rich anglophone countries against which Canada usually compares itself: the United States, the United Kingdom, Australia, New Zealand, Ireland, and Scotland. They make guest appearances (New Zealand and US cities have been doing some interesting zoning experiments; Scotland has a better nonmarket-housing system than many other nations). The Anglosphere is not doing great housing policy these days, and part of the problem is that we're looking to one

Market and nonmarket housing: Market housing is built and managed by the private sector. In Canada, over 95 percent of housing falls in this category. In Singapore, less than 20 percent of housing does.

In contrast, nonmarket housing – which has a dizzying array of synonyms ranging from "social housing" to "community housing" to "nonprofit housing" – is built and managed by the public and nonprofit sectors. In Canada, about 45 percent of nonmarket housing is **public housing.** It's owned by a federal, provincial/territorial, regional, or (most often) municipal government – thus by the public. Another 35 percent, including most of the housing that offers on-site social and health supports, is owned by charitable organizations, such as religious entities and community organizations. Following international practice, I call this **community housing**; if there's on-site services, **supportive housing.** Ten percent is **cooperative housing**, which is "owned" collectively by the households who live in it, and another 10 percent is held by market developers under short-term affordability agreements. Units can't be sold for profit. The most common international term for nonmarket housing is **social housing.**

another instead of elsewhere. I also leave out the Netherlands, which like Sweden has a great nonmarket housing past but an uncertain housing future. I'm most interested in places that have taken a bold approach and succeeded, in many cases across the political divide.

By the end of the book, you'll know more about what is, admittedly, a wickedly complex problem without no magic-bullet solutions. You'll have the tools to understand what can be done to fix Canada's housing and advocate for a better future.

At its heart, good housing policy comes down to a simple message. Homes save lives.

1

What Is a Home?

My friend Barbara Holtmann, who works on violence prevention in South Africa, taught me that the first step in working with diverse people to solve a complex policy problem is to imagine what it looks like when it's fixed.

This is what it looks like when everyone has a good home.

The short film *The Wedding Part II* features a real-life couple. A wedding is being celebrated in David Crombie Park, in downtown Toronto's St. Lawrence neighbourhood. As at any good celebration, guests enjoy food, dancing, and witty repartee. Nancy (a pseudonym) grew up in this mixed-income neighbourhood built on formerly industrial land. She's marrying Inez, who immigrated to Canada in 2012. Of course, because it's Toronto, the first line you hear is, "Weddings are so expensive."

The video was created by Jamii, an arts collective based in St. Lawrence. Jamii, which means "community" in Swahili, is dedicated to "building community and nurturing young women in leadership." Jamii organized sixteen young people to design and paint a mural in the park's basketball court. It coordinates crafts, plays, and choirs and group drumming. It produced an award-winning documentary on the ten thousand citizens who have found a home in St. Lawrence since the neighbourhood was developed as a showpiece project by all three levels of government in the 1970s and 1980s.

Still from *Wedding Part II.* |
By Alejandra Higuera and Ana Maria Higuera.

Jamii's founding members wouldn't have been able to find places to live and celebrate culture in downtown Toronto if it weren't for the fact that two-thirds of St. Lawrence's four thousand homes were created for low- and moderate-income households rather than for speculative profit. Nancy and Inez, both in secure employment, wouldn't be able to afford to live in their three-bedroom townhouse with Nancy's brother Max and their dog, Pudding, if it weren't for cooperative housing, run by and for members. Eleanor, Nancy's mother, wouldn't be living in the same development if disability benefits hadn't made her rent affordable. Eleanor wouldn't be alive if it weren't for nonmarket housing.

When I talked to Eleanor, whom I'd known for over thirty-five years, she was upfront about housing saving her life. In her late twenties, she had severe mental health problems, compounded by postpartum depression. In her early fifties, severe physical health problems forced her to leave the paid workforce. Her nonprofit home gave her long-term security in a supportive community, close to services. Instead of scrabbling year after year to find and pay rent on an apartment big enough for a single mother with two children, Eleanor stayed in the same three-bedroom townhouse for twenty years. When her children left home, she took in housemates who couldn't otherwise afford to live downtown.

Eleanor gets to live near Toronto's central food market. She's an excellent cook and hostess and, by extension, a boon to her many grateful friends and neighbours. Instead of having to own a car, Eleanor can walk or take public transit to her medical appointments. Nancy and Max, both in their early thirties, didn't have to move far from central Toronto to buy or rent an affordable home. They live in the same neighbourhood where they grew up, surrounded by lifelong friends. When Eleanor gets older and can't handle the townhouse stairs, she can move to an accessible apartment in the same co-op.

In the 1980s, urban planners would come from around the world to tour Toronto's innovative affordable housing. Those days are long gone.

The ceiling of Kikékyelc (*right*) was modelled on a traditional pit house, with flags of the Indigenous Nations whose members live there. A mother bird protects her young, by wrapping her wings around them (*bottom*), in a representation of the meaning of the name Kikékyelc.

Home Truths

But this moment of joy and creativity, a mock wedding that is a preamble to a real wedding, is a reminder of what could have been.

Across the country, on a blisteringly hot July day in 2022, another celebration unfolds with food, dancing, and joy: the first Kamloopa Powwow after a two-year pandemic hiatus. Thousands of people have gathered, from dozens of First Nations across Turtle Island, colonially known as North America. The fairgrounds, returned to the Tk'emlúps te Secwépemc First Nation, sit at the bottom of a hill. Atop that hill stands a former Residential School, where for eighty years, from 1890 to 1969, Indigenous children were imprisoned after being torn from their families by the Canadian government. In 2021, with the help of ground-penetrating radar, the unmarked graves of two hundred of those children were discovered, shocking those settler Canadians who had not been paying attention to the Truth and Reconciliation public hearings on the genocidal legacy of this system.

As people enjoy the powwow, I relish the air conditioning at Kikékyelc: A Place of Belonging. This intergenerational project, also in Kamloops, is managed by a Métis family services agency called Lii Michif Otipemisiwak Family and Community Services. It provides studio-sized homes for twenty-six Indigenous youth aged sixteen to twenty-six who have aged out of foster care, along with one-bedroom homes for five Métis Elders who work part-time as mentors to the young people. Kikékyelc is located on land owned by the Tk'emlúps te Secwépemc First Nation and named after the protective wing of a mother bird in that language.

Silas is heading out to work security at the powwow. He has been a resident of Kikékyelc since it opened in September 2020. Before that, as an Indigenous young person in foster care, his future was uncertain. Silas also works at Kikékylec. He works reception, does light housekeeping, and assists his fellow tenants. He's called "Captain" because captains of the hunt oversaw their Métis communities just as he oversees the welfare of his neighbours, young and old. Rather than being a statistic, a descendant of stolen children removed from his family and community as a child, Silas is a leader.

Melissa works weekend and night shifts at reception but lives elsewhere with her children. She's just returned to school for a degree in social work after a dozen years working at the local Dairy Queen. For our interview, she's brought sugar cookies. I munch as we talk. I'm sitting in Kikékyelc's round common room, modelled on a *kekuli*, or pit house, a form of housing before colonization.

Most of the project is supported by a stringent housing-only budget cofunded by BC Housing, the provincial housing agency, and the Canada Mortgage and Housing Corporation. Because the common room is used for Lii Michif Otipemisiwak's youth services, its construction was funded by a different charitable foundation. The meeting room hosts workshops, youth groups, and a weekly communal meal. The wood-panelled ceiling carries the flags of Indigenous Nations whose youths have found a home at Kikékyelc.

Colleen Lucier, the head of Lii Michif Otipemisiwak, chats about Kikékyelc's origins. It took years of struggle with the BC government before the agency was delegated authority for Métis child welfare in 2017. The agency then tried to track down Métis children in care who "got lost" in the system and disappeared after they turned nineteen. The Elders' Council was adamant that housing needed to be created for young people who were no longer under the formal "protection of the state," especially since most had grown up far from their families and communities and lacked those cultural connections.

At some point, Colleen says, Indigenous child welfare systems will work well enough that young adults won't need cultural replenishment and job-skills assistance as they age out of care. They'll find affordable permanent housing, not "transitional" supportive housing, which they must leave after the age of twenty-six. When the systems start to work better, the thirty-one homes in Kikékyelc will be turned over to Métis Elders. But for now, the young people reconnect with culture through informal conversations with Elders, shared meals, and social activities. Several attended the Métis Nation's annual Back to Batoche celebration in Saskatchewan the previous month. They drove thirty-six hours, there and back. On the bulletin board, an ad promotes a workshop on how to bead a wallet.

A young woman who never came out of her room when she first arrived takes a seat on a sofa and chats with us older folks about the powwow. Colleen points out that informal talks in the entranceway are a common form of sociability. Shared spaces are particularly important in buildings with small rooms.

Her insight echoes one made in 1948 by US sociologist Walter Firey, who was appalled that local governments were legislating out rooming houses because the residents didn't fit the norm of the nuclear family. He pointed out that single people living in rooming houses and other small single-room dwellings couldn't afford larger private-market rental apartments, let alone home ownership, a fact equally true today. What rooming-house residents needed, according to Firey, was decent accommodation plus no-cost social spaces where they could meet family and friends. From the 1970s onwards, tens of thousands of rooming houses across Canada were converted into single-family homes or simply torn down. Few new options for low-income single people were developed. Unfortunately, all levels of government have been much better, in this century, at eliminating affordable-housing options than enabling them.

Now that Kikékyelc is open, the agency is working on a new housing development with larger homes and trauma-informed care for Métis families at risk of having their children taken from them. Adequate housing is the most effective health measure this child welfare agency can take, says Colleen. But Kikékyelc is a rarity. Despite repeated promises, a separate "for Indigenous, by Indigenous" housing strategy has yet to be co-developed for the 87 percent of Indigenous people who live off reserve and are much more vulnerable to homelessness and housing precarity.

I tell you these stories for two reasons.

First, Canadian solutions already exist; they just need to be scaled up. We need more Kikékyelcs and St. Lawrences to make sure everyone finds their way home. We need to remedy more than thirty years of policy inaction on low-income housing. A new generation of well-located, accessible, purpose-built, energy-efficient homes affordable to moderate-income households needs to be built. Speculative wealth in homes needs to be spread out more evenly across generations.

Second, a "home" is a lot more than a roof over your head. Good housing has a sense of community, intergenerational support, and access to green space and culture. The slogan "Housing for People, Not Profit" is more than an economic rallying cry – it's a recipe for better neighbourhood design.

■ ■ ■

In 1948, the same year Walter Firey wrote his book condemning policymakers for using terms such as "cancer" and "growth" to describe low-cost accommodation and the people who lived in it, a document co-drafted by Canadian John Peters Humphrey presented a road map to freedom, justice, and peace. This document, the UN's Universal Declaration of Human Rights, was developed in reaction to the fascist ideologies that led to the Second World War. It recognized that abstract rights such as liberty meant little without the basic conditions that allowed people to survive and thrive. Indeed, without these basics – a home, health care, education, social support – societies would be far more likely to turn toward simplistic authoritarian responses, as Germany did after the First World War. The Universal Declaration of Human Rights, like earlier activism for unions and later activism on climate change, was based on the belief that the world had enough collective resources to ensure everyone's basic needs, that problems could be solved through democratic management, that humanity could rise above the impulse toward greed and hatred of the other for the greater good.

Note the emphasis on "collective." Individual and collective rights are often simplified as capitalism versus socialism. But even in the most market-driven capitalist societies, people need collective infrastructure – from roads to sewers to hospitals – to survive. Even the most undemocratic socialist societies allow people to make individual, if constrained, choices about what to eat and wear. Vienna and Singapore are two of the most capitalist cities on earth. Most of their citizens live in public housing. Collective policy decisions can lead to wealthy economies.

I treat housing as a collective infrastructure. The goal is to optimize individual choices within a democratic, rights-based framework. Offering someone a choice between sleeping outdoors in a tent or a night's accommodation in an overcrowded and unsafe shelter where infectious disease runs rampant is not an adequate choice. Deciding whether to rent or own one's home, and where and how to live, should be a real choice, with multiple options. Part of the problem is that choices are still constrained by out-of-date notions:

- Nuclear families are the only normal households.
- The private sector is smarter or more efficient than the public sector.
- Home ownership is the only way to save money and ensure a comfortable retirement.

But in wealthier societies, such as Switzerland, Germany, and Denmark, most people choose to rent, and new ways of living together are being conceived.

Most countries ratified the Universal Declaration of Human Rights, but many rich countries such as Canada ignored its ramifications. In 2019, Canada formally incorporated the right to housing into law with the passage of the National Housing Strategy Act, which committed all levels of government to "progressive realization of the right to adequate housing" with an emphasis on "improving housing outcomes for persons in greatest need."

Canada currently uses an outdated definition of adequate housing, called **core housing need**. This measure ignores key aspects of its housing crisis – accessibility and security of tenure, to name two. It also excludes millions of Canadians who don't live in "private households." It uses a good definition of **homelessness** but doesn't measure it consistently across the country.

Adequate Housing

Adequate housing has a more inclusive definition than "core housing need" and has seven elements: (1) security of tenure, (2) access to basic services, (3) affordability, (4) habitability, (5) accessibility, (6) location, and (7) cultural adequacy.

Although "core housing need" acknowledges two of these concerns (affordability and habitability, including overcrowding), Statistics Canada and the CMHC have not yet enshrined adequate housing in law by consistently measuring housing need in relation to those concerns, let alone a road map to attain adequate housing for all.

Security of tenure. Security of tenure guarantees legal protection against forced evictions, harassment, and other threats. Under international law,

According to the Canada Mortgage and Housing Corporation (CMHC), Statistics Canada uses **core housing need** to measure affordable housing: "A household is in core housing need if its housing does not meet one or more of the adequacy, suitability or affordability standards and it would have to spend 30% or more of its before-tax income to pay the median rent (including utility costs) of alternative local market housing that meets all three standards."

In this definition, **affordability** means housing "costs less than 30 percent of a household's before-tax income." **Adequacy** means there is no need for "major repairs [including] those to defective plumbing or electrical wiring, or structural repairs to walls, floors or ceilings." **Suitability** refers to "enough bedrooms for the size and make-up of resident households."

■ ■ ■

According to the CMHC's website, "**Homelessness** describes the situation of an individual, family or community without stable, safe, permanent, appropriate housing, or the immediate prospect, means and ability of acquiring it. It is often the result of what is known as systemic or societal barriers, including a lack of affordable and appropriate housing, the individual/household's financial, mental, cognitive, behavioural or physical challenges, and/or racism and discrimination." This extends beyond people living without shelter or in emergency shelters. It includes people in institutions, temporarily "doubling up" with friends or family, or living in unsafe homes because of violence or harassment by members of the household or landlords.

The definition of **chronic homelessness** is much more restrictive: "Individuals, often with disabling conditions (e.g. chronic physical or mental illness, substance abuse problems), who are currently homeless and have been homeless for six months or more in the past year (i.e. have spent more than 180 cumulative nights in a shelter or place not fit for human habitation)."

forced evictions of encampments (informal settlements on government land such as parks, increasingly seen in Canadian cities) is a violation of human rights. So, too, is withdrawing renter protections against reno- viction (evicting a household because their home is being renovated) or demoviction (evicting a household because their home is being torn down). The Province of Ontario recently struck down rental protections against renovictions and demovictions in some municipalities, replacing them with weak provisions to compensate evicted tenants. According to the Canadian Human Rights Commission, "Under human rights law, relocation to a more affordable adequate housing unit must be con- sidered as an alternative to eviction and eviction must not result in homelessness."

Access to basic services. According to the UN, "Housing is not ad- equate if its occupants do not have safe drinking water, adequate sanitation, energy for cooking, heating, lighting, food storage or refuse disposal." While many Canadians might assume this isn't an issue in a wealthy country such as theirs, access to clean water continues to be an issue in encampments, on First Nations reserves (whose households were not included in core housing need until 2021), in single-room occupancy hotels in Vancouver's Downtown Eastside, and for migrant farm workers. Many rented homes don't have consistent room temperatures between twenty and twenty-six degrees Celsius, which can lead to overheating in summer and dangerous reliance on space heaters in winter.

Affordability. In the United States, unlike in Canada, there is one standard definition of affordable housing across programs at all three levels of government: 30 percent of before-tax household income. In the context of international human rights law, "housing is not adequate if its cost threatens or compromises the occupants' enjoyment of other human rights" such as food, health care, mobility, and education. This way of calculating affordable housing is more like the residual-income or basic-needs approach than the "30 percent of before-tax household income" rule. The CMHC recommended moving toward a basic-needs approach: "A basic needs approach subtracts from a household's dis- posable (that is, after-tax) income the cost of non-shelter necessities, based on the size and composition of the household type. What is left after basic needs constitutes what is available, and therefore affordable, for shelter."

Habitability. Statistics Canada's definitions of suitable and habitable housing also overlap with the human-rights definition of habitability: "Housing is not adequate if it does not guarantee physical safety or provide adequate space, as well as protection against the cold, damp, heat, rain, wind, other threats to health and structural hazards." Emergency shelters can be dangerous and crowded spaces; people who sleep in them are usually evicted with their belongings every morning. Living in a tent or makeshift dwelling can also mean inadequate protection against cold, damp, heat, and wind. The government's role in that case should be to provide access to basic services such as water, toilets, and heating or cooling stations, rather than forcibly evicting people and putting them in equally inadequate emergency shelters or jails.

Accessibility. To date, accessibility isn't counted as part of core housing need, although the CMHC does include it as a criterion in its grant and loan programs. In this case, international human rights law is vague: "Housing is not adequate if the specific needs of disadvantaged and marginalized groups are not taken into account." The CMHC's definition is more specific and measurable: "Accessibility refers to the manner in which housing is designed, constructed or modified (such as through repair/renovation/renewal or modification of a home), to enable independent living for persons with diverse abilities."

Location. Location is measurable but not included in core housing need. The international human rights definition says, "Housing is not adequate if it is cut off from employment opportunities, health-care services, access to transit, schools, childcare centres and other social facilities, or if located in polluted or dangerous areas." The census measures whether people live more than an hour's commute from work, which is a start. Statistics Canada has mapped access to childcare centres, community centres, grocery stores, health-care services, hospitals, libraries, parks, pharmacies, public schools, and public transit across the country, and the CMHC uses location as a criterion for grants and loans.

Cultural adequacy. Cultural adequacy is difficult but vital to measure: "Housing is not adequate if it does not respect and take into account the expression of cultural identity." Cultural inadequacy has been well defined by Canadian Indigenous scholars such as Jesse Thistle, who describes Indigenous homelessness as "individuals, families and communities isolated from their relationships to land, water, place, family, kin, each other, animals, cultures, languages and identities."

My examples of what housing looks like when it's fixed also provide clues about how to measure cultural adequacy: Can your friends and family visit you in your home? If not, is there a common room where you can meet without spending money, with a modicum of privacy? Can you live with a companion animal such as a dog or cat? Is there a green space nearby large enough that you can "find yourself" in nature?

Apart from cultural adequacy, adequate housing can be measured in an objective, comparable, and replicable way. But with measurement comes obligation: numbers must count. Numbers must influence policy; they must be used to monitor and evaluate its effectiveness. If a proportion of the adult population is illiterate or dying of preventable diseases, education and health-care services should respond. Governments have been staring at unacceptably high and rising core housing need and homelessness numbers for thirty years. Behind every number is a person or group of people facing unnecessary hardship. What are we, as a wealthy society, going to do to help the lives of those whose unmet needs are represented by those numbers?

Home, Dignity, and Caring

As useful as numbers can be, I find the term "adequate housing" to be, well, inadequate to describe a home. "Core housing need" and "adequate housing" focus on negative attributes. To me, a home is characterized by positive qualities. In *Home: A Short History of an Idea* (1986), Witold Rybczynski, a white American architect, explores how "home" came to be associated with attachment, comfort, belonging, refuge, ownership, and affection. As he says, "You leave your house, but you return home." bell hooks, a Black American philosopher, views homeplace as a site of resistance against the racist violence of white society. Homes are where Black women generated "the warmth and comfort of shelter, the feeding of our bodies, the nurturing of our souls. There we learned dignity, integrity of being; there we learned to have faith." In Africville, a Black community in Halifax torn down by civic authorities in the 1960s, residents cocreated self-sufficiency, community, and that essential term "dignity."

Home is a place where you can experience joy and comfort with family and friends or take refuge in solitude. Your belongings surround you. You're happy to return home because you chose where, how, and with whom to live. Home is where you partake in culture (even if it's "only" a favourite TV show after a long workday); where you cook an old family recipe or try a new ingredient; where you sleep comfortably and safely; where you can be your best self. Home is part of a supportive and welcoming community. Even if you don't "own" it (and most Canadian households don't own their homes outright: they either pay landlords or mortgage lenders), you feel like you belong. Home isn't reliant on contingent charity: you don't "earn" it by being sober or sane or reflecting majority values. This is how I understand the term "dignity" – your home is yours because everyone deserves a home, full stop.

Thirty-five years ago, when I first began to advocate for better housing policy with a group called Women Plan Toronto, two books shaped my thinking. In *Redesigning the American Dream: The Future of Housing, Work, and Family Life*, Dolores Hayden talks about alternative models of housing and communities that sprang up in the United States during the Second World War to accommodate the hundreds of thousands of working mothers entering the workforce. These models had already been tested in Vienna, a city that transformed its housing after the First World War to support a more egalitarian society.

Childcare centres, communal laundries, low-rent public housing, and take-home food were part of the package offered in Vanport City, Oregon, to attract Black, Hispanic, and white female industrial workers. But after the war, Levittown, New York, became the dominant model of new housing. Black families were excluded from purchasing homes. Self-contained bungalows with laundry machines and backyards were intended to be the domain of white women and children. White men were expected to drive to work downtown and return to a homecooked meal and domestic tranquility – or that was the myth. There might be a commuter railway, but public transit wasn't provided. Indeed, underpasses blocked New York City buses from driving to public beaches, part of a deliberate strategy to exclude racialized "outsiders" from schools and other services and amenities. Municipal bylaws governing single-family zoning and minimum home sizes served the same goal.

Homes shape gender roles, social and racial inequalities, family dynamics, and community life. Suburban homes isolated from work-places limited options for the increasing number of households who did not fit the narrow twentieth-century family ideal: one male commuting wage-earner, plus one female unpaid caregiver, plus children.

The second book, *Housing as If People Mattered: Site Design Guidelines for Medium-Density Family Housing,* by Clare Cooper Marcus and Wendy Sarkissian, provides detailed, evidence-based instructions for (re)creating more egalitarian models in better-located communities. Again, the emphasis is on seldom-considered but vital design elements such as adequate storage for strollers and bicycles, meeting spaces in buildings, courtyard playgrounds, and neighbourhood centres. The book offers ideas on how communities can help parents and other care-givers cope with the double bind of paid work and unpaid labour. It's still hugely relevant.

The thing that distinguishes Vanport City from Levittown is care: whether it should be organized collectively or made the responsibility of the individual, who, in most cases, is (still) female. Are you solely re-sponsible for taking care of your child or your elderly parent, or are there options that allow you to seek paid work and respite? Do you have to own your own lawnmower and swing set, or can you share a big backyard (after all, what fun is it to play, or garden, alone)? Yes, there are privacy and personal choice issues around cooking, laundry, and entertainment, but there are so many other choices when care is seen as a collective re-sponsibility with viable alternatives.

Wonderful things have been written on home as an infrastructure of care and the many ways homes can help us care for ourselves and others. But most societies – and Canada is at the extreme end of this continuum – see collective care as an issue only for the most needy and vulnerable: children and the elderly. When care is seen as an issue only for a minority, that minority runs the risk of being neglected and mis-treated. While rights talk emphasizes justice, care talk emphasizes inter-dependence – of people, communities, societies, and ecosystems. To be full human beings, we all need to care and be cared for. As Jesse Thistle points out in relation to Indigenous people, the need for belonging can be as important as shelter when it comes to our physical and mental health. Increasing interest in shared housing models – from individuals who have a monetary choice as well as those constrained by low income – suggests a growing desire to think outside the box to create housing options centred on the idea of community care.

Home, community, and care have increasing importance in aging societies, where growing numbers of people no longer fit the norm of marriage from adulthood to death. In 1951, only 5 percent of Canadians lived alone; by 2021, almost 30 percent of households had only one person. By 2030, almost one in four Canadians will be aged over sixty-five. Long-term care homes, also known as nursing homes, are housing of last resort. They're understaffed, underfunded, overcrowded, unaffordable, and poorly maintained and have limited cultural adequacy for people outside the "norm" such as 2SLGBTQ+ elders. Canada had the highest rate of death in long-term care homes in the developed world during COVID-19.

The majority of people who live in long-term care homes have physical and cognitive disabilities that require around-the-clock care. But there are cheaper and more humane possibilities for seniors with less stringent requirements for care: meal delivery, nurses and personal-care workers who can help with laundry and housekeeping, shared housing with an on-site support worker. Near my home in Ottawa, Abbeyfield runs a house where ten senior singles and couples share a twenty-four-hour health support worker. Ottawa has two intergenerational cohousing projects in development: Hygge (from the Danish for "coziness") and Concorde. Childcare, eldercare, and student housing will coexist. These are great ideas, but they need more support and they need to be scaled up through policy that recognizes innovation.

To redress its huge housing deficit, end homelessness, and meet environmental and demographic challenges head on, Canada will need 6 million more homes in the next decade and at least another 12 million homes in the two decades after that. We need homes linked to health care, parks, shops, work, and community. We need to progressively realize the right to housing and the central role that care holds in the idea of home.

2

How Did We Get in This Mess?

The historical trajectory of Canada's housing crisis can be summed up in three points.

First, we're building fewer homes now than we were in the mid-1970s, when our population was half of what it is now. Over a quarter million homes were completed in 1973 and 1977. Just under 220,000 were constructed in 2022, after dipping to a low of 120,000 in 1995.

Since 1971, Canada's population has nearly doubled, from almost 22 million to 40 million people. But families have gotten smaller. Canada's population growth, fuelled mostly by immigration, has been poorly

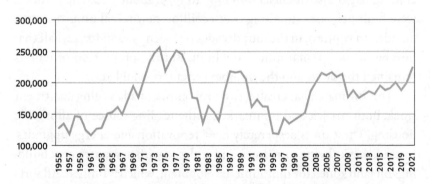

Home completions by year, 1955–2021

Source: Mike Moffatt, "The Federal Government's Big Hairy Audacious Goal (BHAG) to Double the Number of New Homes Built," *Medium* (blog), April 10, 2022.

Federally assisted affordable-housing units, 1946–2020

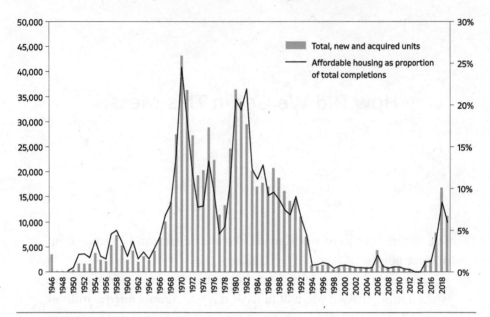

Source: Brian Clifford, based on CMHC Housing Statistics over multiple years.

matched to home completions. This mismatch was particularly bad between 2014 and 2024. If new home construction had stayed at 1970s levels, we'd have an additional 6 to 7 million homes.

Second, in the 1970s we abandoned purpose-built rental stock, including larger apartments. From 1960 to 1979, about 50,000 apartments were built per year – totalling over 1 million new rental units over two decades. In contrast, in the four decades between 1980 and 2022, half that number of new rental units were built. But the proportion of renters remained the same, and the number of renters doubled.

This mismatch has created two problems. Canada's aging apartment stock, both market and nonmarket, is the leading source of affordable housing. These units desperately need renovation and energy upgrades. Instead, they're being torn down and replaced with new apartment buildings on land zoned for multiunit development, which is limited. All sorts of households are trying to rent a limited stock of apartments: students,

Home Truths

downsizing seniors, median-income households who used to buy houses, and low- and moderate-income singles and couples. The result: low vacancy rates and exploitation by unscrupulous landlords and developers. If we take population growth and change since the 1970s into account, Canada has an accumulated deficit of at least 2 million private market rental homes.

Third, we stopped collectively investing in nonmarket housing in the early 1990s. When construction peaked in the early 1970s, up to 25 percent of home completions resulted from federal nonmarket and **regulated affordable-housing programs**, especially public housing. A second peak for nonmarket housing (especially community and cooperative housing) occurred in the early 1980s. But after that, the federal government downloaded responsibility for housing programs to the provinces, and the provinces in many cases downloaded responsibility to municipalities and regions and favoured private-sector, so-called affordable, development.

The decline of nonmarket housing since the 1990s has caused an increase in homelessness. Although the National Housing Strategy of 2017 created a limited stock of new nonmarket housing, most of the homes were not affordable to low-income households. Canada has accumulated

Regulated affordable-housing programs: These are market-sector affordable housing programs, funded by government grants, low-cost financing, and/or tax incentives, usually for a limited time period of affordability (ten to twenty years). As the federal government withdrew from supporting nonmarket housing, the provinces began to rely more and more on private developers and definitions of affordability as a percentage of the "market rate." Most current federal and provincial programs have different definitions of affordability, ranging from 80 percent of average market rent or purchase price to 30 percent of total area income. These rents or purchase prices bear no resemblance to what low- or moderate-income households can afford.

a deficit of nonmarket housing over the past four decades. In the early 1970s and early 1980s, 35,000 to 40,000 nonmarket homes were built per year; between 1994 and 2017, fewer than 4,000 nonmarket homes were built every year, and many more were lost. If construction had stayed at 1970s levels (and rent subsidies had been maintained), we'd have 2 million additional nonmarket homes.

Why did we stop building homes, especially low-cost rental homes?

For thousands of years, the people who lived in what is now called Canada had homes. They might have moved seasonally to hunt or farm, but wherever they were, they erected environmentally and socially appropriate places to live. Whether in an *iglu* (a conical snow house, usually lived in by a multigenerational household), a longhouse (a longer-term rectangular house made of wood and animal skins, usually lived in by multiple households), or another structure, Indigenous homes combined cooking, sleeping, food storage, craft production, child rearing, healing, political decision making, and spiritual practices. Their homes reflected their "relationships to land, water, place, family, kin, each other, animals, cultures, languages and identities."

The notion of one household having a huge home while another went without a home was not part of any Indigenous culture. There might have been people with more food or goods, or times when everyone went hungry, and there were certainly wars and other disputes over territory, but homelessness, with its associated sense of being banished from a community, was rare, reserved as punishment for serious crimes, such as murder.

I'm not telling this story to be nostalgic or to say that we can magically return to presettler Canada. I'm describing a form of housing policy that is sustainable, a framework in which the community decides to create new housing when the population increases or changes to ensure everyone has a home. Housing policy in Turtle Island developed over millennia before it was interrupted.

From the early seventeenth century, Indigenous homes and settlements were stolen to provide homes and livelihoods for newcomers. For a long time, settlers expected to have better homes over time, and they expected the next generation to have better homes than they did.

And indeed, this happened over much of the eighteenth and nineteenth centuries. Just like in the story of the three little pigs, homes made of whatever materials were at hand – mud or straw or wood – were replaced by brick, insulated, and outfitted with electricity, running water, and indoor toilets.

But poor people continued to live in overcrowded, unaffordable, unhealthy conditions, especially in rapidly growing cities. In Montreal, rents doubled between 1889 and 1913 while wages for skilled labourers increased by only 35 percent. Toronto in 1914 had 9,000 residences categorized as overcrowded. Many families lived in single rooms; 447 families lived in cellars or rooms without windows. After the First World War, huge increases in Toronto's land prices drove housing unaffordability. Migrant tenants were afraid to ask for repairs for fear of being demovicted or rents rising. These injustices met with unjust responses that echo today's bad policies.

In his 1911 "slum report," Toronto's medical officer of health, Charles Hastings, focused on the moral dangers of apartment buildings for young white single people rather than windowless bedrooms, overcrowding, or outdoor toilets. He blamed the "feeble-minded foreign element" for ignorance of basic hygiene and posited that lodging houses would lead to child sexual abuse. Instead of advocating for large-scale nonmarket housing, which was being built in the United Kingdom, he wanted zoning to limit apartment buildings to a few areas and stringent regulation of shared accommodations. All for the good of poor people, of course.

Overcrowding persisted. In 1901, about one adult (a person aged fifteen or older) in ten rented a room with meals provided by a landlady or an unrelated family. Those who ran boarding houses couldn't afford to live in their home otherwise. During pre– and post–Second World War housing shortages, almost one in ten households either doubled up with another household or rented a single room. In Toronto in 1951, the proportion was one in five. In 1935, a report recommending the Dominion Housing Act concluded: "There is no apparent prospect of the low income rental need being met through unaided private enterprise building for profit." But the federal government ignored its own research for the next eighty years, leading to at least three lost opportunities.

Lost Opportunity 1: The Curtis Report, 1944

During the Second World War, the Canadian government set out to develop a postwar housing program. Named after its lead author, Clifford Austin Curtis, an economics professor at Queen's University, the Curtis Report defined "affordable" as spending no more than 20 percent of before-tax income on housing and utilities. The idea was a day's work for a week's accommodation – a humane idea from an era that gave us "eight hours for work, eight hours for rest, and eight hours for what you will."

The report factored overcrowding and inadequate repair into its understanding of core housing need. To calculate core housing need, Curtis's team considered accumulated deficits, the replacement of inadequate homes, the need to increase vacancies, and the needs of a growing population. Going well beyond current definitions of core housing need, they considered all nonreserve homes and households and assessed "homeownership, home improvement, slum clearance, low-rental projects, and rural and farm housing." The report concluded that Canada had an accumulated deficit of 320,000 mostly low-cost homes. It recommended a target of 606,000 new or renovated homes and subtargets to fix inadequate housing, address population growth, and provide a slight oversupply to keep rents and home prices low over the next decade. This plan was well-researched and far more extensive in scope and ambitious in its aims than anything produced recently by the federal government. The Curtis Report proposed annual targets of 50,000 homes a year, rising to 100,000 a year by the early 1950s. Today, the equivalent would be a target of 4 million homes in one decade.

What is even more radical by current standards is that the report used income categories to assess and calculate affordability. It divided Canadian households into three income categories: (1) the top third could afford to purchase new homes; (2) the middle third required affordable rentals, including nonprofit cooperatives; and (3) the lowest third required public housing, including operating subsidies. These income-based subtargets are just as relevant today. Many places from Helsinki to Hamburg operate on the "rule of thirds," as should Canada.

To implement its plan, the Curtis Report recommended establishing a federal urban-planning agency, a federal housing agency, and provincial planning agencies to fund and support municipal plans to hit income-based housing targets. Aspiring urban planners, it argued, should have a national curriculum to enable adequate housing. Curtis and colleagues discussed the importance of partnerships among all levels of government but added that "with the current distribution of taxing powers it is inescapable that a major and possibly total part of public investment in housing should come from the Dominion Treasury."

The Curtis Report arrived three years after the federal government instituted national rent controls to stop landlord profiteering during a time of increased demand for urban homes. In 1941, the government scaled up efforts to build homes through a Crown corporation called Wartime Housing Ltd. The Crown corporation bought urban land, entered into contracts with cities to build homes quickly, and used prefabricated materials and scalable home designs. It built almost 40,000 Victory Houses in less than a year. By 1943, the federal government had an acquisitions program that leased, converted, and subdivided buildings for new homes. It banned evictions between October and April. Canada had the capacity to develop a long-term national housing strategy aimed at providing adequate housing for all.

The report led to the establishment of the Canada Mortgage and Housing Corporation (CMHC). The CMHC guaranteed to finance 1.5 million homes for moderate- and middle-income households between 1946 and 1960. Some rental-housing construction was backed by federal mortgage guarantees, and money for land banking and direct grants supported some public housing. But the powerful deputy finance minister, W.C. Clark, did not want Canada to follow the public-housing path paved by England. He was opposed to deficit financing and resisted a recommendation for 2.5 percent mortgages over thirty years for low-cost public and cooperative housing. He preferred the path followed in Levittown and other US suburbs, which were car-dependent and fuelled by the private sector.

The Curtis Report, Canada's biggest housing success, ultimately became its biggest failure. Following the war, national rent controls were quietly dropped. By the late 1940s, most Victory Houses, built for return-ing veterans, were sold rather than rented out. The homes sold for between $6,000 and $7,000 (the equivalent of $80,000 in today's dollars), a price most moderate-income wage-earners could afford. But in 1959, a Toronto Victory House was sold to a second buyer for $19,000. That same house was purchased by a third buyer in an unrenovated condition for $2.1 mil-lion in 2021.

The fate of this Victory House neatly encapsulates the dilemma of subsidizing "affordable" homes in a speculative market: they don't stay affordable after the first sale. A great needs assessment report was met with a fatally flawed policy response, one that has had lasting negative repercussions for all Canadians.

Lost Opportunity 2: Programs in Search of a Policy

Throughout the 1950s and 1960s, the federal government was highly en-gaged in moderate-income housing policy. It insured mortgages to mil-lions of new homeowners through the CMHC and subsidized inexpensive home ownership through land acquisition and industrialized home construction. At the same time, the government supported purpose-built rentals through tax incentives to large developers. For example, the al-lowable tax depreciation rate on rental property was twice the actual rate (accelerated depreciation), and there were additional tax exemptions for wood-framed buildings, which were more environmentally sound than concrete. Individual and corporate investors could use accelerated depreciation to increase the rate of return in the early years of a purpose-built rental-housing project. They could keep the gains after the sale, so long as they invested the proceeds into a building that cost as much, if not more, which encouraged further construction.

In the early 1960s, the federal government finally followed through with a low-income housing program. It granted provinces up to 90 per-cent of the cost of public housing. By the mid-1960s, nonmarket-housing stock had increased tenfold. Ontario set up its own housing corporation in 1962, and most of the other provinces followed. Provincial housing companies focused on land assembly for new suburbs, constructing new public housing, acquiring rental buildings to supplement stock, and providing supplements to ensure low-income households could pay rent.

In 1971, the federal government embraced an ambitious urban strategy that encompassed low-cost housing, public transit, and the first glimmerings of environmental policy. It hired Michael Dennis and Susan Fish, two housing-policy experts, to develop a strategy that would ensure adequate housing for all. Like Curtis, Dennis and Fish were hardly wild-eyed socialists. Dennis went on to head the London and New York offices of Olympia and York, one of the world's biggest market development companies. Fish became an Ontario Conservative cabinet minister. They argued that "at no level of government has there been even mid-term planning for the number, type, distribution, quality etc. of the units produced" and that existing programs were not producing outcomes that met the needs of the "one-third to one half" of households that have low and moderate incomes. Census data indicated that 1 million renters lacked security of tenure and lived far from jobs and services. It was ludicrous to expect the elderly, people with disabilities, and single-parent families to cover their full housing costs. They also condemned poor people's lack of access to decision-making processes. Their analysis talked about the right to adequate housing.

Citing a 1964 federal report recommending 2 million nonmarket homes over the next two decades, Dennis and Fish proposed that 45 percent of new construction over the next decade be federally funded and directed to low- and moderate-income groups. The result would have been over 1 million low-cost homes by 1980 (calculated at the 1971 rate of 260,000 completions per year). Even at the much lower building rates of later decades, this subtarget would have resulted in 5 million more nonmarket homes today.

Dennis and Fish dismissed the idea of demand-side rent supplements. They argued that a guaranteed annual income would be more likely to increase real choices. Rather than supporting large-scale provincial public housing, they recommended a mix of municipal public housing, cooperatives, and housing produced by community-based developers with health and social services. They considered accessibility and environmental standards for all new construction. They wanted to see an expansion of land banking at all levels of government to control price inflation, linked to spiralling land values.

The federal government acted on some of these great ideas, including collaborating with provincial and municipal governments on large-scale nonmarket projects such as the St. Lawrence neighbourhood. But in 1972, the federal government discontinued tax incentives, responsible for hundreds of thousands of moderate- and median-income rental buildings in the late 1950s and 1960s. This had an immediate negative impact on rental construction.

The revisions to the Income Tax Act significantly lowered the after-tax yield on investments in rental property construction; they reduced the liquidity of real estate investment; and they decreased the desirability of investing in rental housing relative to commercial, industrial, and other types of residential property. These tax changes – together with higher interest rates, macroeconomic instability, and new home-ownership subsidies – caused market rental development to plummet.

The same budget introduced a measure to help moderate-income households choose home ownership. Whereas a capital gains tax of 50 percent was brought in for other investments, including rental buildings, the government exempted principal residences (owned homes). At the same time, the Assisted Home Ownership Program was introduced "to bring home ownership within the financial capabilities of families whose incomes do not exceed $7,000." In today's dollars, that would be $55,000 a year, or the low end of moderate-income affordability. The measure boosted condominium development at the expense of purpose-built rental in the limited areas zoned for multiunit buildings. The policy also indirectly supported car-dependent sprawl in suburbs.

The federal government's rationale was clear. After seeing home ownership increase from 40 to 60 percent of households because of government intervention in the 1950s and 1960s, it hoped to further increase home ownership by using tax rebates instead of direct land acquisition and financing mechanisms. Even as it invested in nonmarket rental, the government saw no need to continue tax incentives for market rental, which it treated as a temporary stop-gap until "family" formation led to middle-class status via home ownership. Homeowners were encouraged to treat their homes as equity, to trade up until they cashed in on retirement.

The average life expectancy for men in 1972 was under seventy and for women under seventy-five, which meant five to ten years of living on tax-protected retirement savings from the sale of homes. Today, life expectancy for men is over eighty and almost eighty-five for women. And, of course, without accessible, well-located rental options, affordable retirement for seniors is being eroded.

These two measures – increasing taxes on purpose-built rental while creating a huge tax incentive for homeownership – had a lasting impact on housing supply. By 1974, before rent controls were imposed by every province after a federal directive, private-sector multiunit starts had fallen to 56 percent of their 1969 level while private-sector single-family starts had risen by 45 percent.

Meanwhile, households were changing. Liberalized divorce laws, the decriminalization of homosexuality, improved access to higher education, and support for women in the workplace improved countless lives in the late 1960s and 1970s. But the federal government didn't anticipate the impact these social changes would have on households. Policy-makers assumed baby boomers, entering their twenties and thirties, would marry young and stay married. Government measures failed to meet the rising need for rental apartments from single mothers such as my mother, students like me, and single-person households. Policy-makers didn't consider the housing needs that would accompany the deinstitutionalization of about 400,000 people from psychiatric and chronic care hospitals from the late 1960s onwards. Provincial governments argued that these people's needs could be met by market housing options such as rooming houses, which were starting to disappear.

Throughout the 1970s, the federal government changed its mind about rental construction in almost every budget. In 1974, it reintroduced tax benefits eliminated in 1972 as the Multi-Unit Residential Buildings (MURB) program and extended the benefit to a larger group of investors. The government advertised the program as a short-term stimulus for multiunit residential construction commenced between November 1974 and January 1976. But the government extended the program to the end of 1976 and then, annually, to the end of 1979. Following an ongoing slump in rental starts, Ottawa reinstated the MURB program in October 1980 and cancelled it in December 1981. With each policy reversal, rental construction declined. Developers, whether market or nonmarket, need certainty not flip-flops and one-year programs.

The Assisted Rental Program (ARP) was introduced in 1975, modified in 1976 and 1977, and phased out in 1978. It replaced the Entrepreneurial Low-Rental Housing Program, which subsidized the construction of 100,000 rental units between 1946 and 1975 by providing annual subsidies of up to $600 (later $900) per low-rent home created for five to fifteen years, after which the rents were no longer subject to regulation. When the ARP ended, the federal government had subsidized about 122,000 market rental units affordable to low- and moderate-income households. The MURB program aided an estimated additional 200,000 rental units. Tax measures worked to scale up affordable market rentals, but successive governments ignored the evidence.

They also ignored the disastrous impact of capital gains tax exemptions on home prices. In 1971, over 50 percent of renters between the ages of twenty-five and forty-four could afford to buy an average-priced house. By 1981, only 7 percent were able to do so (the figure is now below 2 percent). By the end of the 1970s, the amount the government spent on indirect tax exemptions was over $5 billion per year, more than twice the amount spent on subsidies for nonmarket-housing construction and low-income rent supplements. The money went directly to property speculation. By not taxing the value of land uplift, a measure to help moderate-income households save for their retirements by "investing" in homes doomed the next generation of moderate-income households to unaffordable homes.

At the same time, restrictive zoning received an energy boost from a new generation of urban reformers concerned with "neighbourhood character" being destroyed by blockbusting apartment developers in the early 1970s. Despite Canada's excellent reputation on the housing file (which led to Vancouver hosting the first UN-Habitat in 1978), reformers saw their environmental mission as protecting neighbourhoods from change, which shifted development toward environmentally harmful suburban sprawl. Most neighbourhoods across Canada were downzoned (lower building heights, fewer units) to prevent apartment construction. Well-located rooming and boarding houses were converted to single-family homes. A 1986 City of Toronto report found that ten thousand downtown rooming-house units had been lost over the previous decade to gentrifying homeowners rather than large developers. Even today, terms such as "neighbourhood character" are applied only to precincts zoned for "single-family" homes, hearkening back to racist, classist, and heterosexist stereotypes. Measures intended to promote "local democracy" locked out the next generation in a manner that can hardly be called democratic.

Across Canada, apartments were limited to retail corridors with heavy car traffic, former industrial districts, low-income areas in need of "urban renewal" (displacing low-income households), and highway front-age. These locations have poor traffic safety and air quality, making them less than ideal for children, people with disabilities, and older people.

Apartments were excluded not only by use-based zoning (e.g., single-unit residential only) but also by a plethora of restrictions, including lot setbacks (the need for front, side, or backyards), parking minimums, height maximums, and heritage-based design guidelines on massing, doors, windows, or materials. Even when multifamily projects are allowed, their design is expected to fit in with single-family homes. Stasis – the inability to change along with households, technologies, and global climate imperatives – was baked into inflexible zoning systems.

From the 1970s onwards, high-rise condominiums replaced apartment buildings in the narrow strips where multiunit housing was permitted. Over the past twenty years, 89 percent of all multiunit housing built in Toronto – almost 120,000 units from 2010 to 2018 alone – has been condominiums. Almost half of rental listings in Toronto are in condominiums rather than purpose-built apartments. Over a third of these apartments are owned by investors who rent them out. Condominium rents are on average 49 percent more expensive than purpose-built rental apartments. Investors frequently flip properties for profit. New owners can evict tenants so a new market rent can be charged. Meanwhile, 73,000 older, larger, and more affordable purpose-built apartments were lost between 2016 and 2021. Most were torn down for new development in the narrow bands of land where multifamily housing was allowed.

Car-dependent suburbs don't meet the needs of new households formed by single mothers, new migrants, students, and older empty nesters. For eighty years, suburbs have been characterized by low-density, single-family low-rise homes that require cars to access employment areas and shopping centres. Low-income, higher-density homes have been zoned out of most of these developments, along with land uses that might support greater walkability (e.g., corner stores) or low-cost commercial start-ups (e.g., hair salons, repair shops). Rural municipalities surrounding big cities used to welcome these new additions to tax rolls. But they incurred bond debt to provide hard infrastructure such as roads, water, sewers, and waste management and then raised property taxes to pay off that debt. Meanwhile, all three levels of government ignore the exclusionary character of these "bedroom communities."

Lost Opportunity 3:
Federal Retrenchment and the National Housing Strategy, 2017

Pundits often say the federal government abandoned nonmarket housing construction and housing policy more generally in the early 1990s. But the rot had set in long before then.

Interest rates soared to nearly 20 percent in the early 1980s, which made any development – market or nonmarket – difficult. The federal government continued to provide thirty-five-year mortgages for nonmarket housing at greatly reduced costs (as low as 2 percent), but subsidizing these mortgages was becoming increasingly expensive. By mid-decade, the government's 1978 target of 30,000 nonmarket homes per year fell apart.

At the same time, neoliberalism took hold as a global ideology. Canada and rich countries around the world equated nonmarket housing with bad urbanism. Public debt was seen as ruinous instead of the best way to finance infrastructure. Meanwhile, governments encouraged private debt through mortgages. The relegation of responsibilities to lower levels of government was presented as a way to encourage so-called innovation rather than as a way to download costs onto local governments, which have fewer powers and revenue sources. Despite fifty years of strong evidence that the private sector could never meet the housing needs of low-income Canadians, the market was seen as the only solution.

By 1991, the federal government had devolved responsibility for housing policy to the provinces. By the end of the decade, Ontario,

Canada's most populous province, had downloaded responsibility to municipalities. The effects of devolution were immediate: increased homelessness, lower nonhousing expenditures by low-income renters, long waiting lists for nonmarket housing, the migration of low- and moderate-income households to sprawling suburbs, and the end of affordable "starter homes" for moderate-income households.

Another negative policy shift in the early 1990s was the imposition of a goods-and-services tax on the full value of new homes. Previously, sales tax was applied only to building materials. The sales tax burden on new rental construction increased by almost 70 percent.

Since the 1990s, environmental concerns have been raised about the irreversible loss of forests, farms, wetlands, wildlife habitats, and other natural environments. The economic folly of inefficient use of scarce land combined with the high costs of infrastructure construction has made it clear that building slightly more affordable housing in the suburbs has had deleterious impacts on society and car-dependent households.

In 2015, when the Trudeau Liberals came to power after a decade of Conservative government, they promised a $120 billion infrastructure investment strategy in affordable housing, public transit, and climate adaptation. Two years later, the National Housing Strategy (NHS) adopted a rights-based approach to prioritize "women fleeing violence, Indigenous people, seniors, people with disabilities etc." The strategy set two headline targets for the 2018–28 period:

- Reduce the number of households in core housing need (nearly 1.7 million, according to the 2016 census) by 530,000.
- Halve the number of people living in chronic homelessness (later amended to "completely eliminating chronic homelessness by 2030").

The government pledged to reach these targets through a "transparent and accountable partnership between the federal government, provinces, territories, municipalities, the social and private sectors, and people with lived experience of housing need." The strategy included supply-side mechanisms to create 100,000 new "affordable" homes and repair or renew 300,000 existing homes. Demand-side mechanisms included Canada Housing Benefits to help 385,000 households cover housing costs.

In 2019, Canada enshrined the right to housing in its national legislation. It named a housing minister for the first time in two decades and created an Office of the Federal Housing Advocate to monitor progress.

But three decades of abandoned housing policies had already impacted the CMHC negatively. Since the NHS's inception, seven federal government evaluations have criticized the CMHC for

- making up a new definition of "affordable housing" for every housing program
- misusing the NHS's budget (which ballooned from $40 to $89 billion) so programs don't address the needs of those who need housing desperately
- failing to track housing program outcomes to reduce core housing need and homelessness
- using an inconsistent definition of homelessness and failing to consistently measure the number of households without adequate homes each year
- using deceptive statistics (e.g., conflating approved projects with completed homes) to inflate poor results.

The CMHC is not a brave Crown corporation speaking truth to power, as was case with the Dennis-Fish report in 1972. The CMHC is a profitable mortgage broker with little housing-policy, research, or evaluation expertise. The decision, made in 2023, to move housing policy to a new Ministry of Housing, Infrastructure and Communities of Canada with direct parliamentary oversight reflected a consensus that the National Housing Strategy led by the CMHC has failed.

Since the 1990s, successive Canadian governments – Liberal and Conservative – have argued that they govern a weak federation in which powers over the four pillars of the welfare state (housing, education, health, and social assistance) have devolved to provincial and territorial governments. Yet there are federal ministers of health, community services, and housing who presumably don't spend their days twiddling their thumbs. Even education, a wholly provincial responsibility, increasingly relies on subsidies from international students granted visas by the federal government. Health, including long-term care and supportive-housing services, is governed by the Canada Health Act, and Canada recently created national standards for long-term care homes. In 2023, the federal government introduced a disability benefit to improve social assistance outcomes for a significant proportion of the homeless.

In Canada's continually evolving constitutional framework, the federal government continues to play a key role in leadership, policy, and cost-sharing. Federal decisions on immigration, infrastructure, taxation, bank rates, climate change, health care, and community services have a profound effect on housing. Canada has responded to housing crises in the past. All levels of government must learn lessons from the past and from initiatives in other countries to work together to develop a sustainable housing approach for future generations.

3

Who's in Charge?

If Canada hopes to fix its housing crisis, all three levels of government need to stop finger pointing and maximize their efforts to help people live healthy and dignified lives. Federalism isn't to blame for Canada's poor record on human rights. But the federal government has failed to lead in terms of establishing rights-based norms. Policy-makers have refused to incorporate international human rights obligations into Canada's bilateral and multilateral agreements with other levels of government (e.g., provincial welfare that doesn't cover rent, and municipalities that won't permit supportive housing in residential neighbourhoods).

Each level of government has its own set of powers, and each one needs a seat at the housing table, alongside other stakeholders: First Nations, Métis, and Inuit leaders; investors, including banks and pension funds; market and nonmarket developers and providers; and affordable-housing advocates, especially those with lived experience of homelessness and inadequate housing. They'll need a big table, and the conversation will be lively. But successful housing strategies can be cocreated and executed, as Sweden's Million Programme has shown.

Sweden's Million Programme, 1965–74

Sweden remained neutral during the Second World War, and its housing stock was less hard hit than its European neighbours. But by the 1950s, housing development in this country of 7.5 million people lagged behind urbanized population growth, partly because of a shortage of construction materials and labour. The country had 3 million homes (one home for every 2.5 people, a ratio similar to Canada's today), but many of the homes were in poor condition in depopulated rural areas. Waiting lists for public housing were seven to ten years long, shorter than Canada's waiting lists today. Like Canada in the 1940s, Sweden instituted national rent control. But unlike Canada in the postwar era, Sweden provided low-interest loans (covering 100 percent of the costs for new rental projects) to municipal housing companies. Even so, these measures didn't work fast enough to meet the nation's needs.

Sweden's Million Programme (Miljonprogrammet), announced in 1965, scaled up these mechanisms to provide housing for the postwar baby boom – 100,000 homes per year over a decade. Strong national leadership and partnerships with local governments, public and market developers, the construction sector, and empowered community associations resulted in success. One million homes in Sweden in 1965–74 would be equivalent to 6 million homes in Canada today.

The program delivered housing on an industrial scale. The national government funded land acquisition and construction, as well as local services, ranging from daycare centres and schools to large parks, trails, roads, and public transit. Planning guidelines developed in Stockholm were put into practice across Sweden. Many towns and cities wanted more homes to encourage industries to relocate and to support local businesses and increase the property tax base. Municipalities retained ultimate planning authority: they chose where and how development would take place. They delivered low-cost homes through municipal housing companies, which operated alongside cooperative housing societies and private developers.

Sweden saw the Million Programme as community building and nation building. The program was an essential pillar in an integrated welfare policy that would improve households and local and national economies and make Sweden's citizens healthier. The goal was to create **15-minute cities**.

Policy-makers often view housing programs as a temporary economic stimulus or brake: short-term tax breaks to get construction moving or temporary eviction moratoriums to cushion an economic downturn.

"15-minute cities" is a term used to describe walkable, bikeable, transit-oriented communities. The average adult can walk four to six kilometres in an hour. But ideal walkable distances are often expressed using 400-metre and 800-metre catchment areas, equivalent to five- and ten-minute walks for children, older people, those with limited mobility, and anyone who must traverse multiple road crossings. These cities offer residents easy access to public transit and walkable access to green spaces, schools, shops, and health services such as pharmacies.

But Sweden's housing policy was **nonsubservient** to economic policy. Unlike many other European countries building public housing at the time – such as England, France, and West Germany – Sweden pursued a **universalist** program for all income levels. Nonprofit homes would be high quality and mixed income, not **residual** housing limited to low-income families (and designed to encourage them to leave as soon as possible). People would live in these homes from birth to old age. Sweden's strong tradition of nonmarket cooperatives ensured a high level of community self-management, including a national tenants' union, which helped set annual rent increases. The Swedes also supported the concept of tenure neutrality – the principle that renters should have the same rights as homeowners.

Swedish cooperatives use a different model than Canadian non-market cooperatives. Residents are required to buy a share (usually 15 percent of the cost of the home). Some households take out bank loans, and many low-income households are shut out. Lease shares can be sold to a new household, although the cooperative retains the title to the home. Swedish cooperatives place less emphasis on subsidized units than in the Canadian model: the Swedes view them as a housing solution for moderate-income households (which is how Canada's Curtis Report also saw them).

Unlike homeowner-dominated resident associations in North America, Sweden's community associations fought to improve their neighbourhoods, not to exclude multifamily homes. Mixed-tenure developments (typically 50 percent public, 30 percent cooperative, and 20 percent privately owned) fostered a culture of inclusivity. The Swedish government imposed rent controls, and annual rent increases were negotiated between the national government, nonprofit and for-profit landlords, and the national tenants' union. The process created the conditions for long-term rental security and community associations that gave an equal voice to renters.

The Million Programme emphasized strong land policy and national government finance instruments coupled with permissive zoning at the municipal level. But the game changer (the element that led to the rapid production of affordable homes) was an evidence-based industrial approach. The Million Programme depended on heightened productivity and mechanization, led by a strong private-sector building industry. Labour shortages and rising wages proved to be a serious obstacle to construction. The solution – state-supported prefabrication.

Sweden, like Canada, has harsh winters that limit on-site construction. The use of standardized, prefabricated construction elements boosted productivity. Walls, floors, ceilings, doors, and windows were assembled in factories, as were three-dimensional kitchens and bathrooms, complete with plumbing fittings. Rail-mounted cranes assembled

Subservient versus nonsubservient housing policy: Housing policy is sometimes treated as a subset of economic or social policy. For instance, Australia's Social Housing Initiative was a three-year program intended to provide employment for construction workers after the Great Recession slowed down housing development. The initiative led to the completion of 20,000 nonmarket homes in three years, but a new government didn't renew the program. Nonsubservient housing policy tends to be associated with long-term programs.

Universalist versus residual programs: Universalist nonmarket-housing programs seek to meet the needs of low-, moderate-, and median-income households. Residual nonmarket-housing programs focus only on the needs of low-income households. They assume that nonmarket housing is merely a stage on the so-called housing ladder.

single detached and multiunit buildings from late spring to autumn. Small construction crews minimized disruptions to existing communities. Prefabrication meant materials had less exposure to rain and snow. Prefabricated windows and doors meant quick weather protection and security from insects and pests. Because Sweden, like Canada, has a strong timber industry, 78 percent of the building materials were locally produced, as compared to 5 percent in most English-speaking countries.

About 45 percent of Sweden's housing is prefabricated, and prefabricated homes are flexible homes. Two two-bedroom homes can be combined into one four-bedroom home with minimal cost – and vice versa. Prefabricated home design also reflected 1960s research into time savings. Ikea, one of the big beneficiaries of the program, created its modular furniture to fit standardized home designs.

Although the Million Programme is associated with slab apartment blocks, it also produced small low-rise houses much like Canada's wartime Victory Houses. All told, between 1961 and 1975, Sweden built 40,000 apartment blocks (low- and high-rise) with about 920,000 homes and 480,000 single-family houses. The three largest cities – Stockholm, Gothenburg, and Malmö – accounted for 35 percent of production, but smaller towns and cities also benefited. Although most of the housing was for narrowly defined nuclear families, thousands of student homes were developed in Stockholm, Lund, Uppsala, and Umeå.

The results of the Million Programme were overwhelmingly positive. In 1960, 34 percent of Swedish households were overcrowded (more than two people per bedroom), and 45 percent had no indoor bathrooms. By 1975, these conditions marked fewer than 5 percent of households. After 1975, landscaping, community gardens, and additional community spaces were added to multifamily apartment neighbourhoods. Nonmarket housing remained mixed income.

But the Million Programme also became a victim of its own success. Municipalities oversubscribed as population growth slowed, leading to high vacancy rates in some projects by the early 1970s. Some criticized the monotonous designs and social infrastructure that failed to keep up with home construction. But homes built by the private sector in postwar suburban Canada faced similar criticisms.

Ultimately, the housing program was associated with the Social Democrat Party. When it lost power in the late 1970s, Sweden moved toward a neoliberal housing system. The government abolished low-interest loans and property tax abatements for public housing. It expected municipal housing companies to run on a for-profit basis. Most public-housing stock was sold off to large-scale financialized firms, which renovicted lower-income tenants. Other public-housing stock was converted to cooperative housing and, after 2009, to condominiums. Tenure neutrality was abandoned as government subsidies encouraged home ownership. Access to mortgages was liberalized, and credit guarantees were given to first-time homebuyers. The government adopted other moves from the neoliberal playbook: tax deductions on mortgage interest, low ceilings on property taxes, a deferred capital gains tax on primary residences, and a ten-year exemption from rent controls for new construction.

About 41 percent of housing in Sweden is still nonmarket, and almost one in five homes is cooperative. But abandoning leadership on housing to the private market has been a massive failure for Sweden – in terms of affordability and supply. Sweden is once again experiencing a housing shortage, particularly for low- and moderate-income households. Its 10.5 million citizens have an unmet demand for at least 70,000 new homes per year. Small towns have housing surpluses, but big cities continue to attract people without enough housing supply. As in Canada, low-income households, especially students and new migrants, are forced into a secondary subletting market, where they face unaffordability, overcrowding, and violations of their rights. Refugees often spend months in heated tents. Demand-side housing allowances are oversubscribed and less adequate than they used to be. Institutional memory loss leads policy-makers to make the same mistakes again and again.

Canada's Governance Failure

I can hear constitutional wonks exclaiming, "Aha! But Canada has three levels of government. It's completely different from two-tier governments such as Sweden's!"

Not really. Canada has a federal government bound by the 2019 National Housing Strategy Act to make the right to adequate housing a reality. The government should be leveraging its considerable fiscal powers to promote affordable housing for groups "most in need." It has the right and the responsibility to set national housing targets (and subtargets) based on consistent definitions. Like Sweden, it should be monitoring the performance of the provinces, territories, and municipalities and linking infrastructure money to their success.

Provincial and territorial governments have the fiscal capacity to provide housing-related health and social supports to those who need them, particularly people with disabilities. They can and should steer land-use planning and zoning, building codes, and cost and size targets to support the national housing supply. They control rent regulations (including evictions) and are responsible for ensuring that everyone has enough money to survive, which is hard to do without a home. If the federal government isn't doing its job, they can fund or cofund the housing that is most needed.

Municipalities are responsible for development decisions that serve the common good, including approving homes rapidly, at the right sizes, tenures, and locations. Their role should include administering and enabling (but not funding or financing) affordable nonmarket and market housing in relation to infrastructure such as roads, public transit, and health centres. Municipalities should coordinate pathways out of homelessness, but they can't be solely responsible for developing low-cost homes with services. Sometimes, municipalities provide public housing directly or through a municipal agency. But expecting municipalities to shoulder most of the costs for nonmarket housing leads to disaster. Disaster also ensues when municipalities are expected to do the right thing when it comes to legalizing abundant housing near transit, jobs, and services without senior government targets.

All levels of government are full of excuses when it comes to why we can't have nice things such as basic human rights, but their roles are clear, and they have failed to fulfill them. The federal government has failed to develop and lead housing strategy, especially over the past three decades. Its current housing strategy doesn't have a strong evidence base. Nor does it have adequate monitoring and evaluation capacity. Despite collecting the lion's share of tax revenues, the federal government refuses to adequately fund and finance housing that low- and moderate-income people can afford.

The federal government doesn't enforce agreements with the provinces to protect the rights of low-income people, who rely on inadequate welfare and wages, who die prematurely in overcrowded long-term care homes or "emergency" shelters, who are denied services to age in place in a dignified manner. The provinces have either stood by or actively encouraged speculative housing developers to tear down or radically increase rents in low-cost housing, forcing people into homelessness. The federal government can and should step in, as it did with rent controls in the 1940s and emergency benefits during COVID-19.

Until 2022, the provinces refused to force municipalities to end exclusionary zoning. Municipalities, often in thrall to wealthy homeowners, have choked off development pipelines, underfunded the maintenance of public housing, and used police officers to criminalize people for the noncrime of not having an adequate home. Voters "fire" these governments often enough, but new governments don't elicit better results. No wonder almost two-thirds of Canadians agree or strongly agree that "politicians can't be trusted."

Federal Powers and Responsibilities

To start with the obvious, Canada is a rich country with enough resources to ensure homes for all. Canada's tax revenues come from four main sources: personal income taxes, pension plans, consumption taxes (primarily the GST), and corporate income taxes. Personal income tax is the single biggest component in Canada, constituting a higher proportion of tax than in most other OECD countries. Personal income tax is **progressive** whereas consumption taxes are **regressive**.

Incomes are highly unequal in Canada. In 2022, the top one hundred CEOs were paid $14.9 million on average, 246 times the average income. And the wealthy have been taxed less over time. The government taxed the highest income bracket up to 70 percent of earnings in the 1950s; they are now taxed less than 50 percent. Stock options, the most common form of executive payment, are taxed at 50 percent of the sale price.

A wealth tax on households with over $10 million could raise over $30 billion a year, enough to fully finance an initiative to end homelessness.

Compared to other countries, Canada has extremely low corporate income tax rates. In 2019, Canada's "marginal effective" corporate tax rate was 13.7 percent, as compared to the OECD average of 18.4 percent. An effective tax rate is the rate corporations pay on profits. An effective rate may differ from legal tax rates because of tax incentives and exemptions and additional taxes such as sales taxes. A marginal effective tax rate is the rate paid on corporate growth or new investment. Over the past two decades, Canada's marginal effective corporate tax rate has declined fourfold. Canada often compares itself favourably to other English-speaking countries such as the United States and the United Kingdom, which allegedly moved faster and further away from being social welfare states under neoliberalism. But the effective corporate income tax rates in the two countries are 18.4 percent and 26.6 percent, respectively.

Reducing corporate income taxes has not spurred business innovation or investment in Canada. Indeed, capital has been locked up in housing and land speculation. In 2019, the OECD predicted Canada would be dead last among industrialized countries in terms of projected GDP growth per capita by the end of the decade. Money that could be going into innovation and labour productivity (e.g., $1.5 trillion in Canadian pension funds) is going to mechanisms such as guaranteeing Big

Bank mortgages. Canada's economic system is less vulnerable to failure than the US system (where speculation in residential mortgages led to the Great Recession), but Canada's economy relies on speculative ownership of housing at the expense of human rights and the environment.

Canada prides itself on being a progressive country, but its social spending on housing, education, health, and social assistance is near the bottom of the industrialized world. Like many other countries, Canada cut social spending in the neoliberal wave of the 1980s and 1990s. Unlike many countries, including those more affected by the Great Recession, its social spending continues to be low: Canada's proportion of expenditures on social spending was 17.3 percent in 2019, considerably below the United States and the United Kingdom and the OECD average of 20.1 percent.

Despite claims from right-wing ideologues that government debt is "out of control," Canada's financial policy has been consistent since the 1990s: minimize national debt by maximizing personal debt, especially through home ownership. Canada did take on considerable debt as part of COVID-19 relief in 2020, but its debt-to-GDP ratio is still the lowest in relation to higher-income countries.

What isn't paid for by government gets paid for by individuals. Even before the spike in home prices, Canadian households had one of the highest per capita household debt figures in the world. The OECD raised concerns about housing speculation harming other aspects of Canada's economy. Household debt is greater than our annual GDP: over $2 trillion. And the biggest source of household debt is speculation in housing, a "shaky palace."

Canada's failure on the housing front must be laid at the feet of a succession of finance ministers, Liberal and Conservative. They have reduced corporate taxes, social spending, and national infrastructure investment and left unaddressed disturbingly high levels of household debt, mostly concentrated in mortgages. The result? A widening wealth gap between renters and homeowners, young households and older ones, women (who are much less likely to own homes) and men, and racialized groups and those considered white.

It's not a lack of funds or Canada's constitution that makes the federal government weak on housing policy. It's cross-party political cowardice.

Provincial and Territorial Housing Powers

One hallmark of neoliberal thinking is the belief that decision-making powers should be devolved to the provinces and territories where a "competition of ideas" can reign. There's only one problem: devolution hasn't worked. Provinces are – and should continue to be – responsible for tenant protection, health and social support, and income security. But they have done a terrible job at these basic tasks and a worse job at providing housing for all.

Rather than telling the stories of each province and territory, I focus on the four most populous provinces. Quebec and British Columbia have been the strongest on the housing front since the federal government devolved housing policy in 1992. But they've simply adopted policies the federal government used successfully in the 1980s. Ontario downloaded responsibilities and costs for nonmarket housing to its municipalities, a policy choice that ended in disaster. Alberta's single-minded focus on reducing homelessness has seen some success, but the rest of its housing portfolio has been neglected.

All provinces rely on roughly the same mix of taxes as the federal government: personal income taxes, sales taxes, and corporate income taxes. In addition, provincial governments levy resource royalties, and some provinces benefit more than others from federal transfers. Personal income taxes in Ontario are low compared to other provinces. But the main source of per capita differences in Ontario, Alberta, and British Columbia is lower federal transfers because of higher resource royalties – a source of considerable resentment, particularly in Alberta.

Expenditures vary wildly. It's not surprising that Ontario, as the most populous province, has the highest number of households in housing need. It is shocking that Ontario, the richest province, has, by a considerable margin, the lowest per capita expenditures, particularly on health and social services. Even before the Conservatives came to power in 2018, program expenditures had been growing at half the rate of the other provinces for nearly a decade. In 2019, Ontario's Financial Accountability Office warned that the government's pledge to reduce its debt while not raising taxes would place additional strain on health care and social assistance.

Why do low levels of health and social support matter? Since the 1990s, the provinces and territories haven't been providing enough housing benefits for low-income households (particularly single mothers and people with disabilities) to cover rent. There's not enough money for support workers to care for people with disabilities and chronic health issues. Nor is there enough money to create and maintain housing with these supports. The people who need health and social support range from people with mental illness, to those in cognitive decline in long-term care homes, to victims of violence. Underfunding feeds homelessness, which, of course, worsens physical and mental health – which costs more in the long run.

Welfare rates should increase with the cost of living, but the only place that mandates this is Yukon. In every other province and territory, from the early 1990s onwards, welfare rates fell in relation to median incomes and inflation. No province or territory maintains a welfare rate above the "poverty line," however it is defined. The closest scenario is a two-adult, two-child household in Quebec, which receives benefits just short of 50 percent of median household income. In Ontario, welfare for single people is 15 percent of median household.

When a country lacks low-cost housing, and when incomes can't keep up in a severely limited market, the result is homelessness.

During the 1960s and 1970s, Ontario was the best province for providing nonmarket housing to low-income people. The Conservative government formed the Ontario Housing Corporation to focus on land assembly and streamline approvals and large-scale public-housing construction. The province granted money and loan guarantees to nonmarket developers, and it gave rehabilitation money to low-income homeowners to add basics such as indoor toilets and better insulation. As in Sweden, the province predicated massive public-housing construction on break-even rents that covered the cost of the building mortgage and expenses such as maintenance, which in turn relied on rising incomes. Public housing was intended for moderate-income seniors and working households whose rent covered operating costs.

By the early 1980s, several problems came to a head. First, gentrification eroded low-cost rental housing in central cities even as the deinstitutionalization of people with disabilities increased demand.

Second, higher interest rates increased construction costs. Third, as welfare rates decreased, poorer households (including single mothers) began to dominate public-housing needs lists, and their rents, geared to income, could not offset operating expenses.

When the 1992 Charlottetown constitutional discussions led the federal government to offload housing to the provinces, it ignored key federal levers such as taxation, interest rates, immigration, and infrastructure funding. Ontario, with 42 percent of nonmarket housing in Canada, saw costs soar: from $150 million per year in 1985 to $1 billion per year in 1995. A publicity campaign by landlords claimed rent supplements would be more efficient than constructing more nonmarket housing. To revitalize the low-cost apartment industry, they argued, the government should end rent controls on new construction. A radical right-wing government, elected in 1995, cut welfare by 20 percent and stopped funding new nonmarket housing. By 2000, the province had downloaded housing to municipal governments and transferred minimal money to maintain the existing stock. Today, 77 percent of nonmarket-housing funding comes from municipalities, 14 percent from the province, and 9 percent from the federal government.

British Columbia went in the opposite direction. It built little public housing during the nonmarket construction heyday from the mid-1960s to the mid-1980s, although it did support the development of about two thousand community and cooperative homes per year. Following devolution in 1992, its provincial agency, BC Housing, unilaterally took over some of the functions of the CMHC: loan underwriting, consulting for nonmarket providers, rent subsidies, and homelessness prevention. It took advantage of small federal grants (e.g., for supportive housing) offered after 2001. From 2000 to 2017, British Columbia built 30,000 of the 91,000 nonmarket homes built in Canada. (Quebec, with almost twice the population, built 40,000.) A drop in the bucket in relation to need, but at least they saved some lives.

Even under a right-of-centre government, BC Housing supported capacity building for nonmarket-housing organizations, including Indigenous-led developers. British Columbia now has the most growth-oriented nonmarket sector in Canada. One BC Housing project helped the United Church take a portfolio approach to its aging assets, including building housing on top of worship halls. Another project supported the development of Housing Central, a partnership between the cooperative and community-housing sectors that allows asset bundling (combining the worth of small projects for financing purposes) under the aegis of the BC Community Land Trust. A third project transferred public housing and associated funding to Indigenous management.

This circle of partnership allowed a new left-of-centre government, cooperatives, community and Indigenous housing providers, and landlord associations to cocreate the best housing-supply policies in Canada. However, supply still trails need. British Columbia now has a large nonmarket-housing acquisition fund and a track record of leasing land for nonmarket housing. After a long, contentious history with municipal governments, the province is tackling exclusionary zoning and approvals issues. Of all the provinces, British Columbia has come the closest to evidence-based decision-making. It has a transparent land-assessment system and relatively standardized needs assessments. But its municipalities have a terrible track record for enabling well-located housing, leading to some of the largest housing shortages – and highest housing costs – in Canada.

Quebec, like British Columbia, took over federal functions such as technical assistance to nonmarket developers, guaranteed financing, and rent supplements. The provincial housing agency provides a grant equivalent to 50 percent of costs: 15 percent comes from other sources (municipal or charitable), and 35 percent is covered by standard mortgages. The province traditionally has the strongest renter protections in Canada, including rent controls, and a strong history of acquiring older rental buildings to prevent gentrification and displacement. Local governments, especially in Montreal, Quebec City, and Gatineau, provide loans, grants, and rent supplements for nonmarket housing.

Until recently, affordable housing was created by partnerships between provincial and municipal governments and nonmarket-housing providers. The provincial government encouraged mergers between smaller regional nonmarket providers to improve the efficiency of housing development. But Quebec's conservative government stripped money from the system. Its contribution is now well below 50 percent. Quebec still has the lowest rates of core housing need and homelessness in the country, partly because of a tenant culture with strong advocacy powers.

Alberta, which has a lower proportion of nonmarket housing than the rest of Canada, took a different approach to chronic homelessness. In 2008, it launched a Housing First program. The province offers permanent subsidized housing with supports, condition-free. The program reached about fifteen thousand people by 2017 and has had relatively stable funding through successive governments. It takes a partnership approach with Alberta's seven largest municipalities, the federal government, and local social services. However, the housing is provided by private landlords with limited security of tenure. Several of the agencies attach sobriety or other conditions, and none are "for Indigenous, by Indigenous." The program needs a nonmarket-housing supply program and a generous social assistance program to meet needs.

Recent audits of provincial and territorial housing policies agree: they aren't doing enough. Yukon doesn't have adequate ways to measure housing needs, particularly in relation to income categories and priority populations. It doesn't adequately fund supports to keep people with disabilities in subsidized housing or to maintain buildings. Programs have inadequate cultural support for Indigenous households, who represent almost 90 percent of the homeless population. In Ontario, funding for supportive and other nonmarket housing has fallen in real dollar terms as demand has risen. In British Columbia, housing need has been undercounted by all levels of government. Devolving housing policy to the provinces and territories has been a disaster.

Municipal and Regional Housing Powers

When I think about who controls what in Canadian housing policy, the Groucho Marx quote comes to mind: "Hey, you big bully! What's the idea of hitting that little bully!" Municipalities and regions (the level of government with the fewest sources of revenue and the weakest powers) should not have sole responsibility for building and maintaining nonmarket housing. That's not fair. They've used their limited powers and remarkably regressive tax structures to create the biggest barriers to building new rental housing in most cities: exclusionary zoning and an unpredictable approvals process. That's not fair, either.

About 70 percent of Canadians live in urban areas, and cities account for 75 percent of GDP. Yet municipalities collect less than 10 percent of total tax revenues. Canadian cities are unusually reliant on property taxes as compared to other countries, where municipalities receive a share of income taxes, sales taxes, and special-purpose taxes such as gas taxes. Having said that, property taxes have many sound principles. They link directly to local benefits, they're difficult to evade, and they can be progressive (e.g., more expensive homes have higher rates), although they aren't in Canada. But property taxes are highly visible. Rather than taking small amounts off wages and goods, governments levy a large amount separately. In response, self-identified ratepayers, usually well-off homeowners, pressure local politicians to avoid reforming a dysfunctional revenue source.

Property taxes are levied directly from homeowners and indirectly from renters. Rental buildings often pay higher multitenant taxes (e.g., in Toronto, double the tax rate for older multitenant buildings), placing an unfair burden on lower-income tenants.

Municipalities can sell municipal bonds to fund infrastructure, including nonmarket housing. But municipal development charges exchange long-term public capital for short-term private capital (with greater costs and lower scrutiny). Direct provision of public goods such as social housing and transit is cheaper and more efficient than private provision underwritten by tax dollars.

Local governments are in a mess partly of their own making. Powerful homeowners' associations advocated for regressive tax systems that reward unearned wealth and punish poor people. Many cities refuse to borrow to fund essential infrastructure and have underfunded services and deteriorating nonmarket housing. Montreal manages 55,000 public homes; only 30 percent of its revenue comes from the federal and provincial governments. Toronto's 60,000 public homes receive not one penny from the provincial government for maintenance. Meanwhile, inadequate welfare and other housing benefits don't cover operating costs. It took a one-time influx of $1 billion in renovation funding from the federal government to stave off the abandonment of much of Toronto's public housing in 2019.

Fixing low-cost housing deficits requires senior government funding and targets. Housing markets in Canada are metropolitan or regional: tiny Tillsonburg on the Niagara Peninsula is affected by the housing market in Toronto almost two hundred kilometres away. Municipalities simply refuse to approve and meet a fair share of regional housing need. Local governments have little to no say when it comes to mortgage-financing rates, support services, and renter protections. They've shown, time and again, that they're incapable of fixing the housing crisis.

■ ■ ■

Canada is a rich country with mostly rich provinces and territories, regions, and cities. We have ample wealth to provide housing for all. Every level of government has heard loud and clear that housing is an urgent issue. Now is the time – morally and politically – for rapid coordinated reform. Every level of government could build on policies proven to work in the areas of taxation and financing, land policy and welfare, and health services. It's up to citizens to become more literate so we can coordinate our demands for a housing system that serves everyone.

4

Who Needs What Homes Where, at What Cost?

In June 2022, the CMHC released *Canada's Housing Supply Shortages*. The report calculated that to bring housing costs down to 2004 levels, 3.5 million additional homes would need to be constructed by 2030, on top of the 2.3 million new homes projected by a business-as-usual approach. That's a total of 725,000 new homes a year, more than triple the Canadian average of 180,000 homes per year completed over the past decade. The report consciously shied away from "targeting a particular level of affordability"; in fact, it doesn't mention the National Housing Strategy's targets on core housing need and homelessness.

Canada's housing supply isn't keeping up with population growth, especially in big cities. If we'd maintained the pace of the 1970s, we'd have 4 million more homes today. When it comes to supply, ignoring factors such as cost, size, location, or type of housing supply is a terrible idea. The best strategies are people-focused and rights-based; the best plans acknowledge diversity and listen to those most in need.

Anti-supply Myths

Some argue that we don't need to triple the supply of homes – we simply need to reallocate existing ones. There's a myth circulating that Canada has 1.3 million vacant homes and 12 million vacant bedrooms. These figures come from the 2016 census. The census includes all "homes that are suitable for year-round occupation but are not occupied by their usual resident." Residences occupied by students or temporary workers are included as vacant, as are duplex apartments recently absorbed into one living space, dwellings whose residents who are travelling, dwellings undergoing renovations, dwellings for sale or rent, and winterized cottages. A dive into metropolitan areas shows an unoccupied rate of between 2 and 10 percent. Kingston and Waterloo have the highest proportion of dwellings "not occupied by usual resident," likely student rentals.

US census data, by contrast, provides reasons for vacancies, such as transactional (units for rent or sale), moving (units sold or rented but not yet occupied), and recreational (units for recreational, seasonal, or occasional use). The United States counts students as real people in need of real homes. A transactional vacancy rate of 4 to 8 percent is considered healthy for a competitive rental-housing market. By that measure, Canada doesn't have enough vacancies in most cities.

But harmful vacancies – homes kept vacant solely for speculative purposes – do exist. And they should be taxed or regulated out of existence. Vancouver's Empty Homes Tax, implemented in 2019, led to a 36 percent decrease in empty homes by 2022. That same year, Vancouver reported a revenue of $68.8 million from the 3 percent tax on the assessed value of the empty homes, mostly condominium apartments used as vacation homes or investments. The most comprehensive recent study of short-term rentals such as Airbnb and Vrbo found 128,000 apartments and homes listed on any given day in Canada, most concentrated in larger cities. The majority were whole homes, not a room in an occupied home. These are disturbingly large numbers, but they're a drop in the bucket in relation to unmet needs.

Canadian homes also tend to be large by international standards. The average home size in Canada is 181 square metres, smaller than in the United States (201 square metres) and Australia (214 square metres) but considerably larger than many countries with better housing policies such as Denmark (137 square metres), France (112 square metres), Japan (95 square metres), and Finland (87 square metres). A 2018 study found that nearly two-thirds of Ontario households were overhoused, to the tune of 5 million extra bedrooms, including 400,000 homes with three or more empty bedrooms. Many of the overhoused are empty nesters who can't find affordable downsizing options to age in place and who may also be dealing with adult children "boomeranging" back home because of unaffordability.

One solution is state control of all housing stock with allocation by household size, something few Canadians, including me, would advocate for. But it's a feature of Singapore's successful public-housing policy; empty nesters there generally find alternative homes in the same building if not the same neighbourhood. The United Kingdom imposed bedroom taxes on public-housing residents who didn't (or couldn't) move to smaller units when their children left. A gentler solution – providing incentives for subdivision of larger homes and scaling up smaller, more accessible options – is possible. But it won't solve inadequate supply.

A better solution is more diverse housing stock so households don't have to suffer overcrowding or overhousing. To be effective, the CMHC's target of more than 6 million homes over a decade would require real strategic planning between all levels of government, along with policies, taxation, and other mechanisms to meet targets pertaining to price, size, and location. Numbers are being thrown in the air without any policy mechanisms to achieve them: a bad sign for Canada. But Sweden achieved ambitious targets over a decade, as did Singapore, a city-state that faced even bigger challenges in the 1960s.

Singapore: Needs, Targets, Action

In 1966, the citizens of Singapore won a political battle to transition from a British colony to an independent nation-state. A large proportion of the 1.6 million residents lived in self-built shacks in informal settlements or in grossly overcrowded and decrepit shophouses (apartments above shops), with multiple families in one room. A needs assessment conducted by the Singapore Housing and Development Board in 1960 calculated the housing deficit (80,000 units), the number of substandard homes that would be lost to redevelopment in the next ten years (20,000 units), and the number of homes that would be needed to account for anticipated population increases (47,000 units). The board determined that they would need a total of 147,000 units to meet housing needs over the next decade. The assessment became the basis for the new government's annual housing targets.

Singapore met those targets over the next decade. Housing security fuelled the development of this powerhouse economy, which has a per capita GDP that easily outpaces Canada's.

As a first step, the Singapore Housing and Development Board expropriated privately held land. The government owned 49 percent of land in 1964; it now owns 90 percent. It created master plans for what would eventually become twenty-three self-contained new towns. The master plans considered the development of homes and communities in a high-density, sustainable transit-based system. The plan was well suited to today's environmental concerns.

It financed the development of high-rise apartments with social and health services, schools, and shops on the ground floor and green space between buildings. Studies have shown that green space has positive physical and mental health impacts; it's more important to have extensive parkland within walking distance of homes than front- or backyards. The actual construction was done by private-sector developers using standardized designs. Construction firms who underbid and delivered shoddy homes were blacklisted; the ones who delivered were awarded merit stars and contracts.

The apartment buildings contained a range of one-to-four-bedroom homes. The designs recognized that people's need for space might change as their lives progressed and that they might want to age in the same community. Flats, as opposed to townhouses, also enhanced accessibility. The flats were basic but relatively spacious; their Cold War–era bomb shelters were eventually converted to storage. Bedrooms, living rooms, and kitchens had windows.

More controversially, from the 1980s onwards, the government mandated a social mix of indigenous Malays and immigrant Chinese and Indian households. It allocated a maximum number for each group in each building. The policy helped prevent ghettoization by ethnicity, which was central to nation building. Residents' associations eventually took over management of the new towns through a quasi-co-op model.

Although Singapore, like Canada, sold its public housing, sales prices were controlled by a ninety-nine-year land lease held by the state, which banned resales for five years. Singapore continues to control house prices through a government land trust model. The government restricts resale prices to keep them the equivalent of two years' wages for an average salary, and it provides subsidies for low-income households. Eighty percent of Singapore's current housing stock was built by the Housing and Development Board in the past sixty years; 95 percent of the flats are owned. At the end of its first ten-year "homes for all" program, Singapore was the second wealthiest country in Asia, after Japan.

Singapore demonstrates the effectiveness of top-down housing models. Granted this is easier in a city-state with one level of government and a strong degree of political consensus (despite opposition parties and regular elections, the same party stayed in power for sixty years). But there are lessons to be learned here. Rapid scaling can happen with a good needs assessment, leading to targets that include maximum affordable-housing costs, backed by a strategy that incorporates government land acquisition and planning, modular construction, and government loan financing.

Elements of a Good Needs Assessment

An international comparison of housing needs assessments concludes that an ideal housing needs assessment includes the same three elements as the 1944 Canadian and the 1965 Singaporean reports:

1 *A deficit figure:* the number of households homeless or in housing need broken down by income category, household size, and underserved populations.
2 *Trends in the net change of affordable-housing stock:* this should be broken down by income category, household size, and underserved populations.
3 *Housing needs related to projected population and demographic changes over the period of a plan:* this should be preferably ten years, although there should be an update every five years or when the policy and program settings, such as immigration quotas, change significantly.

The deficit figure should include not only those who are homeless or in inadequate housing but also groups uncounted in Canadian definitions of housing need: students, migrant workers, and those in congre-

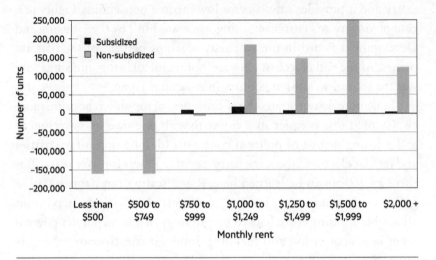

Change in rental stock by rent cost, 2011–16

Source: Steve Pomeroy, "Updating Analysis on Erosion of Lower Rent Stock from 2021 Census," McMaster University Canadian Housing Evidence Collaborative, October 2022.

gate housing such as long-term care and group homes. It should factor in the net loss of younger households to adjacent areas because of affordability concerns and involuntary "doubling up."

Net loss of affordable-housing stock has accelerated in recent years because of factors such as rent and price increases; the end of subsidies for social homes; demolition of older apartment buildings; the eviction of tenants for renovations; and conversions to short-term rentals on platforms such as Airbnb.

Canadian research has shown that between 2011 and 2016, fifteen affordable homes at $750/month or less were lost for every nonmarket home created. But almost four in five households in core housing need earned less than $30,000 a year in 2016 and required rental homes at this maximum cost. The majority of net new rental, including government-subsidized market rental, is unaffordable to low- and moderate-income households. Plans that focus solely on new builds and ignore net loss of affordable housing are likely to result in more homelessness, no matter how many affordable units are developed.

Household growth projections are an inexact science since they involve simultaneously predicting trends in immigration, internal migration between and within provinces and territories, and changes in household formation. Population shifts are often dramatic and influenced by short-term politics. Migration – whether international, interprovincial, or within provinces – doesn't cause housing unaffordability. Refusing to plan for change and population growth causes housing unaffordability.

Immigration has fuelled net population growth – and demand for housing – for most of Canada's history as a settler state. In 2022, 437,180 immigrants and 607,782 nonpermanent residents arrived in Canada, the highest numbers on record. Almost half of these newcomers settled in Ontario, especially in the Greater Toronto and Hamilton Area, and many international students and asylum seekers need low-cost rental housing. Yet the National Housing Strategy's targets have not been adjusted to reflect higher immigration and temporary-resident targets.

When it comes to interprovincial migration within Canada, a COVID-era shift to lower-cost housing and telecommuting led to a net out-migration from Ontario of 108,000 people to other provinces in 2021. Scotiabank, the source of this analysis, again points to housing unaffordability, especially in the Greater Toronto and Hamilton Area, as a key factor.

**Net intraprovincial migration,
children under five, Toronto Economic Region, 2002–21**

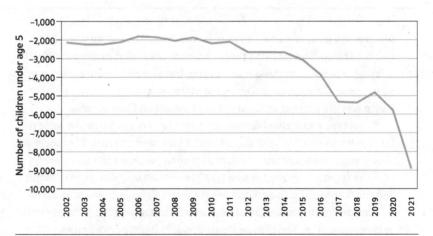

Source: Mike Moffatt, "Ontarians on the Move, 2022 Edition. #2," *Medium* (blog), January 14, 2022.

Finally, there is intraprovincial migration: moving from one community to another within a province or territory. Research reveals a net migration by families with young children out of expensive cities. Nine thousand children aged newborn to four were part of the sixty thousand people who left the Toronto Economic Region for other parts of Ontario in 2021. Inter- and intraprovincial migration from expensive to less-expensive communities is called **suppressed local demand.**

What do these three flows tell us about housing needs? Greater Toronto and Hamilton will probably continue to see high rates of population and household growth fuelled by immigration. At the same time, the region is losing working-age household heads because of inadequate housing choices. The area needs to address the consequences of its large low-cost housing deficit and rapid household growth, including the increasing need for affordable family-sized homes and **suppressed household formation.**

Considering Income Categories

The Curtis Report divided households into three income tertiles – low, medium, and high. But by the 1960s, the CMHC was using five income quintiles to analyze housing needs. It focused on the "low" and

Suppressed local demand, colloquially known as "drive until you qualify," refers to households moving far from where they want to live because of affordability concerns. Now that working from home is more common in white-collar work, those priced out of places such as Toronto and Vancouver are moving as far afield as Montreal and Nova Scotia.

Suppressed household formation refers to people who might want to form independent households but can't because of affordability concerns. This group includes adults who live with their parents and roommates who live together. In 2022, a shortfall of over 400,000 dwellings in Metro Toronto and 130,000 to 200,000 across Metro Vancouver was estimated by comparing the proportion of adults over fifteen who live independently in lower-cost cities like Montreal with those in higher-priced cities.

"moderate" categories, the lowest and second-lowest quintiles. These households require intervention because private market provision may not meet their needs. This is especially true in recent years. Up to 40 percent of Canadians do not have their needs met by market rental and ownership options. Even people in the third income quintile – median-income households – find urban home ownership out of reach. They crowd out lower-income households in the rental market.

Looking at core housing need alone, the Housing Assessment Resource Tools (HART) project analyzed the 1.45 million households in core housing need in the 2021 census by income category and household size. Although some households in core housing need face problems of overcrowding or poor repair, their primary characteristic is the inability to find an adequate, affordable home within their locality. Finding a home for $420/month (the maximum amount a very-low-income household earning 20 percent of Canadian median income can afford) is impossible outside of a rent-geared-to-income nonmarket home. This is true whether you're a single person or a household of five. If you're a larger median-income household in an expensive city, you may also find yourself out of luck if you're looking for a place that costs $2,550 a month in rent or mortgage plus utilities.

All levels of government need to use the standard affordable-housing definition – 30 percent of area median household income – to break down needs and set targets for very-low-income, low-income, moderate-income, and median-income households.

Considering Household Size

According to the 2021 census, 29 percent of private households are one-person, 34 percent are two-person, 15 percent are three-person, 13 percent are four-person, and 8 percent are five-person-plus. But in 2015, only 11 percent of purpose-built rental stock had three or more bedrooms. There's a huge shortage of larger apartments suitable for families. Even assuming many larger households don't live in apartments, a new generation of three-plus-bedroom apartments will be necessary to remedy the family-size home gap for low-, moderate-, and median-income Canadians who can't afford ownership.

Statistics Canada began using the National Occupancy Standard in 1991 as part of the definition of core housing need. It provides a standard of overcrowding based on narrow ideas about families and gender. No more than two people should share a bedroom. Lone parents should have a separate bedroom. Family members aged eighteen and over should have a separate bedroom, except those living as married or common-law couples. Family members under eighteen years of age who are the same sex (not of a different sex) may share a bedroom. Family members under five years of age of a different sex may share a bedroom. There's nothing inherently bad about these standards, but the emphasis on "family" and "nonfamily" households means many households are left out of consideration.

Since the 1980s, there's been a right-wing moral panic about subsidized households being overhoused. Blended stepfamilies are becoming more common: 13 percent of Canadian children live in court-ordered shared-custody arrangements. Boomerang households in which adult children return to their parents' home because of affordability or break-ups are more common. Working from home is possible for up to 40 percent of jobs, leading to inequalities based on the availability of office space (and high-speed internet access). Indigenous families often need accommodation to visit extended family members who come to big cities for medical or educational reasons or to visit reserves for ceremonies or cultural renewal.

Although it wasn't meant for this purpose, the National Occupancy Standard is used to deny accommodation to larger households – new migrant and Indigenous households in particular – and single-parent families. Three-plus-bedroom homes, like every kind of low-cost home, are scarce. A vicious circle of women losing custody of children because of lack of adequate housing then finding it impossible to rent suitable accommodation because they have lost custody is all too common.

In 2021, according to the National Occupancy Standard, most very-low-income households are single people who require only a studio or one-bedroom home. But there are hundreds of thousands of low-income households that require three-plus-bedroom homes for less than $1,050 a month. Until we have more low-cost housing with multiple bedrooms, overcrowding will be unavoidable, and "overcrowding" will continue to be used as an excuse to deny people accommodation. We need a new generation of family-friendly, purpose-built, affordable rentals. Vancouver expects 25 percent of all new rentals to be two-bedroom homes and 10 percent to be three-plus-bedroom homes.

Considering Tenure

Many needs assessments focus on home ownership as a universal goal. But home ownership may not be attainable or even desirable for much of Canada's population. The notion of a housing ladder bears no resemblance to reality for many households.

Almost every housing report at any level of government mentions the housing continuum. According to the CMHC, "housing continuum" denotes a linear progression from homelessness to emergency shelters to transitional housing (none of which are adequate options) to the nirvana of home ownership. The idea that households simply move up a ladder – or rightwards along a continuum from student rental housing, to "affordable" condominiums or townhouses, to "market" ownership of a single-family home – is deeply entrenched in the Canadian psyche and continues to influence policy-makers and developers. In a media release on the 2022 budget, Prime Minister Trudeau promised to "put home ownership in reach for more Canadians" rather than promising an adequate home for all.

As we'll see, many countries with strong renter protections offer better long-term investment options than parking most of your household's assets in a home and expecting its value to rise faster than stocks or bonds. Families with insecure employment or who need to be mobile for work should avoid being tied down by home ownership.

In contrast, the City of Kelowna's wheelhouse model reflects the reality that people's housing needs change over time in a nonlinear fashion. In Kelowna, wildfires and other climate-related disasters have increased the need for emergency shelters and rapid home rebuilding. The city's aging population needs housing with supports such as long-term care. Kelowna is using its wheelhouse analysis to radically change the way it

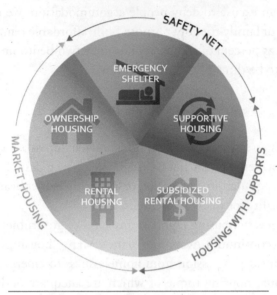

City of Kelowna wheelhouse model

Source: Courtesy of City of Kelowna.

monitors progress and sets income-based targets, including planning permanent nonprofit housing with supports, with senior government support to fill in the gaps.

Considering Priority Populations

Breaking down data by gender, ethnicity, disability, age, and other demographics can reveal patterns of structural inequality. The Canadian government and several provinces and territories have adopted gender-based analysis plus (GBA+), which simply means analyzing the impact of programs on marginalized people.

The CMHC defines twelve groups as priority populations for affordable housing. Although they're not mentioned specifically, women and gender-diverse heads of households (as individuals and single parents) are targeted for a third of funding. Most people don't fall into only one category, and diverse individuals within a household influence housing needs – for instance, one person with mobility impairments within a household requires an accessible home. Furthermore, marginalization

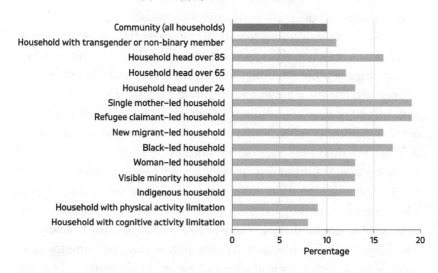

Percentage of households in core housing need by priority population, 2021 census

Priority population	Percentage

(bar chart)

- Community (all households)
- Household with transgender or non-binary member
- Household head over 85
- Household head over 65
- Household head under 24
- Single mother–led household
- Refugee claimant–led household
- New migrant–led household
- Black–led household
- Woman–led household
- Visible minority household
- Indigenous household
- Household with physical activity limitation
- Household with cognitive activity limitation

Percentage (axis: 0, 5, 10, 15, 20)

Source: Housing Assessment Resource Tools project

is intergenerational. For example, I know a Black woman in Vancouver who is married but without children. Her elderly mother, a lifelong low-income renter, lives with her. Finding a secure, accessible two- or three-bedroom rental apartment was increasingly difficult and securing a down payment for a home nearly impossible, even with two professional salaries. Her story reflects the long tail of racism – and ableism – in Canadian society.

Women and children fleeing domestic violence. COVID-19 exacerbated already high levels of violence in Canada. About 50 percent of women reported having at least one experience of physical or sexual violence since the age of sixteen. Most women who face violence in their homes don't access shelters or emergency services such as the police, which makes it difficult to calculate their housing needs. Only 14 percent of the women who leave shelters have access to adequate housing. Women and children fleeing violence may require physical and mental health support services as well as affordable and well-located housing.

Female heads of households and single mothers. In 2016, women led 40 percent of Canadian households. Female-led sole-parent households are almost twice as likely to be in housing need than male-led households: 27 percent versus 16 percent. Single mothers need larger, affordable homes near childcare, schools, and parks and playgrounds.

Seniors. People over sixty-five are the most rapidly growing age group in Canada. A little less than 15 percent of the population is over sixty-five, but by 2041 the proportion may be close to one in four. One-quarter of seniors who live alone are in housing need. They need accessible homes with on-site or nearby health services to age in place. Up to 30 percent of those currently in residential care could be living independently if they had the right health and social supports.

Young adults. Almost one-quarter of young adults aged eighteen to twenty-five who don't live with parents and aren't in postsecondary education are in housing need. Almost three-quarters of the women and 80 percent of gender-diverse young people in core housing need experienced abuse as children. Access to public transit, education, employment services, and health and social services are particularly important for this group.

Indigenous peoples. About 5 percent of the Canadian population self-identifies as Indigenous, and they're one of the fastest-growing populations in Canada. Indigenous peoples experienced a 43 percent population growth between 2006 and 2016. Whether on reserves, in rural and northern areas, or in cities, Indigenous people are much more likely to experience homelessness and inadequate housing.

The 2021 census was the first to investigate housing adequacy on First Nations reserves: the living conditions of almost 120,000 households were counted in core housing need for the first time. Affordability is not the main problem, as in most of Canada. Instead, almost 40 percent of homes are overcrowded or in poor repair, a rate exponentially worse than among non-Indigenous Canadians. At least 48,000 households on reserves need new or substantially improved homes. Bad housing, in turn, forces Indigenous people to move to cities, where they face a greater risk of homelessness.

Indigenous people's homelessness is a direct result of the violence caused by colonial government policy – intergenerational trauma caused by Residential Schools, removing people from their lands and livelihoods, disproportionate imprisonment rates, and climate change, particularly in northern communities. As a result of these policies, Indigenous peoples in Canada experience a high rate of disability (32 percent), twice the national average.

Another form of institutional violence is uncertain jurisdiction when it comes to housing. On-reserve housing is critically underfunded, culturally inappropriate, physically inaccessible, and poorly managed. Off-reserve, non-Indigenous housing services routinely evict Indigenous people if their extended families move in, and they don't provide trauma-informed services. Indigenous seniors are twenty times more likely than non-Indigenous seniors to use emergency shelters. Indigenous children are nine times more likely. One in 15 urban Indigenous people experiences homelessness, as compared to 1 in 128 non-Indigenous people. Indigenous people make up 20 to 50 percent of all homeless people in Canadian cities.

A rights-based approach would be "for Indigenous, by Indigenous," to move from the terrible outcomes provided by non-Indigenous governments and ensure autonomy and increased access to culturally safe housing. Numerous Indigenous-led strategies point the way forward.

Racialized people. The term "racialized" refers to a person or community who faces systemic or other barriers based on racial prejudice. As of the 2021 census, one in four Canadians is of non-European and non-Indigenous origins (4 percent identify as Black), and the proportion is increasing. In 2018, racialized groups were twice as likely to be in housing stress, and during COVID-19, Black and Indigenous people were 2.7 times more likely than nonracialized people to be in rent arrears. The twenty thousand households evicted in Toronto each year are concentrated in predominantly Black neighbourhoods. Few housing providers are by and for racialized Canadians, but Black-managed community land trusts such as Hogan's Alley Society in Vancouver, Black Urbanism Toronto, and Down the Marsh in Nova Scotia show promise.

Recent immigrants, especially refugees. Canada saw the highest number of newcomers (recent immigrants) ever – 1.5 million people – between 2016 and 2021. Almost one-quarter of Canadians are or have been landed immigrants or permanent residents, the highest proportion in post-Confederation history. More than half of these newcomers were admitted under the economic category: people selected for their ability to meet economic needs or create economic opportunities. Smaller proportions – a little over 20 percent each – were admitted under the family-reunification and refugee programs.

Refugees, particularly those not privately sponsored, often struggle to find affordable, suitably sized housing close to mental and physical health services, transit, schools, and places of employment. Across Canada, 14 percent of those using shelters are new migrants, half of whom are asylum seekers. Over 90 percent of asylum seekers end up in big cities, particularly Toronto, Montreal, and Ottawa, where employment, immigration services, and social networks are strong. The lack of low-cost housing (especially for larger households) in these cities hits refugees particularly hard: 40 percent of the people in Toronto shelters, including hundreds of families, self-identify as refugee claimants.

2SLGBTQ+ people. Statistics Canada has been slow to track sexuality and gender identity. A question on gender identity was new to the 2021 census, and although same-sex couples are counted, the census contains no question about sexuality. According to the Canadian Community Health Survey, about 3.3 percent of people self-identify as lesbian, gay, or bisexual, and 0.25 percent identify as transgender or nonbinary. Other research has found that about 10 percent of Canada's population self-identifies as 2SLGBTQ+. Certainly, the proportion of those identifying as 2SLGBTQ+ has increased with each generation. Almost one in three homeless youth identify as 2SLGBTQ+. Older individuals and households also struggle to access affordable and culturally safe homes.

People with physical disabilities. Overall, about 14 percent of the Canadian population has a mobility-related impairment (including chronic illness) that limits their daily activity, and about 18 percent of individuals with a disability are in core housing need. However, these figures don't do justice to the high incidence of disability within very-low-income households: about 45 percent of the chronically homeless have a disability. Lack of access to emergency shelters and low-cost housing has been noted in successive human rights reports. The problem is especially acute for larger households without accessible family-sized apartments. Accessible transit and support services are also important for this group.

People with intellectual or cognitive disabilities and dementia. Between 1 and 3 percent of Canadians live with mild to severe intellectual or cognitive impairments, from autism to developmental disabilities. Among them are at least 13,000 people over the age of thirty who live with their parents and 10,000 people under the age of sixty-five who have been institutionalized in hospitals or long-term care facilities. Most could live in their own homes with adequate support. Many become homeless because of inadequate housing options. A large and growing group of Canadians are living with dementia (25,000 new diagnoses each year). Lack of caregiver support and appropriate low-cost housing options means that many are prematurely hospitalized or placed in long-term care facilities. This segment of the population needs 100,000 more supportive homes.

People with psychosocial disabilities. Around 4 percent of Canadians have severe mental health or addiction issues. They represent almost 50 percent of the homeless. In 2012, the Mental Health Commission called for the creation of 100,000 homes with supports. Between 2012 and 2017, fewer than 3,000 were built. Independent living with adequate supports is the goal of most people with psychosocial disabilities, not life on the streets or in encampments.

Veterans. Veterans became a homelessness-priority group in 2019. Veterans constitute 1.7 percent of the population, a proportion that is expected to decline over time. At least 2.2 percent of the homeless population are veterans, but they constitute a higher proportion (5–7 percent) in some cities.

People who have been incarcerated have not made it into the CMHC's list of priority populations. They're the group with the highest risk of homelessness, but they're almost invisible among policy-makers' concerns. In 2010, the John Howard Society found that of the 363 people jailed in the Greater Toronto Area, almost one-quarter had been homeless prior to incarceration. The average length of incarceration is two months. Almost half said they planned to go to a shelter, live on the street, or couch surf with family or friends after release. The other half didn't know where they'd go; 86 percent expected to be homeless again.

Almost half had severe health impairments. Those who are incarcerated live at the nadir of rights and care.

Considering Location

Canada is an incredibly diverse country bounded by three bodies of water – the Pacific Ocean to the west, the Arctic Ocean to the north, and the Atlantic Ocean to the east. Four types of locations need to be considered in housing policy.

Amenity- and job-rich locations in large cities. Toronto and Vancouver have the worst affordability issues yet continue to attract the most newcomers. They offer employment of all kinds and good-if-overburdened public transit and community services, and top universities and colleges. In the central parts of these cities, people generally live within walking distance of grocery stores, childcare and educational facilities, health services (from pharmacies to hospitals), and parkland. This is more or less true for the other four cities with more than 1 million people: Montreal, Calgary, Edmonton, and Ottawa. It's also true for the twenty-eight middle-tier cities with over 100,000 people. But these areas need to double or triple their housing, particularly for low- to moderate-income young people who want to stay where opportunities are rich.

Spillover suburbs and ex-urban areas. "Drive until you qualify" displacement has enlarged many suburbs and towns near large cities. The fastest-growing municipality between 2016 and 2021 was East Gwillimbury, Ontario, a former agricultural area fifty-six kilometres north of Toronto, near the northernmost interchange of the 404 Highway. It grew by almost 45 percent. The ten most rapidly growing municipalities have similar profiles: they are low-density and car-dependent with low- and moderate-income households. They need affordable housing, but they have huge infrastructure and amenity shortages, ranging from transit to schools. They lack the capacity and experience to steer housing outcomes.

East Gwillimbury, for instance, is in the York Region. The region has had responsibility for social and supportive housing since the late 1990s but is in the process of deamalgamating. Simcoe County, former "cottage country" for Toronto, now has a core housing need of one in seven households, the same as Toronto. Barrie, a city of 150,000 located ninety kilometres north of Toronto, has planning services but has still seen the emergence of encampments. Spillover cities and regions need help with housing strategies and nonmarket housing, especially near commuter transit hubs.

Declining and peripheral areas. Between 2016 and 2021, over one in five communities with a population of over five thousand declined. These communities are mostly located in provinces affected by fluctuations in resource extraction. For instance, Alberta's Athabasca region's population declined 11.6 percent from 2016 to 2021. Many smaller municipalities – in the Atlantic provinces and the Prairies, especially – rely on tourist dollars, but service workers are squeezed out by vacation homes, short-term rentals, and households telecommuting because big cities are too expensive.

For instance, in 2021 Victoria County on the east coast of Cape Breton Island, Nova Scotia, had a population of 7,000. Among them were 255 very-low- and low-income households in core housing need. One-fifth of those households, all single people, required homes with monthly costs of less than $343. In July 2023, Baddeck, the county's sole centre, listed only one room at $600/month. Short-term "vacation rentals" were listed for $600 or more per week. The town's lobster restaurants, souvenir shops, and hotels find it hard to retain staff. These regions need provincial and territorial help to develop housing strategies and nonmarket housing.

Northern and Indigenous communities. Core housing need is higher in Yukon and Northwest Territories than in any province other than British Columbia. In Nunavut, a jaw-dropping one in three households lives in inadequate housing. Housing is much more expensive to build in the North. A home in northern Quebec costs three times as much to build as a house in Montreal. Materials and fuel are difficult to transport, especially in the Eastern Arctic, where there are few roads. Short building seasons are exacerbated by shortages of skilled labour. Foundations and infrastructure are affected by permafrost melting and rising sea levels rising. Communities are tiny, and the federal government has not adequately coordinated or funded housing policy. Inadequate housing and services combined with a lack of educational or job opportunities on reserve force Indigenous people to move to cities.

In 2018, at the time of the launch of the National Housing Strategy, Indigenous organizations created an integrated Urban, Rural and

Northern Indigenous Housing Strategy. It estimated $2.5 billion would be needed annually to meet urgent repair and new building needs. The cost has since blown to $4.3 billion a year. However, the federal government waited until the 2023 budget to announce $4 billion over seven years, starting in 2024–25, a far cry from the $6.3 billion over two years (starting in 2022) recommended by the National Housing Council. In 2023, Indigenous organizations, tired of waiting, created National Indigenous Collaborative Housing Incorporated (NICHI) to support essential needs across the country, but especially in the North. They demanded and received a small amount of start-up money from the federal government to build national capacity. Factory-built housing that can be transported easily would be especially useful in these regions.

The Dream of a Common Language Leading to Effective Action

The science of needs assessments has been well established since the mid-twentieth century. It underpinned successful housing programs in many countries, including Singapore and Sweden.

Unfortunately, Canada has gone backwards in its ability to assess its citizens' needs. The government has stepped away from consistent definitions, income categories, and analysis of trends – the hallmark of needs assessments from the 1940s to the 1980s. The rot starts at the top and extends outwards: the provinces, territories, regions, and municipalities all use different definitions of affordability, monitor different indicators, and ignore population growth and change.

Current "core housing need" statistics don't include most of the people in inadequate housing or at risk of homelessness. These priority populations include the incarcerated, students, migrant agricultural workers, and people in congregate housing such as long-term care and group homes. People locked out of adequately sized and priced homes with the right services in the right locations range from those with cognitive disabilities to families with young children in large cities.

The federal government must provide rights-based data to provinces, territories, regions, and municipalities so that every person "counts." This process would start with analyses that focus housing policy on the people most affected by its failures. It would continue with targets based on income, household size, and priority populations, keeping in mind population growth and change. The targets would be monitored annually. Good data is only the start, but in Canada, we're still just starting.

5

Can Canada End Homelessness?

To address shortfalls dating back to the 1970s, Canada needs to almost triple its housing supply. What if – radical idea alert – we started with the homes most needed by the people who need them the most? What if we started down the road to realizing the right to adequate housing by setting a goal: eradicating chronic homelessness in ten years and attaining **functional zero homelessness** in thirty years? What if we started by creating 200,000 homes with supports for people with cognitive, mental, developmental, and physical disabilities? What if we, as a nation, addressed the inadequate income part of the equation and provided incomes that allowed housing providers to cover operating costs? Let's look at a country that has done just that.

Finland's Housing First Model

During and immediately after the Second World War, Finland was invaded by Germany and the Soviet Union, forced to pay war reparations to the latter, and experienced an influx of over 400,000 Finnish refugees from Karelia, annexed by the Soviets. When neighbouring Sweden wrapped up its Million Programme in 1974, tens of thousands of Finnish households still lived in bomb shelters, refugee barracks, or overcrowded self-built homes.

Yet Finland is the country that has come closest to ending chronic homelessness and reliance on emergency shelters. Since 2008, it has

Functional zero homelessness: a milestone at which episodes of being without permanent shelter are rare (less than 0.01 percent of a community), short (no more than three days), and nonrecurrent (they don't end up without a home again).

fostered a growing political consensus that **Housing First** is the right moral and economic choice. All political parties are committed to housing for all, and evidence-based policy has supported remarkable outcomes.

The housing model had some precedents. The City of Helsinki started to produce housing for seniors and some low-income families in the 1960s. It also encouraged neighbourhoods with a mix of people – renters and homeowners of different incomes. In the late 1980s, when the economy benefited from the global technology boom through companies such as Nokia, Helsinki produced an ambitious plan for the national government to fund land acquisition and new mixed-tenure housing. The government rejected the proposal, but it became the focus of a metropolitan strategy and, eventually, Finnish policy. As we'll also see in Vienna, sometimes great national ideas come from municipal action.

In 1987, Finland's right-of-centre government set a goal to end homelessness. It began with an annual survey of people accessing homelessness services, including emergency shelters: 1,370 homeless families, mostly doubled up in apartments, and 17,110 single homeless persons, half of

The **Housing First** model was developed in New York City by expatriate Canadian Sam Tsemberis. Simply put, it houses people without permanent homes and provides supports to keep them housed. The **staircase model,** by contrast, requires homeless people to "progress" through mental health or addiction treatments in shelters or transitional housing before being "rewarded" with a permanent home.

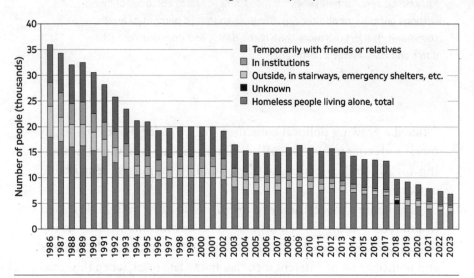

Finland's annual homelessness "census" shows the impact of coordinated government policy

Source: ARA (Housing Finance and Development Centre of Finland), *Homeless People 2022*, Report 2/2023.

whom were sleeping rough or in institutions such as psychiatric hospitals or emergency shelters. During the early 1990s recession, the government subsidized rental construction as an economic stimulus. Some units were earmarked for nonmarket housing. By 1994, the number of people accessing emergency shelters and sleeping rough had been halved. But progress on finding homes for unsheltered individuals had stalled before Housing First became policy.

Before 2008, Finland, like Canada, relied on the **staircase model**. But that year, a group of Finnish experts published a report called "Name on the Door," which argued that eliminating homelessness required a model "where a person does not have to first change their life around in order to earn the basic right to housing. Instead, a ... dwelling is the foundation on which the rest of life is put back together."

In Housing First, a person is offered a low-cost rental home with or without on-site services. They have the right to choose services and supports. The home is theirs for as long as they want it. They pay rent, subsidized by much more generous welfare benefits than in Canada, and

Home Truths

they have the same rights as other tenants. The program is based on a multisectoral partnership that includes the national government, the Association of Finnish Local and Regional Authorities, Finland's five most populous cities, the Evangelical Lutheran Church, the Red Cross, the Confederation of Finnish Construction Industries, the construction trade union, and the Finnish Association of Mental Health. In other words, every potential contributor to the solution has a seat at the table, with leadership from the national government.

Cost-benefit analyses showed that for every homeless person placed in a home with support services, there was an annual savings of CAD$22,000 from money not spent on emergency shelters and institutions, police, and health services.

A Housing First approach requires low-cost housing. The Housing Finance and Development Centre (ARA), which is similar to Canada's CMHC, provides funding to local governments and nonmarket providers to purchase land and create new homes, including purpose-built supportive-housing projects. It also provides funding to purchase existing apartments within larger developments for use as low-cost nonmarket housing. Helsinki has a target of 6,000 new homes a year, a quarter of them nonmarket homes. It's also planning a new harbourfront development called Kalasatama, which will have 20,000 new homes by 2040.

Emergency shelters are converted into permanent housing once better alternatives have been developed. In 1985, Helsinki had 2,121 shelter and hostel beds; by 2016, that number had shrunk to 52. Meanwhile, the number of supportive-housing units grew from 127 to 1,309, and independent rental apartments for homeless people increased from 65 to 2,433. The last big shelter in Helsinki, run by the Salvation Army, had 250 beds. It was renovated in 2012 with a grant from the ARA. It now contains 81 self-enclosed apartments with on-site support staff.

Housing First can't be separated from other aspects of Finnish housing policy. Finland's definition of homelessness is far more extensive than Canada's. It encompasses people temporarily staying with friends and relatives (what in Canada would be considered couch surfing or hidden homelessness) and people in institutions who could be in community-based homes with supports. The ARA's annual standardized count, taken on November 15 each year, engages 209 of 295 municipalities.

Municipalities that don't participate receive no housing funding, but they're mostly very small municipalities.

Finland has a housing policy program with elements that work: annual monitoring with clear targets for up to thirty-five years, top-down planning and financing from the national government combined with bottom-up innovation and land policy from local governments and non-market providers, and a broad-based partnership approach. Whoever is in power, at whatever level of government, has the same goal: adequate housing with an emphasis on those most in need. In Finland, we see the right to housing in action.

Homelessness as an Income Challenge

In contrast to Finland and Sweden, welfare in Canada is a recipe for homelessness. Across Canada, as of the 2021 census, very low-income households, mostly on social assistance, can afford shelter costs of no more than $420 a month. That's not enough to cover the operating costs of any home, market or nonmarket. The inability of welfare and minimum wage to keep up with housing-cost inflation means that governments need to either increase basic income or provide ongoing subsidies through rent supplements.

Canada undertook a "natural experiment" during COVID-19. Core housing need dropped by 250,000 households between the 2016 and 2021 censuses. The drop wasn't because of housing policy. Rather, it resulted from emergency benefits, predominantly the Canada Emergency Response Benefit (CERB). Statistics Canada acknowledged the "CERB bump": "For the 10 percent of renters with the lowest household incomes, their average household income grew by over two-thirds." CERB was $500 a week, less than half the average income of $59,300. But social assistance for a single person in Ontario is $168 a week.

The positive impact of federal emergency income support – rapidly instituted, easy to apply for, more generous than provincial and territorial welfare – suggests that a national guaranteed livable income would help solve many housing, health, and educational inequalities. The Senate produced a report to that effect in 2020. An annual cost of $76 billion

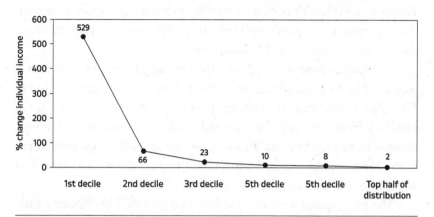

Change in individual incomes between 2019 and 2020, or the CERB bump

Source: Craig E. Jones, Housing Assessment Resource Tools project

would be more than made up for by increased health and productivity, not to mention respect for human rights and viable affordable housing.

The federal government could ensure through bilateral agreements linked to health and social transfers that provinces and territories provide welfare adequate to meet basic needs such as a roof over one's head and food in one's mouth. But even if welfare was doubled or tripled to bring individuals up to the low-income cut-off of 50 percent of the province's median income, we'd still lack a sufficient supply of homes at rents of about $1,000 a month.

Homelessness as a Health Challenge

The relationship between health, disability, and homelessness is circular. An increasing number of individuals and families are homeless simply because they don't have access to affordable housing. But people with disabilities are more likely to have barriers to employment and adequate homes. And being homeless greatly increases the risk of developing poor physical and mental health, including addictions. That's why on-site health and social supports are often necessary to keep people in homes, especially people frequently homeless who move between health and correctional institutions, emergency shelters, and sleeping outdoors. People in poor health need help staying on medications, avoiding overdoses, getting warm meals, and reuniting with family or friends. That's the service component of Housing First.

The federal government tested the Housing First approach. And it worked. But the program was abandoned. From 2009 to 2013, At Home/Chez Soi – a rigorously evaluated, five-city, $110 million project, the world's largest – engaged two thousand moderate- and high-needs homeless participants. They had all lived, on average, without a permanent home for five years. All had a diagnosed mental illness, and most had addictions and chronic physical health issues.

The participants were divided into two groups. The "housing first" group received a subsidized home, either through nonmarket or market rental, and had a choice of supportive services, ranging from mental health to physical health to social support. Each individual was characterized as either "high needs" or "moderate needs" and received appropriate support. By contrast, the "treatment as usual" group could access existing housing and support services in their communities.

Eighteen months later, the "housing first" group retained housing at twice the rate as the "treatment as usual" group. Every $10.00 invested in Housing First services resulted in an average savings of $21.72 because of lower costs for psychiatric hospital stays, general hospital stays, jail or prison terms, police contacts, emergency room visits, and emergency shelter stays.

The program worked, but the federal government didn't expand upon it or even continue it. It passed the buck to provincial governments. The most active province, Alberta, refused to address the issue of affordable housing supply and limited homes to the most "deserving."

This highlights the difference between a narrow definition of Housing First used in At Home/Chez Soi and the more comprehensive approach used in Finland. Finland's program includes some scattered market rental homes, but new purpose-built supportive housing is the norm, particularly for people with mental health or addiction issues who require on-site support. In contrast, At Home/Chez Soi was developed as a mental health intervention. Creating new housing supply was not part of its mandate.

A decade after At Home/Chez Soi, women's homelessness service providers in Montreal and its affordable-housing office are still bitter about the pilot program. Social workers had to spend most of their days driving to pay short visits to scattered sites. Conditions in the market housing were poor, and tenants were evicted after the housing subsidy provided by the pilot ended. And the program's emphasis on chronic homelessness (on the street or in shelters for more than six months) excluded women living in unsafe accommodation but not "on the street."

Housing First, in its original New York City version, is not an upstream approach. It only helps people who have been homeless for a long period, with all the physical and mental damage homelessness causes. Finland has refined its Housing First approach to emphasize preventing homelessness through mechanisms such as rent banks – short-term loans to tenants threatened by eviction. It focuses on those in common entry points to homelessness: being discharged from an institution (a prison, jail, hospital, or mental health or addictions facility); escaping partner or family violence; exiting children and youth services; and new arrivals such as asylum seekers. The program certainly doesn't wait six months until people are labelled "chronically homeless." Most importantly, it has created a stock of nonmarket housing with long-term cost savings.

Coordination and Information

At Home/Chez Soi's successor initiative – Built for Zero – is supported by the federal government's Reaching Home: Canada's Homelessness Strategy. The aim of Built for Zero is to work toward functional zero homelessness. Instead of relying on annual point-in-time counts, Built for Zero uses by-name lists – real-time lists of all known people experiencing homelessness (unsheltered, in emergency shelters, or in temporary housing such as doubling up with family or friends). These lists are maintained by a system coordinator who is part of the local government or a service agency who aggregates information with shelters, health and social service organizations, the police, and housing providers. By-name lists support coordinated access. They prioritize services at the household level and are based on knowledge of homelessness at the system level.

They can be used to evaluate the impact of programs, for advocacy, and to set reliable homelessness counts.

But only forty communities with populations over 5,000 have signed on to Built for Zero. And the program prioritizes veterans experiencing chronic homelessness, because they're "a small and well-defined population ... and an area with clear federal accountability." Built for Zero does not have Finland's coordinated, inclusive, and comprehensive approach.

Medicine Hat, Alberta, a city of 63,000 people, in March 2021 became the first Canadian city to achieve functional zero homelessness. In 2009, the city created a five-year plan, the first step in its commitment to end homelessness. Since then, more than 1,675 people have been housed, including 424 children. The intake form used in its Built for Zero approach isn't onerous or retraumatizing: it focuses on the last permanent residence, whether the household has pets, and physical or mental health issues. The city's 2019 progress report found that it costs between $12,000 and $34,000 annually to provide housing and support per individual; by contrast, the cost of providing resources to people on the street can cost up to $120,000 a year.

Medicine Hat has only one permanent supportive-housing project with thirty homes, so the municipal coordinator works with market landlords. The task was easier in 2009 when Medicine Hat's rental vacancy rate was 10 percent, not 2.4 percent as it was in 2021. In late 2021, when COVID-19 relief measures ended and rents increased, homelessness numbers began to rise. As they say in Finland, you can't have Housing First without housing, first.

Creating Housing

The City of Vancouver, assisted by the BC government, has taken an ambitious approach to creating permanent supportive housing: promote affordability by upgrading inadequate single-room occupancy hotels and creating new modular housing.

Single-room occupancy hotels date from the early twentieth century, when resource workers such as loggers or miners needed temporary accommodation during the off-season. In 2017, 7,000 units remained as "housing of last resort" for low-income households, mostly in the Downtown Eastside. About 4,000 of them were privately owned. The rooms are small, bathrooms and kitchens are shared, and the conditions are generally grossly inadequate, including risk of fire, violence, and exploitation (sometimes by market landlords who double as pimps). Upgrading these hotels while keeping rents affordable was considered impossible without senior government investment. Many tenants have mental and physical health needs and require supportive housing. Private hotels were at risk of being demolished or redeveloped as high-income studio suites.

Between 2007 and 2009, BC Housing purchased thirteen hotels with about 1,000 units and renovated them over the next decade. They required extensive renovations. Tenants were provided with alternative accommodation and support services, and they had the "right of return" to tiny studio units of twenty square metres with their own bathrooms and kitchenettes. The buildings were turned over to nonmarket supportive-housing providers, who agreed to manage them for the next fifteen years, including maintenance costs.

As with At Home/Chez Soi, the initiative didn't expand beyond this effort. Six thousand single-occupancy hotel units continue to have minimal staffing in overcrowded, unsafe buildings; people "choose" encampments over living in these hotels or emergency shelters.

Vancouver's experiment with temporary modular housing has a better record. With only $1.5 million from the CMHC and $3 million in municipal funds, the city piloted a factory-built, quickly erected, three-storey, forty-unit studio building on a downtown site intended for later development. The temporary building had a ten-year free lease on government land.

Impressed with the speed of construction (less than six months from permit to move in) and the quality of design, the BC government committed $66 million toward building 600 more units in Vancouver: $111,000 per studio or one-bedroom apartment. It exceeded the target in three years because of city land and funding, provincial capital funding and operational support, and inexpensive and replicable designs. As of April 2020, there were 663 units on ten sites. One of the sites is operated by an Indigenous provider with culturally adequate services; others engage both Indigenous and Black community services. The BC government rolled the idea out across the province to build 2,000 homes by 2022. The program inspired the CMHC's 2020 Rapid Housing Initiative, which included 250 modular homes in Toronto.

This is a rare Canadian example of ongoing learning and improvement making a good idea better. Vancouver's original building on Terminal Avenue had minimal common space, no support services, and no elevator. The studio apartments were only about twenty-four square metres, and accessible units were limited to the ground floor. Later buildings were four storeys with an elevator. The accessible design allowed for a first floor devoted to common spaces and offices for support services. The total number of homes varies between thirty and fifty, depending on the number of one-bedroom homes for couples, and the size of studios has increased to thirty square metres. The modular construction company, NRB Modular Solutions, adopted this building prototype for Ontario. There's nothing temporary about the housing other than its location on government-owned land slated for redevelopment. While built to last, modular housing can be easily taken down and rebuilt or modified to make larger homes, as was the case in Sweden.

But there's another lesson here: the five-year lease of one of Vancouver's first modular apartment buildings expired, and the building sits on land slated for the new Vancouver Art Gallery. Although the "temporary" land-use designation can make homes possible, it can also lead to the displacement of low-income tenants to locations with fewer resources. Modular supportive housing should be built on sites intended for permanent use.

The Vancouver-based planning and engagement consultancy Happy City worked with residents and workers in several modular buildings to develop recommendations on design and programming for these spaces. Although they recognized that communal spaces take away interior space that could be used for desperately needed housing, their discussions reinforced Walter Firey's conclusions in 1948: when private spaces are small, shared spaces are essential. When a hot meal is shared in a communal setting, a large kitchen and combined dining or meeting room offer a vital site of social interaction and nutrition for isolated single people. Outdoor spaces, even if they're as simple as raised garden beds or benches, are as important to mental health as they are to physical health. Particularly in Indigenous housing, one unit should be set aside for visiting families, and larger three-bedroom homes would help parents seeking to regain custody of their children. Smaller or flexible communal spaces in separately ventilated rooms that won't trigger fire alarms might be necessary for healing ceremonies such as smudging.

McCurdy Place in Kelowna, British Columbia, includes forty-five studio and four one-bedroom homes. One floor is set aside for young people aging out of foster care. Operated by the local branch of the Canadian Mental Health Association, it's supportive housing with a barrier to entry: no drugs are allowed, and tenants must commit to "recovery." On the day I visited, the front office was distributing bus tickets and lollipops, lasagna was on the menu, and the outdoor seating area had several smokers. (I had to wait for a smoking shift change to avoid photographing people.) The youth hangout room on the second floor was colourful, but folks were gathered for a sad occasion. One of the young people had recently died of an off-site overdose. Residents were creating a memorial poster.

Like many newly built homes, supportive housing often looks institutional, and many residents have had traumatic experiences in institutions. But it only takes a bit of money and adequate staffing to add pops of colour, paint doors to personalize them, add a message board, and consult with residents about activities, food, and their concerns. Unfortunately, the BC government has fallen behind on staffing supportive housing, including the new modular buildings. It's difficult to attract and retain staff for low-barrier housing because of the frequency of drug overdoses. But if tenancy agreements specify no drug use or limit visitors, these activities will simply move to less safe places, as was the case with the young person from McCurdy Place.

At Home/Chez Soi and British Columbia's experiments with renovating single-occupancy hotels and modular housing are examples of successful "pilot" projects that saved lives and money but were abandoned before they became scaled up to end homelessness. A fourth recent example of this start-stop approach is the Rapid Housing Initiative. Announced as COVID-era emergency funding and intended to address overcrowding in shelters, the federal program provided funding to

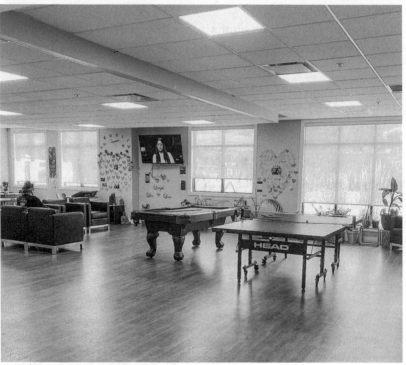

FACING PAGE
McCurdy Place, exterior (*top*) and common room/ dining area (*bottom*).

McCurdy Place's youth space with social worker (*right*) and outdoor area (*bottom*).

municipalities and Indigenous communities to use their land to create low-income housing in less than a year (18 months in rural and northern areas). A high proportion of the projects used factory-built modular housing.

The Rapid Housing Initiative was the only National Housing Strategy supply-side program to target people who were homeless or had very low income. In three rounds of funding (2020, 2021, and 2022), $3.5 billion was designated to build 14,500 homes – 30 percent for women and gender-diverse individuals or household heads and 41 percent for Indigenous peoples. However, only 1,500 homes had been completed by January 2023, two years after the first round was awarded for 4,000 homes. Onerous local public consultation requirements led to delays (one project in Toronto was held up for over three years by an ultimately unsuccessful appeal by a NIMBY group), and the provinces' reluctance to fund on-site services and provide adequate welfare caused budget shortfalls. The program also lacked long-term, stable funding.

At a Rapid Housing Initiative–funded building in London, Ontario, Indwell, a religious-based supportive housing developer, provides one hot meal a day plus medications and addictions support to high-needs tenants who live in sixty-six one-bedroom homes. These services require on-site staff twenty-four seven. Some tenants spent decades in institutional settings and rely heavily on staff interaction because they have no contact with friends or family. Other tenants, with less acute needs, live there because the rents are geared to their excessively low incomes on social assistance. This mix makes it essential to have high levels of support along with private, self-contained homes with no-cost amenities such as parks and libraries nearby. The homes aren't sufficiently subsidized to peg rent to income, so a base rent of $500 per month subsumes more than 50 percent of some people's income, leaving little money to hang out in a coffee shop, let alone see a movie or take public transit to work or see a family member.

Despite these limitations, after eighteen months, rates of severe mental illness and addictions among the tenants decreased to moderate levels. A report on the Indwell initiative ends with four simple recommendations:

- The province should increase welfare to levels that cover rent.
- The federal government should create a purpose-built supportive-housing building stream in the National Housing Strategy, based on the short-term Rapid Housing Initiative.
- A federal-provincial agreement should ensure adequate levels of on-site staff support.
- Specialized addictions and mental health counselling, in addition to more generalized tenant support, needs to be adequately funded.

Supportive Housing for the Elderly

Assisted living for older people – including "retirement homes" with on-site services and nursing or long-term care homes with twenty-four-hour care – are part of the continuum of supportive housing. Without adequate and affordable housing, seniors with declining cognitive and physical health may end up in hospitals or even prisons. Canada's population is aging. The grey wave will require nearly a quarter million new seniors' living spaces by 2046. Without a lot of new supportive homes, these seniors will face homelessness and dangerously inadequate living conditions.

Like other forms of health care and social services, living conditions for seniors fall to the provincial and territorial governments, and they've signally failed to uphold the rights to health and housing. Nonmarket long-term care homes are operated by municipalities and service organizations. But the expansion of market-based seniors' housing has been exponential, particularly in Ontario. In 1997, the first seniors-housing **real estate investment trust (REIT)** launched with twelve homes. By 2020, financialized market firms controlled about 28 percent of seniors' housing in Canada, including 17 percent of long-term care homes and 38 percent of retirement homes. In Ontario, for-profit companies own 54 percent of long-term-care beds, which had 73 percent of deaths in COVID's first wave. Nonmarket homes, by contrast, had 20 percent of beds but only 6 percent of deaths. Financialized firms that advertised high yields to investors had death rates five times higher than nonmarket homes. In response, the federal government stepped in with national standards for long-term care. Health transfer payments to the provinces (for facility improvements and staffing) were linked to resident ratios. Supportive housing is an inappropriate place for market providers focused on profit.

The dementia village concept, pioneered in the Netherlands in 2009, is a model of safe and culturally appropriate housing for seniors. The Hogewyck Dementia Village has twenty-three houses for 152 seniors. The village has a bar, restaurant, theatre, grocery store, and streets and gardens. It's publicly funded and runs on a budget comparable to conventional long-term care homes.

In Comox, British Columbia, a dementia village inspired by Hogewyck is under construction on the site of a former hospital. Funded by BC Housing, Together by the Sea will have 156 individual rooms in clusters of twelve, each with a bathroom and kitchen area. The complex is replacing an older and much more institutional centre. A large enclosed courtyard with planter boxes will allow for freedom of movement but will prevent residents from wandering off. The cluster concept allows residents to help with food preparation and laundry. A childcare centre is also planned to promote intergenerational mixing (and better services for staff). The site may eventually have other nonmarket affordable-housing options for seniors with fewer needs, making it a more complete community.

Long-term care is a difficult issue for many people. Like services for people with mental health and addictions, or housing for former prisoners, it can elicit discomfort, which all too often translates into opposition. But safe and dignified homes for all people have been neglected for far too long, creating huge unmet deficits. Supportive housing is where the rubber hits the road when it comes to financialization. Should housing for the most vulnerable members of our society be a site for profit maximization?

What Would It Take to End Homelessness?

Homelessness is, in its most basic form, the absence of a home. But it's impossible to look at ending homelessness without considering two other aspects of a basic social safety net: income and health care. A systems approach to ending homelessness must consider how much income it takes to pay for housing and how much money is left over for basics such as food and transportation. It accepts that some people need support to access and retain their homes, meaning that on-site health and social-support services are part of low-cost housing. Finally, it enables coordination to meet the often complex needs of people without homes.

To end homelessness, Canada would need

- to commit to a target of 200,000 new or renovated deeply affordable supportive homes over the next decade
- to systematize the Rapid Housing Initiative by including agreements with provincial governments for income and health- and social-service supports at a rate of ten tenants per support worker (for those with the greatest needs)
- to use land leased from all levels of government
- to ensure that initiatives are, at minimum, 20 percent "for Indigenous, by Indigenous"
- to provide permanent housing, as some people (especially seniors, those with cognitive disabilities, and some people with mental illness) have chronic support needs
- to have very-low-cost options without in-house supports so that people who recover aren't returned to homelessness.

For people who are not in the paid workforce because of disability or other barriers, social assistance incomes are simply not enough to cover the operating costs of an adequate home. Canada as a nation has two income choices:

1 A guaranteed living income for all provided by the federal government in lieu of transfers to provinces or territories. The Canadian Senate estimated this would cost $67 billion a year in 2020.
2 Adequate social assistance, including housing benefits, provided by the provinces and territories as a condition of social and health transfer payments from the federal government.

Even with a guaranteed living income equal to 50 percent of an area's median income, there would still be a need for supportive housing for people with disabilities and addictions. Supportive housing is far less expensive than emergency shelters or incarceration. And a by-name list approach to preventing and addressing homelessness should be a condition of transfer payments to the municipalities. If municipalities are willing to provide service and housing benefits but the provinces are not, perhaps housing and health support could be paid by the federal government and clawed back from provincial health transfers in a transparent and accountable fashion.

With these strategies and measures, ending homelessness is possible. But it requires political will.

6

Why Start with Nonmarket Housing?

There's a reason why the 1944 Curtis Report said one-third of new homes should be public housing and another third rent-regulated or cooperative. Today, about 3 million very-low- and low-income households need homes for less than $1,000 a month (in 2021 dollars). For almost a century in Canada (and longer elsewhere) it has been acknowledged that profit-oriented developments can't produce adequate housing for low-income people as efficiently as nonmarket housing. At some point, some level of government will need to step in and provide more generous and plentiful rent supplements or directly support low-cost supply (or both). But the evidence is clear: subsidies are much less efficient than direct support for nonmarket housing.

Affordable housing is critical infrastructure, much like hospitals, schools, libraries, public transit, sewer lines, or bridges. The same concerns about public-private partnerships arise again and again: Should the emphasis be on social return on investment or profits for private investors and developers? If we want to prioritize energy-efficient, accessible, innovative choices, why not fund them directly and let them be the essential cornerstones of communities? Would scaling up nonmarket housing to a third of all new construction set the bar for the housing we need? Other places have done just that. Vienna has a one-hundred-year history of directly building affordable housing, with a huge social return on investment.

Vienna: A Century of Innovative Nonmarket Housing

Like Singapore following independence, Vienna was a disaster in 1920. The population had grown from 440,000 residents in 1840 to 2 million people by 1919. Even before the First World War, most Viennese households lived in overcrowded, poorly ventilated tenement blocks. Ninety-five percent of apartments didn't have indoor toilets or running water. One in four one-room apartments contained six or more people, and the beds were often rented out in shifts. By the end of the war, 90,000 people were homeless, sleeping in former hospitals and military barracks. Mortality rates were three times greater in low-income than in high-income districts (much like we see a ten-year life expectancy difference between districts in Vancouver today). Tuberculosis, an infectious lung disease endemic in overcrowded housing, was called the Vienna Disease.

But out of the chaos associated with the end of an Austro-Hungarian Empire came an opportunity for radical change. Vienna became an autonomous state in the new nation of Austria, and a social democratic government was elected in 1919 (a social democratic government has been re-elected, with one ten-year interruption in 1934, for over a century). It embarked on an ambitious housing strategy. As in Singapore, Vienna's housing policy led to a healthy, prosperous society and remarkable political stability.

The government put a progressive levy on property wealth and earmarked revenues for large-scale residential construction. The levy was 2 percent of prewar rent for low-income residents and up to 37 percent of the value of luxury estates. Eighty percent of lower-income households contributed only 20 percent of the levy, while the wealthiest 0.5 percent of households contributed 45 percent of the total. A luxury food tax replaced a regressive grocery tax, and levies were placed on events such as balls and horse races. Unused land was also heavily taxed. The city-owned developer was named Wohnfonds Wien (Vienna Housing Fund) in recognition of the central role municipal finance would play in the development of nonmarket homes.

Vienna used the funds to purchase vacant lands or lands with substandard tenements. In 1920, it owned 5,487 hectares; by the end of the decade, it controlled 2.6 million hectares, about a third of the built-up area. This was a wise move since local and foreign property speculators were interested in Viennese real estate. A mission-oriented landowner got there first.

Viennese residents were already building their own homes in allotment gardens and unclaimed lands. Brickworks and door and window manufacturers contracted with the city to supply building materials. A strong tradition of cooperative development emerged from these practices.

From the beginning, Vienna's goals included design excellence and community development alongside affordability. And the city had an ambitious building target: 25,000 new public homes between 1923 and 1928, alongside private development. Over two hundred architects worked on public housing during the 1920s, some on up to forty different projects.

Vienna met its target by 1927 and set a second five-year target of 30,000 homes. For a decade, the Viennese housing authority built 5,000 to 6,000 homes per year (the equivalent of 120,000 a year in Canada today). It's a myth that the city only "allowed" nonmarket housing. Its nonmarket housing catered to low- and moderate-income households, many of whom would have been homeless otherwise. Market homes simply had to compete.

Building on an existing apartment typology, Vienna perfected an architectural model called the superblock. Most Wohnfonds Wien complexes joined together smaller apartment buildings of between three and nine storeys. They had hundreds of homes but usually fewer than a dozen per entranceway. The Karl-Marx-Hof consists of almost one hundred "point access" blocks of five to six apartments, each separated by soundproof fire walls, along a 1,100-metre facade (yes, a kilometre of joined-up apartments). Apartment buildings were generally arranged around large courtyards, with communal laundries, bathhouses, libraries, childcare centres, meeting rooms, educational workshops, health centres, sports halls, libraries, and workshops at the base. Housing built to support US industrial women workers during the Second World War and Toronto's St. Lawrence neighbourhood were both inspired by the Vienna model. Designers understood that single women needed to work outside the home and viewed child and elder care as a collective domestic responsibility.

A new development in Vienna showing the influence
of "superblock" thinking – joined up separate apartments
linked by an interior courtyard.

By the end of the first phase (1920–34), about 200,000 people, 10
percent of Vienna's population, lived in public housing. And public
housing was universalist: 80 percent of the population, all but the highest income quintile, could apply. Those who were homeless or lived in
extremely unaffordable, overcrowded, or poorly repaired homes took
precedence. Most of these people were industrial workers. They paid

only for operating, maintenance, and administrative costs, and their rents were 5 to 8 percent of an industrial worker's wage. The apartments were very small: 75 percent were 38 square metres and consisted of an entrance-way, kitchen, bedroom, and toilet but no bath or shower. About 25 percent were 45 square metres and had a small second bedroom. (For context: In London today, the current minimum size for a new studio apartment is 37 square metres.)

After the Second World War, the population decreased to 1.5 million, and construction picked up to a steady rate of 4,200 new public homes a year. The size of apartments increased to today's average of 75 square metres (equivalent to a small three-bedroom flat). The tradition of public art on walls and in gardens continued, as did the integration of public transit into new developments. Architectural innovation abounded. The whimsical Hundertwasser House, completed in 1986, consisted of 52 apartments with 250 bushes and trees incorporated into its colourful facade. The development quickly became one of the city's top tourist attractions, with over 1 million visitors a year. Factory-built modular con-struction, the hallmark of Swedish public housing, was also extensively used in Vienna. Most importantly, the certainty of long-term and consist-ent planning rules and financing, combined with public ownership of the land, kept costs and rents low.

There are many lessons to learn from Vienna. First, the city's example shows the long-term advantage of a supply-side infrastructure approach. After the Second World War, the city charged a 1 percent payroll-based housing tax, and employers and employees contributed equally. Rents were set to cover costs, including routine maintenance and energy or accessibility upgrades. If costs were over 25 percent of a household's in-come, rent was subsidized further. Wohnfonds Wien's current budget is CAD\$650 million per year, and its payroll-based subsidy is offset by cost-based rents. It has enough funding to renovate older buildings on a thirty-year timeline and to create about 4,000 municipal and 10,000 other nonmarket (mostly cooperative) homes a year for a population of 2 mil-lion. Austria, with 23 percent nonmarket housing, pays less per capita for affordable housing than New Zealand, which has traditionally relied on demand-size housing subsidies and has less than 4 percent nonmarket housing.

Second, Vienna demonstrates the importance of long-term targets. Wohnfonds Wien consistently maintained multiyear targets for non-market homes within its overall annual housing targets. This long-term strategy is still evolving. To maintain its current proportion of 60 percent nonmarket housing, in 2019 the city's planning department created a "subsidized housing" zoning overlay on (1) residential construction in all former industrial or commercial areas, (2) when density is being increased in residential or mixed-use zones, or (3) on high-rises over ten storeys. In these zones, at least two-thirds of all floor space must be nonmarket housing. As the Vienna housing commissioner states in the 2018–19 housing annual report, "Just as the state is responsible for educational or healthcare facilities or roads, it's also essential to frame conditions for affordable housing."

Vienna has subtargets for homeless, refugee, and student households, who are given priority on waiting lists. Most households spend less than two years on the waitlist. A household must have a year's residency in Vienna before going on the waitlist, but the requirement is waived for asylum seekers. Vienna's Housing First model, developed in 2000, emphasized meeting the housing needs of refugee families by using modular housing.

Despite heavy regulation, market developers continue to provide 40 percent of housing, both owned and rental. Low rates of land speculation and rent control mean that market rental and ownership costs are low as well. In 2021, Viennese who lived in market housing spent an average of 26 percent of their post-tax income on rent and energy costs, not much more than social-housing residents, who paid an average of 22 percent of their income on housing. In Toronto, average rents are now 74 percent of average rental household income; in Vancouver, the figure is 75 percent.

Meanwhile, international headlines complained that Vienna is at the "epicentre of Europe's housing woes" because its house prices dropped over 12 percent between 2022 and 2023 when most other European cities saw house prices increase by the same proportion. But a "woe" for ownership speculation is a "win" for people seeking an inexpensive place to live. The average house price in Vienna is half that of Paris or Munich, about CAD$1 million for a four-bedroom, centrally located home. Austria has a high mortgage stress test; it expects a down payment of at least 20 percent of the price. But housing analysts claim the city's lower prices stem from the city's affordable rental market, which gives little incentive for people to buy. Vienna is a prime example of trickle-up housing economics: supplying large numbers of low-cost, high-quality nonmarket housing leads to competition and to stable, if not decreasing, rents and home prices.

Industrial-scale housing technology and land policies are the hallmarks of Vienna's approach. Wohnfonds Wien's focus on large-scale land ownership allows for strategic land-pooling and quality control of development. In contrast to neoliberal beliefs, providing financing to one major public developer fostered diversity and innovation. In 2018, Wohnfonds Wien had thirteen competition developments with at least five hundred homes each in development. Housing competitions stress themes such as intergenerational living, new family forms, and environmental sustainability. Wolfganggasse is built on a former rail depot and has a nursing home, workshops, a hostel for apprentices, a kindergarten, and a supermarket. Five buildings aimed at low-income single parents have 850 homes and plentiful indoor and outdoor spaces for children. Käthe-Dorsch-Gasse is aimed at single parents and older people. Located on Austrian Federal Railway land, it includes 253 subsidized rental flats, 116 deeply affordable flats (for students and very low-income households, including asylum seekers), 97 privately financed dwellings, and 54 assisted-living units – for a total of 520 homes. There's a shared courtyard for passive activities with benches and community gardens, an intergenerational courtyard, and a sports courtyard. Campus Wien West adjoins the development, offering a kindergarten, primary school, middle school, and music school.

The new suburb of Aspern Seestadt, a former airfield, will offer 10,500 homes and 20,000 jobs over a decade. A rail station and feeder buses came first, then schools and shops. When I visited the growing suburb on a hot day in May 2022, the lake and beachfront were bursting with young families (who also had access to swimming pools in their buildings), and an ice cream shop had a line down the block. An exhibit on feminist planning also had a queue. Suburban Viennese are passionate about design in the urban realm.

Stereotypes assign monolithic top-down management to public housing, but Vienna takes a partnership approach. The *Mietermit-bestimmungsstatut,* or tenant participation statute, governs the 220,000 households in public housing. It legally guarantees tenants participatory budgeting rights in relation to maintenance costs, the erection and maintenance of elevators, common utilities, and housing management. Leases are for two to five years, and community activities receive generous funding.

Vienna has large-scale nonmarket housing that is low cost, energy efficient, universally accessible, well designed, and respectful of tenant rights. Why can't Canada do this?

A Target of 2 Million Nonmarket Homes

A needs-based target for Canada would include a least 500,000 homes available to rent for $420 a month (in 2021 dollars) over the next decade. These half million homes would be divided into 300,000 student residences and 200,000 units of supportive housing for seniors and other very-low-income individuals on fixed incomes such as welfare and pensions. Some of the housing could be congregate, with private bedrooms and shared kitchens, bathrooms, and common spaces. But very-low-income Canadians also need studios and one-bedroom apartments for couples.

Canada needs another 1.5 million homes at rents between $421 and $1,050 for households reliant on minimum wage. One-third would need two or more bedrooms for larger households. Even if the minimum wage were doubled to account for doubled housing costs in recent years, there would still be a huge deficit of low-cost market and nonmarket rental housing. Even a target of 2 million homes in a decade at less than $1,050 a month wouldn't end homelessness or inadequate housing. It will take at least three decades to catch up with policy failures since the 1970s.

Need-based targets run up against the reality of nonmarket housing in Canada. Nonmarket home production shrunk to fewer than 1,000 homes a year from 1994 to 2017. Even with the National Housing Strategy, the bulk of so-called affordable-housing grants and financing has gone to homes renting for $1,600 to $3,000 a month, unaffordable to most low- and moderate-income households. Only the Rapid Housing Initiative produces or acquires about 1,000 genuinely low-cost homes per year. Both the Canadian Housing and Renewal Association and Scotiabank recommend doubling the stock of nonmarket homes from 894,000 in 2021 to almost 1.8 million in 2031, a rate of 90,000 homes a year. Within the current policy setting, most homes would, at best, meet the needs of moderate-income households or low-income households spending 50 to 70 percent of their income on housing. Little would be left over for food, transportation, education, and other costs.

Whether 90,000 homes a year or 200,000, a "big target" must take advantage of economies of scale. Nonmarket development has almost the same costs as market development and almost the same potential sources of cost savings: free or low-cost land, long-term and low-rate financing, tax incentives, rapid and predictable approvals (which reduce both financing risks and the "holding costs" of the land), and construction efficiencies.

But the financial advantage of nonmarket development is the removal of the profit element. Developers who sell properties upfront (to individual buyers or a rental provider) have an expected return on investment of 12 percent to 38 percent, depending on the risk level. For rental properties, an annual return of 5 to 10 percent is expected. Property speculators who flip properties for profit expect annual rates of return of over 20 percent (with, of course, greater risk). Nonmarket developers and providers can have small annual surpluses, but they don't have to return profits to investors or shareholders. The cost of marketing the homes is also smaller since residents come from waiting lists.

Despite similar costs, nonmarket development has long-term payoffs. A comparison of similarly sized and situated rental apartments in five Canadian cities built in the 1970s and 1980s found that the rents in nonmarket housing were 25 percent cheaper after two decades and 33 percent cheaper after three decades. Tenure is generally more secure in nonmarket housing, and tenants often have more say in how the housing is managed.

But nonmarket housing can cost more per square metre if the project is small and undertaken by small developers reliant on stop-start government funding. In 2017, there were only ten nonmarket providers, mostly municipal public-housing companies, with more than 10,000 homes each. In Ontario, over 500 providers had fewer than 100 homes each. In British Columbia, the figure was over 600. It's difficult to attract and retain good development, management, and finance staff within such a fragmented system.

A report by global management consulting firm McKinsey prioritizes four key interventions to address the global affordable-housing challenge: (1) unlocking land in the right locations, (2) reducing construction costs through the industrialization of housing, (3) reducing operations and maintenance costs through industrial efficiencies, and (4) reducing financing costs. These four measures could reduce housing costs by up to 48 percent, allowing affordable housing without government subsidies for moderate-income households. Reiterating a century of housing analysis, the report concludes that adequately housing those in the lowest 20 percent of household incomes would require a combination of direct government grants, below-market financing, and ongoing rent subsidies, measures best carried out by nonmarket actors.

In contrast to Canada's history of programs with different targets, mechanisms, and definitions of affordability, countries such as France have had consistent municipal nonmarket-housing targets since 2000, which allows nonmarket developers and providers to take an industrial approach. France's targets, which include acquisitions and new builds, started at 20 percent of total stock for all municipalities but were increased to 25 percent in 2016. Penalties for municipalities that failed to meet targets increased. In addition to using a stick, France provides a carrot: stable low-cost financing through a payroll tax (like Austria) and rent subsidies. Paris, with nonmarket targets of 30 percent, has also benefited from national changes to zoning and building regulations.

France, like Canada, has a three-tier governance system. Housing policy devolved to the regions before 2000, but devolution didn't work. Nonmarket housing was concentrated in a few suburban municipalities and insufficient to meet needs. So France created a national accountability system and stuck to it through political shifts in government. France produces 110,000 nonmarket homes a year, which would equate to 60,000 a year in Canada – more in one year than the total number of nonmarket homes created in Canada between 2000 and 2024.

But let me be clear: even 2 million new, acquired, and upgraded nonmarket homes wouldn't fix Canada's thirty-year housing deficit. This "rule of thirds" program would need to continue for at least two more decades to achieve this goal. Two million nonmarket homes would move Canada closer to functional zero homelessness and substantially reduce housing need. It would refocus the National Housing Strategy on evidence-based targets.

Finance and Land

In Sweden, Singapore, Finland, France, and Austria, nonmarket-housing development relies on free-leased government land. Most of these countries use land banking to support social housing. Land banking occurs either through the reuse of existing government land or through the purchase or expropriation of private property. Land banking allows governments to work with preferred developers for desired ends, such as permanently affordable housing with parks, schools, and cultural spaces. Leasing rather than selling land allows governments to retain a say in the long-term future of housing, especially when or if providers default. However, some governments prefer to gift land to a **community land trust**, which can keep the housing affordable, even when politics change.

Austria, France, and Finland also use low-cost financing to support nonmarket homes. In Austria, approximately 40 percent of a typical project is financed through bank mortgage loans with a maturity of

Community land trusts: Nonprofit organizations, usually based in a community, that focus on acquiring properties, both land and buildings, to hold them permanently in trust and out of the private market. Many trusts directly provide affordable housing; others represent the bundled assets of several organizations, which may borrow money together or communally provide financial or maintenance services. Some trusts operate commercial properties or provide community gardens and other enterprises.

twenty-five years at a 1.5 percent interest rate. The remainder is financed with public loans with a thirty-five-year maturity and 0.5 to 1.5 percent interest rate. Although housing associations are expected to make equity contributions, these countries allow social-housing providers to run up surpluses and reinvest them. (Canada, historically, has not allowed this.) Pension funds and other sources in nonmarket housing provide returns of 3.5 percent, based on rents, and the profits are reinvested in new development. Social-housing providers are exempt from sales and corporate taxes. Denmark's National Building Fund provides forty-five-year mortgages. The first thirty years are to pay off building costs; the next fifteen years fund new projects.

Public Housing

There are three main forms of nonmarket housing in Canada: public, community, and cooperative. I'll illustrate the pros and cons of each through examples.

Public housing is owned by a government – usually provincial, territorial, regional, or municipal. Half of all nonmarket housing in Canada is public housing. Some providers rely solely on rent-geared-to-income approaches, while other municipal housing companies charge cost-based rents or subsidize some units with market rents or sales. In British Columbia, the Whistler Housing Authority is a corporation tasked with planning, building, and managing new housing stock for the municipality's 14,000 residents and the thousands of seasonal workers who maintain the ski resort's 2 million annual visitors. The housing authority was created by the municipality in the 1990s in response to rising real estate prices, which led to concerns about the ability of service workers to live there. Even in the 1990s, resort workers were spending up to $1,000 a month for a shared room. Whistler introduced a bylaw that requires companies to build housing for their workers or contribute to a fund to that end.

Whistler Housing Authority learned as it grew. At first, it encouraged resort operators to sell housing below cost. Allocation was decided on a lottery system. But as was the case with Canada's postwar housing programs, residents "won the lottery" when they resold homes. The

Limited-equity home ownership: A nonmarket provider retains ownership of a share of the value of the home, usually the land (through a community land trust or public ownership of the land). The buyer buys only part of the property, and the profit on resale is shared between the seller and the provider.

housing authority received no return on the investment. Whistler then used $6 million in business contributions to build 232 rental homes. Because of good service-sector wages, these homes were returning $2 million in annual revenues by 2010. That year, Whistler inherited over 500 homes from the 2010 Winter Olympics Athlete's Village. Its waiting list decreased to fewer than 450 households. Whistler now provides 82 percent of workers' housing through a mix of short-term dormitory-type rentals and longer-term rentals and **limited-equity home ownership**.

In a move strongly reminiscent of Singapore, Whistler retains land leases and now sells affordable homes with a long-term covenant. At first, it linked sale prices to surrounding market rates. But market rates rose so quickly in the Lower Mainland that homes were no longer affordable to workers. In response, the housing authority limited price increases on homes to the consumer price index and restricted sales to local workers who didn't own properties elsewhere. Condominiums in 2017 cost $241,000, with a down payment of $12,000, half the cost of surrounding market condominiums. Two-thirds of local households could afford them. But larger townhouses (half the cost of their market equivalent) were affordable to only a third of local households, pointing to the need for more rentals geared to income.

Outside of First Nations, Whistler is a unique case of housing being publicly planned and provided. Unlike on reserve, Whistler's public housing is well designed and climate appropriate. As in Singapore, adequate housing has led to remarkable political stability: in contrast to surrounding communities in the Lower Mainland, voters tend to elect mayors by acclamation, and every council since 2000 has promised to continue the Whistler Housing Authority.

Whistler benefits from a small number of cashed-up businesses that have seen the advantage of worker housing. Fewer than 1 percent of households are very low income, meaning that rents can generally cover operating costs. But even with its high proportion of nonmarket housing, Whistler had 905 households in core housing need in 2016. Half the households were under the age of twenty-five, and they included over 40 percent of single-mother households. Even in a best-case scenario, it's difficult to provide enough affordable and adequate housing without subsidies from senior governments.

Community Housing

Community housing, which makes up 28 percent of social housing, is provided by nonprofit organizations, often affiliated with a religious or social service provider. Most supportive housing is provided by community-housing providers. Other community-housing providers focus on nonmarket housing without on-site services; many are focused on neighbourhood development.

Centretown Citizens Ottawa Corporation (CCOC) grew out of the downtown resident activism of the early 1970s. Resistance to a downtown highway and "blockbusting" high-rises transformed into a community plan to make 25 percent of new housing nonmarket. In 1974, when the CMHC moved away from funding solely public housing to allow community organizations to access grants and loans, CCOC was one of the first beneficiaries. It purchased a dozen rooming houses and other properties at risk of losing affordability. In 1978, it purchased an eleven-storey building with almost 90 apartments. It constructed its first apartment building in 1979.

Although CCOC had dedicated housing development staff, it wasn't interested in providing supportive housing. Instead, it partnered with service agencies and offered one of the first buildings to Bruce House, which provides supports to people living with HIV/AIDS. Faced with drying up federal and provincial funds in the early 1990s, it innovated in terms of land and financing. In the early 2000s, the City of Ottawa "gifted" it a former tavern whose owner had defaulted on mortgage and property tax obligations. It converted the tavern into ten apartments. (The project is kitty-corner to where I wrote this book.)

Similarly, it turned a former federal government barracks, bought at a below-market rate, into a large mixed-use, mixed-income development in 2012. Beaver Barracks illustrates the best of community-housing innovation and its common pitfalls. It has 254 homes in five buildings around a central courtyard. One of the homes is on top of an ambulance station. There are two commercial spaces and a large meeting room. Thirty-eight homes are supportive housing for formerly homeless people, who receive services from specialized mental health and disability agencies. Fifteen of these homes are fully accessible, and 90 percent can be visited by people with mobility impairments because of elevators, wide hallways, and a preponderance of single-storey flats. A further 76 homes have rents geared to income for low-income households, and 39 have below-market rents that make them affordable to moderate-income households. The remaining 101 homes are rented at market rates affordable only to median- or higher-income households. Homes range in size and include 50 three-bedroom homes for families with children.

Beaver Barracks, which includes geothermal heating and other environmental innovations, was developed at a difficult time for nonmarket housing. The financing brought together ten federal, provincial, and municipal government housing and environmental grants (about 35 percent of total costs). It had a low-rate mortgage guaranteed by the CMHC based on the CCOC's strong equity in its properties. The total budget was $85 million a dozen years ago. While 80 percent of revenues come from tenant rents, 30 percent of those households are supported with ongoing housing subsidies, and fewer than half the homes have rents geared to income. As the Whistler Housing Authority discovered, nonmarket housing can't meet the needs of low-income households without senior government funding or cross-subsidies from median- and higher-income households.

CCOC, which has over 1,500 homes, is a rare example of a large community-housing provider. But it waited almost a decade before taking on a large project after Beaver Barracks. Many community-housing providers can't scale up to the extent Canadians need.

Cooperative Housing

Cooperatives tend to be the smallest scale nonmarket-housing providers, making up 11 percent of the social-housing sector. In Canada, cooperative housing originated in the Antigonish Movement, a Catholic social justice initiative to end poverty and outmigration from the Maritime provinces in the early twentieth century. By 1938, credit unions, co-op fisheries, and farmers' cobuying clubs had 10,000 members. Small self-built housing cooperatives were established in communities such as Reserve Mines, Sydney, and Glace Bay, totalling 71 homes by the end of the Second World War, with 170 more under construction.

University of Toronto students established a housing cooperative in 1936, and students at Queen's University established **nonmarket student housing** in 1944. The Canadian Labour Congress helped establish the Co-operative Housing Federation of Canada in 1968. By the mid-1970s, changes to CMHC funding that benefited community housing also benefited cooperatives. Over 68,000 cooperative homes were developed over the next fifteen years.

Most cooperatives are small, housing an average of forty households. Households become members by paying a small amount, usually equivalent to the first and last month's rent. They can't sell their membership, so no household equity is required. The Antigonish Movement's principles of self-government still prevail. Boards are made up solely of household members, but most cooperatives hire management and maintenance staff.

Nonmarket student housing: Canada used to treat students as a group in need of subsidized housing. Colleges and universities were funded as community-housing providers. Between 1960 and 1967, the federal government covered up to 90 percent of the cost of student residences through 176 projects worth $220 million ($2 billion in 2023 dollars). The result: dorm rooms for over 38,000 single students and larger apartments for about 2,000 married students.

Home Truths

Many cooperatives begin with a group of like-minded individuals. Les Artistes du Ruisseau, for instance, is a housing co-op in Gatineau, Quebec's third-largest city. According to its website, its mission is to create live-work spaces for artists. The co-op includes a studio and performance space on the ground floor and forty-nine homes above. Ten of the homes are for singles with one bedroom; the others – including ten three-bedrooms – are reserved for families. Half the households receive a rent supplement that allows them to pay 25 percent of their income for housing. (Quebec has a more generous rent-geared-to-income program than the rest of Canada.) The financing, dating from 2016–17, included a $3.4 million federal-provincial grant, a mortgage guarantee, $1.3 million from the City of Gatineau (mostly for the artistic spaces), $83,000 a year for five years for rent subsidies from the province, and a further $131,000 for environmental sustainability measures.

As in Europe, co-op rents (called housing charges) reflect the cost of building and maintenance. Unlike many European co-ops, most Canadian co-ops don't expect members to contribute to construction costs. Government support generally comes in the form of start-up grants, low-cost long-term mortgages of thirty-five to fifty years, and ongoing subsidies that provide low-income affordability for about a quarter of households. In the 1970s and 1980s, there was start-up grant assistance for both community and cooperative housing. The grant recognized that it can take up to two years and millions of dollars to find and purchase suitable land and prepare designs and other development requirements.

In 2022, the federal government promised a new codesigned cooperative housing program. But it's difficult to expand the cooperative model because there's an absence of pooled equity to provide start-up funding or assure mortgages. According to its website, the Co-operative Housing Federation of BC pooled the assets of 260 co-ops to create $4 billion in shared equity in its Community Land Trust. It created or renovated 2,300 homes over the past decade through this model.

Compass Housing NS was established in 2017 to accomplish the same end. Shared equity began with four small co-ops with a total of thirty-nine homes that were no longer financially viable and were in the care of a liquidator. Other co-ops joined, and the federal government and small municipalities provided land for development. A Black-led co-op is being developed in Halifax, where the destruction of the Africville community in the 1960s led to a new generation of housing activism in the province where Canadian co-op housing began.

What Would It Take to Scale Up Nonmarket Housing?

The rapid expansion of community and cooperative housing in the 1970s and 1980s shows that with the right targets, developmental assistance, land policies, finance settings, and approach, nonmarket housing could be a third of total construction.

Public housing, mostly in the form of municipal housing companies, tends to be the biggest provider with the most access to finance capital. However, public housing has a history of top-down management. Community housing can be small-scale and sometimes poorly managed, but at their best, these projects respond well to community needs, particularly in the case of supportive housing. Cooperatives are the most democratically self-managed (members are co-owners rather than landlords and tenants) but tend to be the smallest providers. All three types of nonmarket-housing developers and providers can work together effectively on larger sites, as was the case fifty years ago in Toronto's St. Lawrence neighbourhood and through BC's Community Land Trust today.

Moving toward adequate homes for all is feasible. But nonmarket homes would need to be scaled up ten-fold over the next thirty years – 20 percent of all homes in an expanded universe of 27 million homes. A purpose-built nonmarket housing program would work backwards from rents affordable to low-income households to determine grants and guarantee long-term financing that would allow housing to be built, acquired, and renovated on a break-even basis. Like most countries that have successfully scaled up nonmarket housing, the federal government would need to help cities acquire public land, and local governments would need to quickly approve apartment buildings, flats, and supportive housing.

The benefits? Directly meeting the needs of households who can't be served by the market. Modelling the kinds of transit-oriented, sustainable, and people-centred housing that Canadian communities need. Whistler's land trust model, Beaver Barracks' energy efficiency, and Les Artistes du Ruisseau's mix of domestic and artistic workspaces demonstrate the same kind of city-building innovation showcased in Vienna. Freed from the profit-maximizing logic of Canada's market housing, nonmarket housing can create exemplary homes – and communities – for the future.

7

Can Housing
Become Abundant Again?

In the 1960s and 1970s, market- and nonmarket-housing development created homes for households young and old. Families with moderate incomes could afford to rent or own "starter" homes. Can Canada once again become a place where abundant, affordable, and secure homes are the norm?

Nonmarket housing must be scaled up to end homelessness and meet the needs of low-income families. But market housing can also meet the needs of low-income households, particularly in communities with lower land values. (Most low-income households live in market housing, especially older high-rises. But the apartments tend to be un-affordable, overcrowded, insecure, and inaccessible.) The universalist approach used in Vienna, France, and Singapore works. Nonmarket developments will have a mix of income levels because as households age, incomes tend to increase. The most important thing is to produce affordable, abundant, well-located homes with secure tenure. At this point in Canadian history, rental homes can fit that bill. Ownership homes can't – not unless they sell at a fraction of their current price.

Keep in mind the households who need rental housing, especially in big cities:

- newcomers, including large migrant families and temporary migrants, particularly students

- young households, including singles and couples who wish to have children but are locked out of home ownership
- older households, including empty nesters who might want to downsize in their neighbourhoods and people who have rented their entire lives.

A high proportion of these households are single people or couples. But households with children need two or more bedrooms, as do people who want to share homes for economic or personal reasons or who work from home. The rental universe should be about 25 percent two-bedroom homes and 10 percent three-plus-bedroom homes.

Here, I reverse-engineer policy settings to meet a target of 2 million new market homes with affordable monthly rents of $1,050 to $2,500 (in 2021 dollars) for moderate- and median-income households (adjusted for inflation and median incomes in metropolitan markets). It's as ambitious a target as 2 million social and supportive homes for very-low- and low-income households described in the last two chapters. But both targets are necessary if Canada hopes to reduce greenhouse gas emissions to zero and realize adequate, affordable homes for all.

I've already explored ways to save construction costs, but taxation and regulation, particularly at the municipal level, are also powerful determinants of construction costs – and delays. Standardizing and simplifying zoning, building regulations, and approvals will help unlock the kinds of prices Canadians need.

Ending Exclusionary Zoning and Regulations

Land, especially well-located land, is a spatially fixed and limited resource. **Zoning** controls the use of this limited resource. Zoning generally protects those who have more power and wealth from uses – and people – that pose a perceived threat to the value of their property. In Canada, zoning makes well-located land a scarce resource – and in a market-based economy, scarcity breeds profiteering.

A century ago, zoning was advertised as a public health measure to shield middle-class residents from noxious industries. But it became a tool to segregate districts with good public transit, schools, parks, health care, and job opportunities from lower-income and racialized households. Removing exclusionary zoning is a necessary, though insufficient, way to provide adequate housing.

Until recently, most neighbourhoods in Canadian cities excluded all but the highest household income quintile (people who can afford to buy detached homes). In Toronto, 64 percent of land was, until recently, zoned for detached houses exclusively. In Vancouver, it was 81 percent of the land, but laneway houses and secondary suites have been allowed on larger lots for a decade. In Calgary and Edmonton, the figures were 68 percent and 69 percent, respectively. Montreal is an outlier: more than three-quarters of its residential and mixed-use land is zoned for apartments in duplexes or triplexes, rowhouses, semi-detached houses, or buildings with fewer than five storeys. Unsurprisingly, Montreal has a lower proportion of households living in core housing need or homelessness than Toronto and Vancouver.

Zoning tends to prioritize housing cars rather than people. A single underground parking space is estimated to add an average of CAD$71,000 per unit in multifamily apartment buildings. Parking takes up 27 percent of the costs in low-income projects. The typical parking space required for a two-bedroom apartment in many large North American cities is

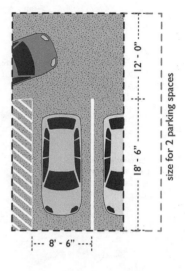

2 BEDROOMS
900 SQUARE FEET

1.5 SPACES
488 SQUARE FEET
INCLUDING AISLES

MEDIAN REQUIRED PARKING
FOR AN **APARTMENT**
AMONG LARGE U.S. CITIES

Housing people versus housing cars. |
Courtesy of Seth Goodman, graphingparking.com.

more than half the size of the apartment itself. Their embodied carbon is about seventeen tons per stall.

Parking provisions are unjust to those who need affordable housing the most. The 2005 Canadian Social Survey found that 81 percent of Canadian men aged eighteen and over drove at least once a day, whereas only 66 percent of women did. Women-led households are three times more likely to be in housing need than male-led households. People aged forty-five to fifty-four are 2.5 times more likely to drive on any given day than people aged eighteen to twenty-four. The latter are much more likely to be renters. Younger people are also more likely to use car-sharing and ride-hailing services. These services are much less expensive than

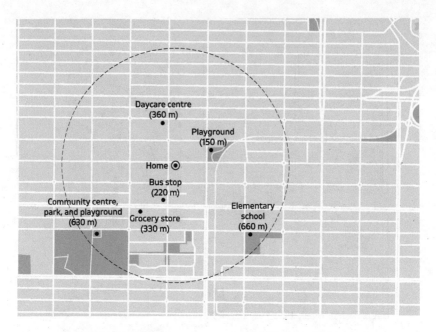

Elements of a 15-minute city, as described in Vancouver's 1992
High-Density Housing for Families with Children Guidelines.

paying the fixed costs for a car, insurance, and parking, particularly when that parking reflects the true cost of scarce urban land and cars are parked 96 percent of the time.

Higher-density housing with nearby transit, services, and amenities supports **15-minute cities** (see page 48). Accessibility is a component of adequate housing, and definitions of "accessibility" need to extend beyond elevators or wheelchair-accessible shower stalls to neighbourhoods that have shops, parks, and transit within a short and safe walking (or rolling) distance to homes.

One of Canada's earliest planning efforts to enable 15-minute cities was the City of Vancouver's 1992 *High-Density Housing for Families with Children Guidelines.* The guidelines were intended for new market and nonmarket developments in the central area, and at least 25 percent of developments were to have two or more bedrooms for families with young children. The guidelines emphasized proximate services for children and parents. Elementary schools and their outdoor play areas, daycare centres, after-school care facilities, community centres, and grocery shopping should be within 800 "effective" metres (that is, along existing streets rather than a straight line). Playgrounds and a public transit stop should be within 400 metres.

Guidelines are great, but an analysis of Shanghai's 15-minute city strategy, adopted in 2016, found that neighbourhoods with a large proportion of young children or low-income undocumented workers were the least likely to have walkable access to services and amenities. In China, as in Canada, reducing sociospatial inequalities needs to be central to any 15-minute city strategy. The Shanghai case study concluded that the provision of affordable housing in high-amenity neighbourhoods needed to be improved, while low-income areas needed to be retrofitted with better amenities.

This Shanghai study draws on international research to argue that a population density of 10,000 to 30,000 people per square kilometre could easily support a 15-minute city. Paris and Barcelona, the cities that have gone the furthest in 15-minute thinking, have population densities within that range throughout their built-up areas. This density was achieved through consistent, adjacent six- to eight-storey apartment buildings located throughout the city rather than a few high-rises downtown. Vancouver and Toronto have dense downtowns, but the density gradient declines rapidly outside of these areas. Five kilometres from downtown, Toronto's population density per square kilometre falls from 16,608 to 6,836, and Vancouver's from 18,837 to 4,884. If you travel thirty minutes from downtown via public transit, population densities are under 500 people per square kilometre. Montreal, in contrast, has a lower-density downtown, but the city has a consistent landscape of adjacent triplexes.

Transit-oriented development: Coined by Peter Calthorpe in 1993, "transit-oriented development" refers to a mixed-use community within walking distance of a frequent transit stop. It usually incorporates residential, retail, office, and public space and associated social infrastructure such as schools, childcare centres, and libraries.

Montreal's zoning and building rules are conducive to a 15-minute city and the allied concept of **transit-oriented development.**

Zoning reform has taken off in many Canadian cities over the past few years. Toronto and British Columbia are instituting multiplex zoning that will allow a baseline of up to four homes – including triplexes, laneway homes, and basement apartments – on a single lot. But these "gentle density" zoning reforms don't lead to affordable rental apartment buildings, let alone the kinds of mixed uses that promote walkable neighbourhoods. To increase low-cost homes through zoning, we must look at an entirely different planning playbook.

In Praise of Japanese Zoning

In sharp contrast to zoning in the Anglosphere, which treats every development not centred on detached homes with suspicion, Japanese zoning is permissive. Planners and local councils rarely say no to a proposed urban development.

Ottawa has 120 residential zones in a city of 1 million; Japan has 13 residential, commercial, agricultural, and industrial zones in a nation of 126 million. Even in the most restrictive Japanese residential zone – low-rise residential, reserved for narrow roads and laneways – there's no limit on the number of units and few restrictions on land use. In Japan, on "residential" streets, single-family homes stand next to apartment buildings with small shops or offices on the ground floor. Elementary and junior high schools are permitted. Height limits are based on the width of the street, with heights three times the width of the road. Lanes tend to be three metres wide, and many streets have one lane with no street parking and no sidewalks. This three-metre standard has been recommended to increase space for sidewalks, bike lanes, and trees in Canada. If we apply the standard to Canada, we'd allow six- to seven-storey buildings on narrow two-lane streets and twelve- to fourteen-storeys on four-lane streets.

In the most common Japanese zone – mid- to high-rise residential, which covers half of cities – hospitals, shopping centres, and office buildings are allowed as of right. The only nonresidential uses considered nuisances are hotels and bars with karaoke machines, and even these are included in most residential zones. Residential uses are encouraged in all commercial zones, as are restaurants and cinemas. Residences are even allowed in areas zoned for light industry (but schools and hospitals are not). There's one heavy industrial zone reserved exclusively for uses that "considerably worsen the environment" and one agricultural zone for food production.

In other words, Japanese zoning isn't driven by racist and classist concerns such as "neighbourhood character." It's driven by a desire to limit nuisances, primarily noise pollution and heavy truck traffic, while recognizing that all areas must have an element of nuisance in the form of noise and traffic.

Japanese zoning is three-dimensional in that it assumes mixed-use in almost all zones. In contrast, zoning in the Anglosphere is based on the notion that there can only be a single use on most lots. If you're building a low-rise office building or a commercial centre, why aren't you building housing on top? One-third of the revenue of Japan's big six rail companies comes from residential, office, and commercial space on top of their stations. These spaces create a built-in commuter base for transit, and passengers disembarking from a train can pick up groceries or take-away meals before they continue on foot, pick up their bicycles, or take a bus home. There's no reason why provincially owned commuter rail networks in Canada can't take on this model. There's no reason why federal infrastructure money for new light and heavy rail can't be contingent on high-rise housing above stations.

Japan has an extensive communal transit network, including high-speed trains between cities and subways within most large cities. From the 1960s onwards, it recognized the relationship between car dependence and sprawl and between extensive public transit systems and density. For that reason, there's no overnight on-street parking in most Japanese cities. To register your car, you need to prove you have a parking space each time you move. Parking spaces are most often found in automated, commercial, multistorey neighbourhood garages. There are no minimum parking restrictions attached to zoning or building codes. Some people need state-subsidized homes, but car parking is provided solely by the market. It's not subsidized by taxpayers.

The City of Tokyo has 13.5 million people within a metropolitan area of 37.3 million people. That's a little less than the population of Canada within a land area the size of Prince Edward Island. The City of Tokyo's residential densities are much lower than downtown Toronto and Vancouver at 6,158 people per square kilometre. However, homes are spread consistently throughout the entire urban area. The City of Tokyo's housing completions per individual aged over fifteen were higher in 2018 than Ontario's in 2023, even though Tokyo is growing at a fraction of Ontario's growth rate. The average rent of a two-bedroom flat in Tokyo in 2018 was about CAD$1,000, affordable to a low-income household. Abundance leads to low rents.

This was not always the case. Japan, like Canada, has had active neighbourhood associations since the early twentieth century. During the 1970s, there was a backlash against high-rises; governments stepped back from public housing, sold off public land to corporate developers, and loosened restrictions on agricultural land. By the mid-1980s, cashed-up corporations stepped up speculation in office and commercial real estate, vastly increasing land prices and housing costs. In central Tokyo, the share of land owned by corporations increased from 59 to 69 percent, and the share owned by individuals decreased from 41 to 31 percent. Tokyo's housing costs – to own and rent – increased by 70 percent. As is now the case in Canada, financialized firms were taking advantage of a housing shortage.

In reaction, the Japanese government enacted the Basic Land Act in 1989. The act enshrined four principles that should inform land policy in Canada:

- Public welfare should be given priority over private profit in the ownership and use of land.
- Land should be used efficiently, with an emphasis on using existing built-up areas rather than sprawl.
- Land should not be an object of speculation.
- Landowners should return part of their profits to the public through taxes.

A land-value tax was imposed, but exemptions for some large corporate landholders watered down the impact. The Japanese government also began to once again purchase land for public housing. By the 1990s, it

　　　　　　　　　　　　　　　　　　　　　　　　Home Truths

was reviewing zoning and building codes to encourage more small-scale development. Japan continues to have a strong network of resident associations. They focus on neighbourhood amenities: improving parks, streetscapes, shrines, community infrastructure, and waste management rather than on refusing to have more neighbours.

The Movement to End Exclusionary Zoning in New Zealand and the United States

Exclusionary zoning is like the fossil fuel industry. Given how harmful it is to environmental outcomes (let alone affordability), it's amazing it continues. In 2016, Auckland, New Zealand, became the first large city to eliminate single-family zoning, after three years of discussion and six years after several municipalities were amalgamated into a city of 1.6 million. Three-quarters of the urban land was upzoned to allow buildings of modest height (maximum of five storeys). The emphasis was on increasing the number of well-located homes by increasing floor area ratios and eliminating minimum house sizes.

By 2021, five years after implementation, the number of building permits had doubled. There was also a substantial increase in the number of attached or multifamily dwellings (from approximately 9,000 to 35,000). An additional 4 percent of homes, over and above previous completion rates, were added to the housing stock. Development on agricultural or natural land outside Auckland decreased while permits near the downtown and rail lines increased.

Upzoning had a positive impact on rent affordability. In 2015, Auckland had the highest rents in the country. By 2023, rent increases were below the national average. The rent benefit also extended to low-income households. Between 2010 and 2017, before the impacts of upzoning, lower-quartile rents saw a growth of approximately 38 percent, but from 2017 to 2023 rents increased by only 14 percent, roughly the same rate as incomes. Like most Canadian cities, Auckland still has unaffordable rents and ownership costs, but rent increases are least keeping pace with income increases. Upzoning was extremely unpopular when it was introduced, but a 2021 poll found that fewer than a third of Auckland residents opposed the zoning changes.

Auckland's reforms were taken up by national policy-makers. New Zealand cities are now required to allow buildings of up to three storeys and up to three units on every residential lot. Higher densities are permitted near public transit. A cost-benefit analysis projected that the net benefit, mostly in the form of curbing sprawl, would be CAD$11.7 billion (about $9,600 per household in added disposable income) by 2043. The total cumulative value of better-located affordable homes for moderate-income households was estimated at $161 billion.

In 2019, Minneapolis became the first North American city to end single-family zoning. At the same time, concerned about the potential displacement impacts of upzoning, it doubled funding for homelessness prevention. Compared to similarly sized midwestern US cities such as Milwaukee, Indianapolis, and Madison, where rents increased by 30 percent in relation to incomes, Minneapolis has seen rents increase at the same rate as incomes since 2017. Homelessness has also decreased compared to these other cities. Zoning reforms followed in other states, most notably California, but not always with the critical component of preventing the displacement of low-income households in older homes and rental properties being redeveloped.

So how did Auckland and Minneapolis bring about a political consensus on zoning reform? First, YIMBY (yes in my backyard) advocates – from private and nonmarket-housing developers to environmental activists – focused on the benefits. They argued that ending single-family zoning would help their cities hit climate-change reduction targets (by reducing commutes), address inequalities caused by racial and economic segregation, and improve overall housing affordability. Second, both cities based their strategies on solid needs assessment. Minneapolis had built 64,000 new homes since 2010 but added 83,000 households. With too many residents chasing too few housing options, the city had a dangerously low apartment vacancy rate of 2.2 percent (a 4 to 8 percent vacancy rate is recommended by economists to reduce rent inflation). More than half of Minneapolis's residents are renters, and half of those renters are in housing stress (as in Toronto). Based on business-as-usual projections, Minneapolis was on track to deliver only 75 percent of the homes needed, mostly at the wrong price points, between 2020 and 2030. Third, planners went big: instead of concentrating change in a few neighbourhoods (which would inflame local councillors), they focused on a simple and dramatic zoning change.

Auckland and Minneapolis have used zoning reform to increase rental supply and stabilize rent increases. Some cities are using an affordability lens and providing density bonuses and modifying regulations to encourage affordable rentals. Austin's Affordability Unlocked Development Bonus Program, in effect since 2019, is part of an effort to create 60,000 affordable homes in eight years in a city of fewer than 1 million people. It offers extensive waivers and modifications to regulations – particularly in relation to heights, parking minimums, and setbacks. In exchange, developers must designate at least 50 percent of the units to affordable housing for a minimum of forty years (for rental units) or ninety-nine years (for ownership units). In addition, 20 percent of the units must be either two-plus-bedrooms or supportive or seniors' housing. Rental affordability in Austin is defined as less than 30 percent of pretax income for households earning less than 60 percent of the area median household income; ownership affordability means that mortgage payments and other housing costs are affordable to households earning less than 80 percent of median household income. This program was just one aspect of Austin's strategy, which included a $250 million affordable-housing bond and renter protections against "no fault" evictions.

Within the first year, there were 2,700 new homes, 2,400 of which were affordable to low- and moderate-income households. The high ratio of deeply affordable homes signalled uptake from nonmarket developers. With limited grant programs at both the national and state levels, one nonmarket provider reported that the difference between nine storeys and no parking requirement versus seven storeys and one parking spot for twenty-six seniors' homes made the difference between viability and nonviability.

The City of Austin now recognizes it should have applied these rules to all lots, instead of instituting a 165-metre minimum "buffer zone" around single-family homes. City staff expressed frustration with piecemeal amendments to gradually reduce this barrier and a preference for a holistic approach to upzoning everywhere.

The City of Portland, population 650,000, also offers density bonuses as part of its ban on single-family zoning. Any lot can now include two to four homes as of right (depending on the size of the lot and the proposed homes). The "deeper affordability" option allows for six homes if at least half are available to low-income households at affordable prices with rent control and universal-access features. These six-plexes come in different forms, including three-storey apartment buildings and cottage clusters of six tiny houses. Portland also has measures to promote affordable accessory dwelling units (ADUs, small homes constructed on laneways) such as waiving development charges. Dramatically, the city reduced maximum new house sizes from 622 square metres to 232 square metres to decrease knockdown rebuilds (tearing down older, smaller homes to build large luxury homes).

The City of Cambridge, Massachusetts, instituted its 100%-Affordable Housing Overlay in 2020. All new housing development must be 100 percent affordable to those earning very low to median household incomes. Cambridge has two major universities (Harvard and MIT) and virtually no undeveloped government land. The government had literally run out of options to develop new affordable housing. The high cost of land and property made acquiring existing private rentals and land-banking strategies unfeasible. The city also felt its discretionary permit system introduced too much uncertainty and delay to the planning process. This bylaw overrides existing zoning restrictions. In one example, a nonmarket-housing developer provided a concept plan for a four-storey extension on an existing six-unit building, which would increase the number of homes to twenty-one, making it eligible for state and federal construction subsidies. Pre-existing maximum unit counts make it nearly impossible to build nonmarket housing. Cambridge works backwards from affordable rents to the regulations that might enable them.

Ending Exclusionary Zoning in Canada

In Canada, changes have not been as radical nor as focused on making low- and moderate-income rental housing affordable. In 2020, Edmonton became the first city to waive minimum parking requirements for both residential and commercial developments, citing evidence that fewer than 50 percent of spaces are being used at any given time. New Westminster, Burnaby, Vancouver, and Victoria all took another approach after the BC government enabled it in 2018. They ended exclusionary zoning but also developed rental overlays that required developments near rapid transit stations to be rental only, and they protected rental buildings from being converted into condominiums. Within a year, Burnaby's new rental pipeline had 9,600 proposed homes, 6,700 of them nonmarket. City-owned lands were leased for nonmarket rentals, and the province increased funding for nonmarket housing. Victoria not only ended single-family zoning – in 2021, it eliminated public hearings for all nonmarket-housing rezonings.

Zoning reform is a newer idea than Housing First. The evidence of its impact is more contested, and the idea meets with local resistance, including from some rights-based housing campaigners who argue that YIMBYs are "development shills." But zoning reform enhances moderate- and median-income rental affordability (in Austin and Cambridge, it enabled low-income nonmarket affordability), and the idea is spreading fast throughout North America. In Canada, Ontario and British Columbia, the provinces with the most housing need, are ending single-family zoning. And the US and Canadian governments are creating infrastructure incentive programs linked to targets. As part of its $4 billion Housing Accelerator Fund, the Canadian government recommends a four-storey minimum for all residential zones and a ten-storey minimum within 1.5 kilometres of rapid transit.

Zoning reform can decrease rent hikes in relation to income and increase well-located land supply, including for nonmarket housing. The federal government should provide national zoning and building code recommendations, which are linked to infrastructure funding incentives and renter protections against demoviction. Japan's example demonstrates the importance of scaling up issues such as the right to housing and climate change to the highest level of government, so it can provide consistency and predictability.

Cities can promote public engagement. For example, in British Columbia, the Urbanarium held a Missing Middle Competition. Architects envisaged how an existing block in Burnaby could be reimagined with flexible home sharing, multigenerational living, and commercial uses added to the ground floors of three-storey houses. In Edmonton, the winner of another Missing Middle Competition was commissioned to design five parcels of city-owned land. As is the case with Housing First, there's enough evidence to move from pilot project to a national program without debating its worth in every community in Canada.

Lessons from recent practice suggest the need for a transformative approach to zoning based on three principles: simplicity, affordability, and scalability.

- No residential or mixed-use zone in any city of over 5,000 people should restrict low-rise mixed-use buildings of four storeys. If 100 percent of such buildings is affordable rental aimed at very-low- to median-income households with a ninety-nine-year affordability covenant, then a density bonus of an additional 50 percent (two storeys) should be added.
- Apartments should be encouraged over townhouses, as they're more accessible if they have an elevator.
- Building codes should allow point-block access up to six storeys or the height of the highest firefighting ladder, whichever is higher.
- There should be no minimum parking requirements.
- There should be no maximum limit on units, to allow for student housing, group homes, long-term care, and other multitenant housing in all areas.
- There should be targets of 25 percent two-bedrooms and 10 percent three-plus-bedrooms on all developments over twenty homes, except those intended solely for students, supportive housing, or seniors.
- Other design requirements or considerations should be limited to accessibility or energy efficiency; the need for nearby green space should be met by parkettes within 400 metres of homes.
- Mid-rise zones of eight storeys (twelve, if affordable) should be allowed within 400 metres of frequent bus stops or rapid transit stations.
- High-rise zones of twenty storeys (thirty, if affordable) should be allowed within 400 metres of major bus or rapid transit interchanges.
- If municipalities wish to put a 100-percent rental, affordable, or non-market housing overlay on zones, they should be allowed to do so.
- Municipalities should be encouraged to implement legislation to end demoviction and support the large-scale redevelopment of existing apartment buildings with minimal tenant disruption.

- To speed up approvals and end undemocratic NIMBY (not in my backyard) dominance over housing decisions. decisions should be made by planning staff rather than requiring public hearings or going to council.

Ending NIMBYism

From the 1980s onwards, the term "NIMBY" has been used to describe the opposition of residents, usually homeowners, to proposed new developments. Exclusionary zoning is policed through NIMBYism. NIMBY rhetoric about nonmarket-housing development often reflects fear and ignorance about potential residents, based on racism, classism, and ableism. There's a hierarchy of acceptance: market duplexes or triplexes are considered more acceptable than a group home for people with intellectual disabilities, which is less likely to provoke opposition than housing for people who have become homeless, particularly if there is a drug or alcohol treatment or ex-offender aspect to support services. The Advocacy Centre for Tenants Ontario characterizes opposition to rooming houses, shelters, supportive housing, and group homes as people zoning, not use zoning, and thus in conflict with human rights legislation.

Decision making based on zoning and other regulations usually provokes a rhetorical shift from opposition based on people to opposition based on design concerns: parking, traffic, heights, or the number of units. Sometimes NIMBY groups wrap themselves in the cloak of environmentalism or affordable housing and argue that new homes will be too expensive or will pave over a tree. Affordable housing is often seen as a threat to property values, but NIMBY arguments tend to be based on criteria such as school capacity, public safety, and potential impact on infrastructure and amenities. While "social mix" is often argued in opposition to affordable housing ("there are already too many poor people living here"), the obverse is rarely argued in relation to exclusionary amenity-rich areas ("there are already too many rich people living here").

There are underlying psychological themes to NIMBY opposition. The uncertainty of new development can contrast with the implicit certainty of "no change," especially when there are strong emotions associated with a sense of place. Generalized distrust of government can be a strong driver of NIMBYism. There's almost always a generational inequality element. Gen Z and millennial renters increasingly locked out of high-amenity areas are more likely to support land use and social mix than their boomer homeowner parents.

Wealthy areas with low proportions of nonmarket housing tend to be more resistant to affordable-housing proposals than areas with more social mix. NIMBY campaigns are usually led by residents' associations, also known as neighbourhood or ratepayers' associations. These are voluntary groups whose membership is drawn from a geographically delimited residential district and whose activities centre on that area. In Toronto and Vancouver, for example, members are more likely to be white, older, highly educated, and homeowners than in other neighbourhoods. Residents' associations share the general population's political affiliations but have different priorities. NIMBY advocates can sway local politicians to emphasize issues and perspectives that differ from those of most residents. Far from being representatives of local democracy, NIMBY groups distort municipal politics to the detriment of our right to adequate housing.

The impacts of NIMBYism can be severe. While opposition to affordable housing usually takes the form of petitions and deputations at public hearings, NIMBYism can escalate to harassment and lawsuits. A council meeting to gain "community input" on 127 supportive homes over thirteen storeys, one block from a rapid transit station in the wealthy Vancouver neighbourhood of Kitsilano, took over six days; one meeting went past midnight and had numerous altercations outside the council chambers. The future residents of the supportive housing were called a criminal threat to women and children rather than people who needed a home. The residents' association then took the City of Vancouver to court, delaying the project by another year. They also filed a lawsuit against Sḵwx̱wú7mesh Úxwumixw (the Squamish Nation) and the City of Vancouver to block water and sewage lines to a proposed 6,500-home rental development.

Because of the tendency for rezoning applications to become "hostage situations," the Canada–British Columbia Expert Panel on the Future of Housing Supply and Affordability recommended blanket upzoning to reduce reliance on site-by-site public hearings and council approvals.

A US survey of over seventy affordable and nonmarket-housing developers found that 70 percent experienced opposition from neighbourhood associations on multiple grounds, including crime and safety, the impact on local schools, and "environmental" concerns. Tactics included using media, door-to-door campaigns and petitions, lobbying politicians, and deputations to councils. One-quarter of social-housing providers faced legal challenges, and 23 percent had experienced picketing at their offices or the housing site. In 62 percent of cases, NIMBY opposition led to construction delays and cost increases. In a quarter of cases, the number of affordable homes was reduced. Five developers said they had to cancel projects because of opposition. These tactics led nonmarket-housing providers to prefer lower-income and amenity-poor areas where there would be less opposition, reinforcing spatial disparities. A Canadian review of twelve nonmarket-housing providers found that the costs of confronting NIMBY opposition through formal planning and provincial appeal boards could exceed their resources, capacity, and expertise. Every provider spoke of the cost of NIMBYism, not only on the viability of projects but also on the mental health of staff and homeless people forced to fight for their right to housing against hostile neighbours.

There's no way affordable, accessible, and well-located housing can be scaled up across Canada without a new approach that limits public hearings and council decisions on every multifamily proposal. The acceptance of third-party rights – the right of neighbours to object to nearby development – is a distinctive and harmful feature of Anglosphere planning, which prioritizes property ownership over the right to housing. In Germany, third parties can take legal action on planning decisions only if the new development directly infringes on their property boundary. Japan takes a similarly stringent approach to third-party objections. In Sweden, third parties can object only if the development takes place in an area with "special" environmental or cultural value, a small minority of urban locations.

Permissive zoning codes would help obviate the need to rezone most multiunit developments. So would housing targets based on neighbourhood income and tenure. Edmonton, as part of its equity-based Infill Roadmap, set neighbourhood targets for 16 percent of all new development to be nonmarket multiunit housing. The Infill Roadmap is framed in terms of legal obligations under Treaty 6, signed by settlers, Cree, Assiniboine, and Ojibwa Nations in 1876: "Since then we have all, as Treaty people, held the responsibility of ensuring that the opportunities for prosperity are shared and enjoyed by everyone." The twenty-five actions were phased in over four years and ranged from ending minimum parking requirements, to eliminating unit-number limits, to enabling more group homes, to facilitating land assembly of multiple lots for apartment development. The plan includes "a publicly available map of optimal infill development locations for medium, high scale and mixed-use developments based on best evidence and neighbourhood level indicators." Rather than giving residents a forum to "accept" or "reject" potential neighbours, Edmonton is opening constructive debates on the community infrastructure necessary for a range of people in a changing neighbourhood to thrive. Stasis is no longer an option.

Building Code Reform

We aren't going to "duplex or triplex" our way out of a decades-long housing shortage and a looming climate crisis. In 2021, 667,000 homes changed hands across Canada: a remarkable 4 percent of all homes, 30 percent higher than the ten-year average. Even if 10 percent of the single-unit homes sold were converted into two or three units, we would still need more homes to bring down prices to affordable levels. Canada desperately needs tens of thousands of well-located four- to twelve-storey apartment buildings on existing lots on every street in every neighbourhood. But building codes make small apartment buildings nearly impossible to develop.

In contrast to the "plex" culture in Quebec, which emphasizes single-storey flats, English Canada, with its legacy of single-unit homes, has relied on townhouses for affordable three-plus-bedroom homes. But townhouses lack accessibility, and a large proportion of their usable area is consumed by staircases. Townhouses aren't appropriate for an aging population, people with mobility impairment, or small children. These people require elevators.

Industrializing housing production (already discussed in relation to four-storey modular supportive homes) can be applied to four-, six-, eight-, and twelve-storey prototype apartment buildings that could be fitted onto typical urban and suburban lots. Mike Eliason, an architect who worked on this concept for the City of Vancouver, talks about the importance of the "big dumb box" as an essential component in large-scale projects such as Helsinki's Kalasatama, Hamburg's Oberbillwerder, and Vienna's Aspern Seestadt. Before zoning and building codes, most houses didn't have recesses, height setbacks, or modulated facades. The simple bungalows known as "strawberry boxes" that made up the majority of Canada's postwar Victory Houses, row houses on streets from St. John's to Winnipeg, and most early apartment buildings were square boxes that covered most of their lots.

For an example of stupid form-based zoning, look no further than the City of Toronto. Even though an eleven-storey building is allowed on an avenue with public transit, it must have four setbacks (the distance the building must be from a property line or street) to avoid shading the opposite sidewalk and to "fit in" with three-storey height limits on the side street. This "angular plane" makes building more than six storeys unfeasible and adds to construction costs and energy inefficiencies. Every time a building must turn a corner, costs are added. Roofs and foundations become more complex, weathering and durability risks increase, and homes become harder to heat or cool efficiently.

Perhaps the biggest barrier to large household-friendly apartment buildings is the requirement for a double-loaded corridor (two stairwells), a stipulation of outdated fire regulations. In Canada, the National Building Code is the basis for provincial and municipal codes. Most codes limit single-stair buildings to two storeys. In contrast, most building codes in Europe and Asia allow single-stair buildings of up to ten storeys or even higher, depending on the length of aerial-rescue ladders on fire trucks. Single-stair buildings unlock single-lot multifamily development. One to six apartments on each floor are clustered around a stairwell and elevator. The buildings can be combined, as they are in Vienna, to create a series of buildings, each one accessed through a central staircase and elevator.

Because of the requirement for double-loaded corridors, most apartments in North America are designed like hotels. Apartments have windows only on one wall. Because bedrooms legally require windows,

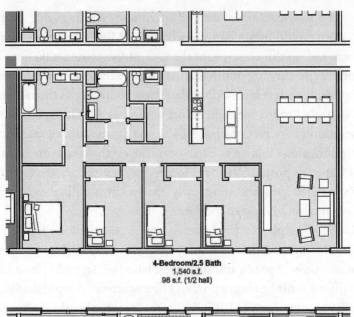

4-Bedroom/2.5 Bath
1,540 s.f.
98 s.f. (1/2 hall)

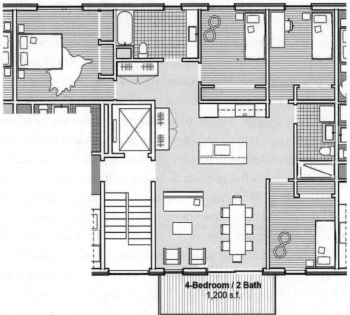

4-Bedroom / 2 Bath
1,200 s.f.

A four-bedroom, 2.5-bathroom apartment along a double-loaded corridor (*top*) and a four-bedroom, 2-bathroom unit in a single-stair block apartment (*bottom*). | Plan by Michael Eliason, for the Center for Building in North America, courtesy of Stephen Smith.

bathrooms and kitchens may be windowless. The typical layout of a larger apartment is deep and inefficient, with extra closets and bathrooms added to fill up space. Illustrations of a typical European four-bedroom apartment compared with a hypothetical North American four-bedroom (they're rarely built) give a sense of the additional light, air circulation, and flow that can be gained.

The single-stair block apartment not only has more natural light in the living/dining area, but at 111 square metres, it's almost 25 percent more compact than the double-loaded corridor apartment (143 square metres). At a construction cost of at least $2,500/square metre, that's a big savings of $80,000 per apartment. For a six-storey building with twenty-one larger homes, the developer could save $1,680,000. Compactness also reduces embodied carbon and carbon emissions.

Another advantage of the single-stair building is flexibility: a single story can accommodate anything from six studio apartments to a four-bedroom apartment and a three-bedroom apartment. Units have daylight on multiple sides, reducing the need for powered lighting. Cross-ventilation lowers the need for active cooling systems such as air conditioners. Dumb boxes also limit heat loss and the amount of heating required. Dumb boxes are a smart way to scale up affordable, energy-efficient, and healthy apartments.

■ ■ ■

To make cities environmentally sustainable, economically resilient, and socially just, the rhetoric of intensification – part of planning discourse since the 1990s – needs to be matched by a national commitment to overcome local barriers to housing development near jobs and services. Reforming zoning and building codes to emphasize affordability, accessibility, and energy efficiency will open up space for small- and large-scale developments. Building more rental apartments – nonmarket and market – is the first step in providing adequate housing for all. The second step is treating renters as right-holders.

8

How Can Renters Have the Same Rights as Owners?

What would it look like if tenants – 35 percent of "private" households, and a proportion that is increasing every year – were given the same rights as homeowners? What taxation and regulatory mechanisms would need to change to level the playing field between renters and those who have gained unearned windfall wealth from escalating land prices?

Curbing Financialization to Close the Rights Gap

The National Housing Strategy Act, which enshrines the right to housing in Canadian law, created an Office of the Federal Housing Advocate to address systemic barriers to the right to adequate housing. The first set of public hearings in 2023 was on the topic of financialization, the process by which "finance capital has come to dominate the economy and everyday life, and in which money is increasingly made through financial channels, rather than by making things."

In the context of Canadian housing, well-located land is relatively scarce, population growth is often rapid, and homebuilding is relatively inelastic, meaning it takes a lot of time, money, and labour to produce homes. These three factors are exacerbated by taxation and regulation policies at all three levels of government that favour homeowners and landlords over tenants. It's easier to make money by buying and selling scarce existing homes than creating new homes. The cost of housing gets bid up, and households spend money on rent or mortgage costs rather

"Housing for People, Not Profit" is an international tenant slogan, with Germany having some of the most effective campaigns. This poster was for a Housing Action Day in Hamburg in May 2022.

than on food, education, or leisure activities that would generate local employment. This trend maximizes the money going to banks or landlords. Investment capital that could be used to produce new technologies or develop new housing is diverted into bidding up the prices of existing homes. Speculation benefits a lot of people who invest, but it harms those who are most vulnerable and increases wealth disparities.

In Canada, home ownership is treated as a household's primary pension fund. A household is expected to go into debt to get on the property ladder, trade homes like stocks as they move up the ladder, and then reap the reward of a nest egg for retirement. Renting is treated as a low and temporary rung on the housing ladder, and renters are treated as second-class citizens with fewer rights to secure tenure.

That model worked for many households from the 1950s to the 2000s. But for the past two decades, the housing ladder (which never worked for low-income households) has lost too many rungs to work for the majority of those born after 1990. Homes are now transferred among the wealthy and their children, cutting out moderate-income new households. Younger moderate- and median-income households are locked out from home ownership. The main beneficiaries of financialization in Canada are older homeowners in big cities.

Meanwhile, pension funds – including union funds that serve teachers, nurses, and public-sector workers – have invested heavily in market rental speculation through real estate investment trusts (REITs, see page 100) and other investment instruments. Large investment funds that hold rental properties raise rents well above incomes and evict people on moderate incomes such as teachers, nurses, and public-sector workers. Everyone becomes an agent of financialization, as governments, companies, union pension funds, and households pursue the highest investment profits while neglecting the basic needs of fellow citizens, including members of their own families.

Herongate is a twenty-two-hectare apartment and townhouse complex built by apartment developer Minto in Ottawa in the 1960s. In 2011, it had over 4,000 residents, 90 percent of whom were racialized immigrants from the Horn of Africa, the Middle East, Asia, and the Caribbean. In 2007, it was sold to a REIT called TransGlobe for $180 to 200 million. The complex was flipped at least once more before being sold to Timbercreek in 2013. In the meantime, repairs were neglected, and bedbugs, cockroaches, and mould spread unchecked. Timbercreek evicted two hundred people from 80 homes in the winter of 2016 to demolish one block of properties; it evicted another five hundred low-income tenants from 150 homes in 2018 for further demolition. One tenant activist received an eviction notice with a one-time offer of $1,500 for relocation (less than a month's rent) the same week she was diagnosed with cancer.

Herongate is part-owned by Manitoba's Teachers' Retirement Allowances Fund. Timbercreek, which changed its name to Hazelview to escape negative publicity, grew by 34 percent in five years between 2015 and 2020, from 16,055 to 21,580 homes.

Similarly, PSP Investments (a Crown corporation that manages a federal pension fund) and Starlight (one of Canada's largest real estate firms) co-own 21,000 rental units, most of them in the Greater Toronto Area. PSP Investments, like many other pension funds, is legally required to maximize shareholder profits and stymie members advocating for more ethical investment. In 2021, its $870 million investment in Pretium, a US private equity firm seeking to evict 1,700 renters during a COVID-19 eviction moratorium, came to light.

Meanwhile, Starlight was encouraging "building repositioning" by neglecting essential repairs and applying for above-guideline rent increases to price tenants out. Rent control hasn't applied to vacant units in Ontario since 1996, so rent eviction allowed Starlight to raise rents with new tenants. Starlight, which is a private company, isn't required to make its earnings public, but Northview Residential REIT, a publicly traded company Starlight acquired in 2020, posted a net operating income of almost $113 million that year. Canadian Apartment Properties REIT, the single largest Canadian financialized landlord, posted a net operating income of nearly $750 million for the first nine months of 2021. It made 115 applications for above-guideline rent increases over the same period, affecting 22,600 households.

REITs owned no apartment stock in 1996. They now own 200,000 homes, about 20 percent of purpose-built rental stock across Canada. That proportion increases to 80 percent in Northwest Territories and 74 percent in Nunavut. REITs are increasing wealth for many Canadians but bringing misery for many others. It's simpler to buy REIT shares than to flip properties. It's more lucrative to squeeze every penny out of "undervalued" property than to build homes. Everyone with a pension fund gets to be a landlord, but if you're not investing in Canada's future infrastructure, who is?

Tenants occasionally fight back. For instance, a May 2017 rent strike by 1,200 tenants in fourteen buildings in Parkdale, Toronto, was called after years of rent increases with no basic maintenance. The buildings were owned by AIMCo, the Alberta government's pension fund. Tenants who received eviction notices picketed AIMCo's Toronto offices and created a website that allowed people to send emails to public service unions with pension funds in AIMCo. By August 2017, the tenants had secured an agreement to reduce that year's rent increase, won a maintenance plan, and established a fund to support tenants on income assistance from being evicted.

But big landlords, in most cases, win. They have legal teams and the power to make tenants' lives miserable and unsafe. They neglect essential repairs and send eviction notices that may or may not have validity. Legal Aid Ontario faced a 30 percent budget cut in 2019 as provincial and federal governments argued over who was responsible for services ranging from tenant to immigration law. The result: tenants can't obtain legal advice or representation in eviction hearings.

Disallowing large investment firms from purchasing certain types of properties – from nonmarket housing to mobile homes to long-term care – would take windfall profits out of consideration when they affect vulnerable groups. The federal government could also link taxation benefits for investments (such as capital gains exemptions to shareholders) to affordability for household income categories. The growing interest in ethical and environmental investment funds could help shareholders exclude REITs with business models based on tenant turnover and promote investment in building homes. Investment funds could be required to include specific wording about housing rights and definitions of affordability, and they could refer to the United Nations Sustainable Development Goal of all people having adequate homes by 2030. As part of their due diligence, potential investors could request data on tenant turnover and rent increases.

Evictions: The Worst Actors Aren't Who You Might Think

As disturbing as these actions by large financialized landlords are, they're only one symptom of a larger rights imbalance between renters and owners. Almost 6 percent of tenants (243,000 households) were evicted in Canada from 2016 to 2021. British Columbia is the capital of evictions, with more than one in ten households forced to move in five years. Across the country, Indigenous households were almost twice as likely to be evicted. And over two-thirds of those evictions (85 percent in British Columbia) had nothing to do with tenants' "fault" – that is, their inability to pay rent or their record of creating a nuisance. One-third of evictions stemmed from landlords selling their property, a quarter from landlords wanting their property for their own use, and 7.5 percent from a stated desire to renovate, repair, or demolish the property. Only about one in twenty evictions was caused by late or nonpayment of rent; two in ten were related to the tenants' behaviour. What this data points to are many small landlords, primarily investors with multiple homes, evicting tenants from "secondary rental" units such as houses, suites, or condos.

Tenants have been evicted for as little as being in arrears by two dollars (in Quebec) and five dollars (in Saskatchewan). The EU Commission on Human Rights has developed a legal framework called proportionality, under which evictions are limited to those situations that meet the following criteria: (1) the eviction must have a legitimate objective, (2) eviction must be necessary to achieve the objective, (3) there must be no reasonable alternative, and (4) the consequences of eviction must be proportionate to the objective. Provinces and territories should operate under national guidelines to enact proportionality and ensure adjudicators are trained in exploring alternatives to eviction.

Between 2011 and 2021, the number of rented condominiums in Canada almost doubled, from 419,000 to 800,000. In Toronto alone, the number increased from 81,000 to 178,000. Collectively, small investors own four times the housing stock held by REITs. Rented condominiums make up close to 50 percent of rental stock in large cities. It's easy for an individual house flipper to argue that they need vacant possession of a property, or that they or a family member plans to move into a rental home. Not all big market landlords are evil, nor are all small landlords. But whoever the landlord is, renters in Canada have limited rights to secure permanent homes.

Overall, nonmarket landlords perform better, with one-third the rate of evictions of market rental homes. This isn't surprising. In nonmarket housing, rents are generally more affordable, and rent increases are often collectively negotiated (certainly in cooperative housing and often in community housing). Nonmarket-housing providers have a mission to make housing affordable rather than to maximize profits. Practices such as emergency loans and access to housing subsidies prevent evictions and homelessness.

Market renters need similar protections.

First-time home ownership is impossible for most young households. Home ownership is limited to high-income households, investors, repeat buyers, and those reliant on the "Bank of Mom and Dad." Faced with this reality, how can renters get long-term tenure security? Canada needs a charter of renter rights to protect tenants against discriminatory rental practices (rejecting tenants because of gender, race, or sexuality or for being on welfare), evictions, and double-digit rent increases.

Once again, let's learn from a place that's doing it right.

Denmark: Curbing Financialization through Renter Protections

In 2022, I visited a friend in Copenhagen. She'd just moved into her place and told me she'd just gone to a tenants' meeting where they decided next year's rent.

"I didn't know you lived in a co-op," I said.

"We don't," she said. "We're negotiating with the landlord."

Denmark's nonmarket-housing history began, like Vienna's, after the First World War. But unlike Singapore's and Vienna's public-housing programs, Denmark's focused on cooperative housing and embraced the notion of tenant democracy at the heart of the co-op model.

About 20 percent of Danish homes today consist of nonmarket housing, mostly cooperatives, and rents are based on costs and near-universal access (most households can apply). Cost-based rents can create affordable homes for low-income households in countries with generous social assistance, such as Denmark. In countries such as Canada, additional subsidies for low-income households – or better yet, a basic income – would have to make up the difference between cost and affordability.

In Denmark, almost eight hundred housing associations own over half a million homes in a country of a little under 6 million people. Nonmarket housing is subsidized by low-interest, long-term government mortgages that cover almost 90 percent of costs. Tenants buy a 2-percent share in a co-op, and municipalities cover the remaining 8 percent of building costs. The government gives nonmarket housing providers tax-free status. After the mortgage period ends, usually after thirty years, housing associations continue to pay the same amount to the Danish government for ten years to make up for the mortgage subsidy, then continue to pay into the National Building Fund for Social Housing, which finances renovations and new nonmarket housing for an additional ten years.

Denmark, along with Finland, Austria, and Slovakia, has a national bank aimed at nonmarket lending. Other countries, such as Ireland and

Australia, have established special-purpose lending banks – the Housing Finance Agency and the National Housing Finance and Investment Corporation, respectively – to fund nonmarket and affordable market housing and energy retrofits. Individuals and unions place their pension funds in these banks.

Affordable housing is treated as essential infrastructure, and energy upgrades working toward net zero emissions are a national priority in Denmark. The National Building Fund pledged to invest $8.6 billion from 2021 to 2026 for green renovations of social housing. Seventy thousand homes were renovated in 2021 alone. Municipalities such as Copenhagen own a large proportion of urban land and have a 25-percent target for nonmarket housing. Like in Helsinki and Vienna, nonmarket housing is made possible through large-scale projects, such as Ørestad, a suburb of Copenhagen with four metro stops and ten thousand homes planned for 2025.

While cooperative housing is universal (available to all household incomes except those in the highest income quintile), about one-quarter of tenants (one-third in Copenhagen) are drawn from municipal waiting lists. As is the case in Canadian cooperatives, the tenants of each Danish housing estate, whether public or cooperative, elect a tenant board at an annual meeting, where they also decide the next year's rent and budget, approve major refurbishment and maintenance projects, and set estate rules.

Remarkably, market rents are decided in a similar manner. Thirty percent of Danish households live in private rental homes. Under Danish law, rents can't exceed an amount that covers "necessary operating expenses" and a "return on the value of the property." The latter is defined as a strict percentage of the property value pinned to the year the property was built. This cost-determined rent governs the market and the cooperative sector.

Information on costs is transparent and available online through the national statistics agency, Statbank, which publishes information on rents and house sales monthly. Landlords are allowed to charge roughly 7 percent above costs to cover profit, a competitive rate of return compared to other investments. In 2022, a typical thirty-year-old, 100-square-metre private market apartment (a large three-bedroom) in Copenhagen would rent for about CAD$1,299 – moderate-income affordability in both Canada and Denmark. Rents are often decided, as was the case for my friend, in annual building meetings, just like in co-ops. Copenhagen's tenants' union has thirty-three staff and advises tenants on negotiating with landlords on repairs, rents, and evictions. Average annual rent yields are 3.28 percent on costs. Average rent yields in Canadian cities range from 3.45 percent in Vancouver to 5.17 percent in Ottawa, all termed "really acceptable yields" by the *Global Property Guide.* I suggest that stable rent yields might be a better investment for many landlords than high but consistently risky rent yields in less regulated economies such as Canada.

However, until recent reforms were adopted, Denmark's rent-control legislation specified two important exemptions: the rules didn't apply to buildings built since 1992 or to older buildings that had undergone extensive improvements, mostly in relation to energy efficiency. Enter Blackstone.

Blackstone is the biggest landlord in the world. It has residential stock valued at CAD$1.2 trillion, including rented apartments, detached homes, long-term care homes, and student residences. Its twenty-six offices in North America, Europe, and Asia analyze property markets; they can quickly leverage $225 billion in available capital to buy up "undervalued" housing. After the Global Financial Crisis, it bought up 82,000 homes in the United States, jacked rents, evicted homeowners in mortgage default, and sold off its shares in 2019. In Spain, it bought 1,800 publicly owned homes in 2013, neglected essential repairs, evicted tenants, jacked up rents, and sold off the stock in 2019.

Then it turned to Sweden. Several decades of low rental supply after the abandonment of the Million Programme had created a potentially lucrative market of desperate renters. In 2016, Blackstone bought 16,000 apartments, including privatized public housing, from Sweden's largest real estate firm. By 2019, it had bought 5,000 more apartments. It renovated 1,000 of them and jacked rents by an average of 42 percent. It neglected the other homes. The Swedish tenants' union studied two buildings on the same estate in North Stockholm, one owned by Hembla (the name Blackstone chose for its Swedish subsidiary; *hem* means "home" in Swedish), the other owned by the local authority. The Hembla half had broken playground equipment and holes in the walls; the public-housing half was much cleaner and better maintained.

Blackstone met its match in Denmark, where it started buying apartments in late 2018. Blackstone, like other REITs, is hard to track. Individual buildings are listed under separate company names; groups of property companies have separate holding company names; holding companies are owned by companies with other names, based in the tax haven of Luxembourg. Still, enough homes were bought by the friendly sounding Kereby (Danish for "caring city") to alert the Copenhagen tenants' union, especially when emails and voice messages began to pour in from tenants.

Reports of tenant mistreatment and harassment included scaffolds blocking entrances without notice, roofs being left open mid-repair, rain coming into apartments, work crews entering homes at 6:00 a.m. without permission, multiple reminders about late rent being sent to households who paid on time, time-limited offers to vacate, and new rents being more than double the previous rent. A grassroots advocacy campaign to stop financialization grew. Political allies on the left called for tenants' rights; political allies on the right called for less foreign investment.

In July 2020, new legislation to curb financialization came into effect. Among its provisions was a clause that rent-increase exemptions can only be sought five years after a building has changed ownership. The exemptions are only applicable to buildings with a high energy rating, and they must be in line with the building's value (whereas before they could be 10 percent above the building's value). The legislation made it illegal for an owner to offer a tenant a financial incentive to vacate a dwelling. Tenants who face higher charges, or additional charges, can sue their landlords for up to thirty-six months of excess back rent. These measures were in response to the growth of all kinds of landlord malfeasance, but Blackstone was the poster child for predatory "overseas" landlords.

This victory was dampened by the fact that the Danish government is privatizing its limited public housing on the grounds that it leads to a concentration of poor and racialized people. Areas with 40 percent public housing are being targeted. In contrast to minimum nonmarket-housing targets in France, which became a way to spread public housing more evenly, social-housing regional maximums have become an excuse to dehouse low-income households. Public housing is being sold to private investors, usually with the backing of pension funds. The head of the Copenhagen tenants' union pointed out that higher retirement savings returns shouldn't be bought at the expense of the right to housing.

Rent Regulation Systems

The Danes combatted financialization by supporting transparent rent systems, long-term tenure, and tenants' rights to organize as a union, just like workers in a company. Denmark correctly treats precipitous and arbitrary rent increases as a form of eviction.

In Canada, net loss of affordable rental stock is a major cause of tenants losing their homes. Canada lost half a million homes affordable to low-income households between 2011 and 2021. Tenants were de facto evicted when rents became too much for them to afford. Landlords can then set new rents that bear no resemblance to previous rents or the costs of maintenance. Net affordable rental loss has also been exacerbated by evictions based on rental-to-ownership conversions, demolitions, and renovations.

Rent regulations are the responsibility of the provinces and territories. All have some form of rent regulation, but the rules vary. Alberta is often described as a province without rent control. And there is indeed no limit on how much a landlord can increase rent. But the landlord can only increase rent once a year, they must provide three months' notice of a rent increase, and they can't increase rents midway through a fixed-term lease agreement. There are similar rules in place in New Brunswick, Saskatchewan, and Newfoundland, but in Newfoundland, the landlord must provide six months' notice of a rent increase.

Ontario, Quebec, and British Columbia, Canada's three largest provinces, have rent stabilization, which means that landlords can only increase rents by a set amount each year, usually based on the inflation rate. However, rent controls have limitations. Ontario doesn't stabilize rents for homes built after 2018. Landlords can increase rents by any amount if the tenant changes, a process called "vacancy decontrol" and a powerful incentive to force tenants to move. All three provinces have

Home Truths

processes whereby landlords can increase rents above the set amount (in Ontario, a "guideline"). In British Columbia, reasons include repairs or renovations that could not have been foreseen or a landlord's financial loss. Ontario allows rent increases for repairs on the building. In Quebec, where tenant protections are stronger, a landlord must send a notice to tenants to increase rent above the recommended percentage, and tenants have a month to dispute this notice. Manitoba and PEI have rent stabilization combined with vacancy control. Even if a tenant moves, the unit is still covered by limits on rent increases.

Rent regulation thus comes in many forms. During the Second World War, the federal government froze rents at 1941 prices to protect renters' rights during an era of scarcity, to minimize disruption and displacement, and to allow the economy to function. The rent freezes lasted until 1949. (At the onset of COVID-19, several provinces enacted temporary rent freezes.)

A second generation of rent stabilization or control was enacted in all provinces and territories in 1975 to align with federal anti-inflation measures. Annual rent increases were capped, with provisions for additional costs such as unexpected repairs. But most provinces eroded rent controls in the ensuing decades, leaving behind a confusing patchwork of rules. Perhaps the most harmful change is vacancy decontrol, which gives landlords a powerful incentive to evict tenants. Reinstituting vacancy control might be the most direct way for provinces such as Ontario to support low-income renters and prevent homelessness.

Another method of rent regulation – described already in relation to Denmark – is cost-based rents. Rents are set by a relatively transparent and publicly accessible process based on inflation; the age, size, and location of the building; the costs of upkeep, including predictable capital upgrades; and a set profit rate for private landlords. Both landlords and tenant unions have a seat at the table when the annual rent matrix is negotiated, and buildings can also negotiate rent increases (for instance, if they decide to upgrade heating or cooling systems). Tenants can find out what the previous tenant paid through a public database, and rents are vacancy controlled (as in Manitoba and PEI). The goal in Denmark is to promote tenure neutrality: to give tenants the same rights as homeowners. It's real local democracy in action.

Orthodox economic theory is opposed to rent controls for the same reason that orthodox economic theory is opposed to minimum wages and generous welfare systems: people's rights get in the way of the sacred laws of supply and demand. According to this theory, if investors see profits being curtailed by regulation, they'll invest elsewhere. If low rents influence tenants to keep renting instead of buying homes, then the price of homes will be artificially depressed and rental demand will increase beyond supply. If rents don't cover repairs, then buildings will deteriorate.

Evidence suggests that Canadian home prices are the opposite of artificially depressed, and investment in rental properties thrives despite regulation in Quebec. Buildings deteriorate when speculation leads to windfall profits, and providing an adequate home does not. So perhaps the answer lies in addressing housing and land speculation and tearing down barriers to affordable supply, and not in eroding renters' rights.

Rent control is the main reason developers provide for the decline of purpose-built rentals in the early 1970s. But the argument doesn't hold up against the evidence. In Ontario, there were 45,000 purpose-built rental construction starts in 1972 and 25,000 in 1974. By the time rent control was imposed in 1975, there were only 8,000. The number increased after the introduction of rent controls – to 10,000 in 1976 and 12,000 in 1977. In 1992, the Ontario government lifted rent controls on new construction for five years. In 1998, it introduced vacancy decontrol and lifted rent controls on new construction until 2014. Rental starts continued to decline. From 30 percent of all new starts in the late 1960s, new purpose-built rentals declined to less than 5 percent of all new starts from 1996 to 2001.

In other words, inadequate supply may have allowed landlords to increase rents with relative impunity, but rent controls didn't affect rental construction, at least in Ontario. Other factors played a role: high land prices, exclusionary zoning for multiunit construction, taxation systems that favour ownership properties over purpose-built rental, and the absence of a national nonmarket rental construction program.

The main goal of rent regulation is to support renters' rights. In Canada, homeowners are protected from being forced to leave their homes against their will. During the job losses and slowdowns of COVID-19, the CMHC assured homeowners that their mortgage insurance meant that they could defer mortgage payments or extend their mortgage. As interest rates climbed post-COVID, the CMHC ensured that mortgage holders could extend their mortgages. If low-income senior homeowners can't pay property taxes or water bills, they're entitled to defer their payments in most Canadian cities.

In contrast, more than six thousand eviction orders were received by Ontario's Landlord Tenant Board between March and July 2020, during the COVID eviction moratorium. Four years after rent controls ended in Massachusetts in 1994, rents had jumped by an average of more than 50 percent, and rent decontrol was linked to shorter renter stays (two years as opposed to six).

Rent control isn't the only form of regulation to protect tenants. From 1991 to 1997, the Ontario Rental Housing Protection Act prohibited the loss of apartment units for condo construction. During those six years, Toronto lost only 276 rental homes. The following year, after the legislation's repeal, the city received 954 condo applications that required the loss of rental homes (roughly the same number of rental homes that had been constructed in the previous six years).

Following the legislation's repeal, the City of Toronto spent over a decade in the courts trying to establish its own bylaw. In 2007, the city adopted the Residential and Rental Property Demolition and Conversion Control bylaw. If a property owner planned to demolish, renovate, alter, or convert to other uses six or more residential rental units, they had to replace the homes with similarly sized homes at similarly sized rents and give the displaced tenants the "right of first refusal" for the new homes. A density bonus was included as a sweetener for the developer. Between 2013 and 2015, over eight hundred affordable apartments in demolished buildings were replaced by new condos. However, this protection didn't apply to rooming houses. Local rental replacement provisions were replaced by provincial protections in 2023.

In 2019, the BC government allowed municipalities to prevent landlords from evicting tenants without permits, evicting without relocating tenants, failing to provide a relocation agreement or relocation documentation, and implementing an excessive rent increase. Vancouver, Burnaby, and New Westminster passed similar bylaws and successfully weathered court challenges from landlords. The trick here (not yet implemented by British Columbia) is to open up more areas for apartment construction through zoning reform so that there is less pressure on older apartment buildings with affordable rents.

While most rental leases in Canada are for a year, leases in many European countries last much longer. In France, where most metropolitan areas have rent controls, anyone renting an unfurnished property from an individual landlord receives a three-year lease, after which three-year renewals are common. Those renting from institutional landlords receive six-year leases. Evictions require six months' notice and are not allowed during the winter months of November to March. Renters get the right of first refusal if a landlord wants to sell the home.

France's housing benefits are much more generous than Canada's. In 2020, the annual budget for French housing benefits was CAD$20 billion, six times the per-capita amount the Canadian government expended on housing benefits that year. About half of French renter households received rental assistance in 2018, and benefits covered between one-third and one-half of their rent. In 2021, Canada's Parliamentary Budget Office estimated that over the period of 2021 to 2025, affordable-housing funding would average 16 percent of the projected affordability gap and about $63 per month per household in housing need.

After two years as a renter in Denmark, you can live in your home as a tenant indefinitely. If a landlord claims they want to live in the home (the only reason for a "no fault" eviction), they must give you a year's notice. This is true tenure neutrality: long-term leases with locked-in rents that increase with costs based on a transparent, negotiated process. If necessary, rents are supplemented by government benefits. Keep in mind that France, Denmark, and Germany all spend 0.7 percent of their GDP on rent supplements. Canada spends less on all housing-related expenditures, including its incentive programs for market rental construction (which is unaffordable to low- and moderate-income households and often displaced by exclusionary zoning and inadequate renter protections).

A rights-based housing system in Canada would protect renters from evictions and give renters the same rights as owners. Coupled with transparent land ownership, renter protections would lead to lower rents, longer leases, adequate housing, and tenure neutrality.

Regulating Short-Term Rentals

Canada's loss of affordable rental housing has been fuelled by short-term rentals. By definition, a short-term rental is a dwelling unit, usually furnished, that is rented out for less than twenty-eight days at a time. In 2015, short-term rentals – in Canada and abroad – were almost universally illegal, except for licenced bed and breakfasts. But this illegality didn't stop their rapid growth. Informal vacation rentals – a second home such as a lakeside cottage or a temporary sublet of a home or part of a home – joined the internet in the 1990s when Vacation Rentals by Owner (now Vrbo) and later Booking.com allowed people from around the world to browse listings and book via credit card. Airbnb, founded in 2008, initially focused on rooms in people's homes; a decade later, it had 6 million listings around the world, most of them entire vacant homes.

In Canada, nearly half of short-term rentals are in the country's three most populous metropolitan areas. In contrast to Airbnb's origins as a way for individual owners or renters to sublet or subsidize their rent, twenty-five "hosts" were estimated to have hundreds of listings with gross revenues of over $1 million per landlord per year, and 84 percent of revenues came from "entire home" listings. Airbnb removed an estimated 17,000 to 45,000 rental apartments from the long-term rental market by 2018. Toronto and Montreal lost about 7,000 homes each, and Vancouver 5,000.

In 2016, Quebec became the first Canadian jurisdiction to introduce a law regulating short-term rentals. Hosts had to register with the province and pay an accommodation tax. However, fewer than 5 percent of reported listings were certified the following year. British Columbia and Ontario followed with agreements to gain millions in taxes by treating short-term rentals as hotel accommodation.

Municipalities have been more interested in stemming the loss of well-located long-term rental homes. Toronto, like many other local governments, bans the rental of apartments that aren't primary residences; it allows primary residences to be rented for a maximum of 28 days, for a total of 180 days in the year. But Airbnb, after promising to enforce licensing, left it to cities to find illegal units by contracting third parties to scrape through listings. Airbnb allowed 8,400 listings to be listed for longer than 28 days without converting to long-term leases. Plan A, a Vancouver company that rents three hundred furnished apartments with two-to-four-month leases, has engaged in numerous battles with the BC Residential Tenancy Branch for misrepresenting the condition of its apartments, hiking laundry machine costs from $3.25 to $14.25 overnight, and setting arbitrary move-out dates for tenants. Plan A argues that tenants of furnished apartments with short-term leases do not have the same rights as tenants with long-term leases.

To be clear, licenced hosts should be allowed to rent parts of their homes on a short-term (or long-term) basis as an affordability mechanism. And there need to be monthly leases for short-term residents, including those staying in a city for medical or employment reasons. But if the goal is to decrease home prices and rents, then licensing and limiting short-term rentals is part of the solution.

Transparent Ownership and Licenced Landlords

Transparent ownership would expose predatory practices by some landlords and support better affordable housing policy. Large-scale housing investors are often adept at hiding their holdings. So are governments.

In the United States, any developer who receives low-income housing tax credits must display the costs of construction. In Canada, the CMHC doesn't provide any information on rents from projects subsidized by its $89 billion affordable-housing programs, which mostly go to the private sector.

One form of transparency is licensing landlords, just as restaurants, childcare centres, or any other business is licenced. In British Columbia, most municipalities register long-term and short-term landlords. The City of Vancouver, for instance, requires the business licence to be displayed, along with the name and contact information of the landlord or their agent, a phone number for inspection complaints, and the contact information for the Renter Office, which supports tenants with health and safety issues. An open database lists buildings with five or more properties that have unresolved health or safety bylaw infractions. The cost to the landlord is hardly onerous: $84 per unit per year.

Toronto's RentSafeTO, developed in 2017, registers all landlords who own more than ten units or operate a building over three storeys. Landlords are required to post contact information and outstanding bylaw enforcement issues. They must register capital plans for major building repairs, electrical maintenance, cleaning, and waste management. Buildings are audited once every three years. As of 2020, only 3,472 buildings were registered, but audits showed improvement in building maintenance over the previous three years.

Montreal introduced a landlord registry in 2023 that targeted 250,000 homes in 12,000 buildings of more than eight units. Landlords must submit a report every five years on conditions and rents. The program is being phased in over four years, starting with the largest buildings.

The City of New Westminster in Metro Vancouver has gone a step further, creating a system of fines and potential loss of licences for landlords who evict tenants without relocating them or who implement excessive rent increases.

In these examples, it's grassroots tenant unions and provincial and national advocacy groups such as RentSafe who have led the way. In New Westminster, an Instagram star, a cat named BenBen, helped attract attention to poor rental conditions and evictions. For some reason, companion animals appeal to voters more than humans in need.

A spin-off advantage of widespread landlord licensing is that it would help keep track of rents and building conditions across the country in real time. The CMHC doesn't generally keep track of rents outside of purpose-built rental, which means that its "average market rent" measure is generally much lower than reality. Landlord associations complain about onerous licensing costs passed on to tenants, and tenants complain that there aren't enough inspection officers to follow up on complaints. One possibility, of course, is turning market rentals into nonmarket rentals through acquisitions.

Acquisitions Programs and Tenant Rights

There are over 1 million older high-rise rental homes across Canada, the biggest market source of affordable housing in cities. The federal social-housing programs of the 1970s and 1980s included an acquisition component: nonmarket providers could purchase rooming houses and other private rental buildings at risk of becoming unaffordable. The National Housing Strategy has focused on new construction, except for the Rapid Housing Initiative, which allows commercial buildings such as hotels to be converted into housing. Nonmarket providers and the Federation of Canadian Municipalities want federal programs to have an acquisitions component.

A successful acquisition program would identify buildings at risk of losing affordability in neighbourhoods that are undergoing rapid change. It would purchase private properties as soon as they go up for sale and have deep pockets for essential upgrades. It would minimize disruptions for existing tenants while ensuring that new tenants are in need of affordable housing.

Milton-Parc in Montreal is a tenant-led acquisition initiative from the early 1980s that transformed six hundred private rental buildings on six city blocks into nonmarket housing on a community land trust. The properties were bought by the federal government and leased by the municipal government to community-housing providers and new cooperatives.

In Vancouver, when it came to acquiring single-room accommodation hotels, BC Housing rapidly purchased properties, but it failed to make timely essential repairs or provide social and health supports to those in the greatest need. The BC government needs to bite the bullet, greatly increase social assistance, and accept that providing adequate supportive housing will take billions of dollars in upgrades that will never be recouped in rents. Acquiring and renovating properties is not cheap, but it's less expensive than continually tearing down encampments.

Quebec continued to support acquisitions after the federal government abandoned its affordable-housing policy in 1992. In the 1980s and 1990s, Quebec's housing agency, Société d'habitation du Québec, funded the purchase and renovation of apartment buildings that were transferred to nonmarket providers. It provided funding to preemptively purchase buildings before other funding was committed. Montreal's public-housing authority acquired 3,080 apartment units and 398 rooming-house rooms. More recently, in 2016, the province allowed

Montreal and other municipalities to directly purchase and expropriate housing. Montreal recently used its new powers of "right of first refusal" to identify 447 multiunit apartment buildings at risk of losing their affordability. However, because of cutbacks to provincial housing budgets, only one purchase has occurred thus far, a six-storey building for $6.5 million in 2022. It had been bought by a developer in 2017, who evicted the tenants for a renovation that never occurred.

Two other provinces have recently created acquisition funds. Nova Scotia developed a Community Housing Acquisition Program in 2022 to offer up to $10 million in low-interest loans to municipalities or non-market providers to purchase properties with at least five homes (including rooming houses). It had several successful acquisitions in its first year. The Housing Trust of Nova Scotia borrowed $5.6 million, which it leveraged into a $30 million loan from the Bank of Montreal to purchase five properties with a total of 295 homes, along with $445,000 in waived charges, including land-transfer taxes, from the City of Halifax. The loans also support $15 million in energy-efficient renovations. The Bank of Montreal said the Nova Scotia government's creditworthiness informed its decision to provide a large loan to a new organization. The tenants, some of whom have lived in the buildings for thirty to forty years, have been promised rents of no more than $1,247 a month, which is low- to moderate-income affordability.

British Columbia announced a much larger ($500 million) Rental Protection Fund in 2023. It has some innovative aspects, including an arms-length agency that can provide rapid grants to nonmarket providers and the potential for social investors to provide "patient capital" loans with a 2-percent annual payback from rents.

Acquisitions, like renter protections and zoning- and building-code amendments, are programs that desperately need national leadership and tripartite collaboration between levels of government. One issue is that apartment neighbourhoods have had their zoning frozen to 1960s standards. Minimum parking requirements created for mobile middle-class singles and couples no longer meet the needs of lower-income families with children, older people, and new migrants, all heavily reliant on transit. Large underutilized surface parking lots could become sites for new shops and services or infill housing, if any of those uses were allowed. But health centres, childcare and educational facilities, large grocery stores, public services, places of worship, cafés and restaurants, and ATMs or banks aren't allowed. Meanwhile, tenants face the awful "choice" of remaining in overcrowded, poorly maintained homes or being evicted by large landlords who see a "rent gap" in well-located areas zoned for high-rises.

A Better Future for Renters

When assigning blame, it's tempting to look to "others" (developers, foreign buyers, new migrants) rather than looking inwards to a housing system we've taken for granted for far too long. Canada's housing system was built on a foundation that is no longer socially, economically, or environmentally sound – or morally just. It supports property speculation as a way to save for retirement. The result is an increasingly impoverished nation that rewards car-dependent sprawl and discourages innovation. The system is deeply unfair to low- and moderate-income renters, who are punished for not fitting into out-of-date expectations for families, work, and life.

Renters need the right to tenure security. They need predictability about rent increases. They need homes that are well maintained, well heated in the winter and cooled in the summer, without having to pay "extra" for the right to a habitable home. Most of all, they shouldn't have to subsidize homeowners through an exploitative rental system that feeds pension funds by denying people their rights.

9

Is There a Future for Affordable Home Ownership?

Many cities – Paris, Helsinki, Copenhagen – have committed to making 25 to 35 percent of total housing nonmarket rentals, with an emphasis on large-scale, mixed-tenure development. Other places, such as Vienna, have become wealthy while keeping most of their homes nonmarket rentals. The idea that home ownership is the only route to household wealth or even tenure security must be uncoupled from Canadian housing policy.

Even if Canada were to commit for the next three decades to a rule of thirds for new developments – one-third each nonmarket rental, regulated market rental, and ownership homes – home ownership would remain the majority form of tenure. Canada has 15 million private homes, for a population of 40 million. That's an average household size of 2.7 people. Two-thirds of homes, about 10 million, are lived in by the owner; 4.5 million homes, a little over 30 percent, are market rental (either purpose-built or secondary), and 894,000 are nonmarket rental, about 5 percent.

In 2056, Canada's population is projected to be 60 million. If we hope to end homelessness and meet the needs of low-income households, we'd need to build 18 million homes, more than doubling our current stock. Even if the new stock were to use the rule of thirds, as of 2056, 20 percent of the total stock would be nonmarket rental, 30 percent market rental, and 50 percent market owned homes. The average household size would be 1.8, reflecting the higher numbers of single people, especially at the younger end (students and others in their twenties) and older end (seniors, especially those over eighty-five). The best-case scenario is that new ownership homes (mostly condominiums in apartment buildings) will be affordable to median- and higher-income households in higher-density urban areas, with some moderate-income affordability in smaller communities. Regardless of location, attention should be paid to shared spaces, necessary to combat the social isolation that can accompany living alone. How can we make this happen?

Addressing Wealth Maximization and
Generational Inequalities

The most insidious aspect of financialization is the widening wealth gap between homeowners and tenants. In 2021, the average homeowner born between 1955 and 1964 was worth more than $1.4 million, 6.3 times the wealth of tenants born in the same era. In 2005, the wealth gap between homeowners and renters for the same cohort was less than half that amount. What is more, the wealth gap is intergenerational: a 2020 Ontario poll found that 41 percent of parents with children under thirty-eight helped their children purchase a home. The average gift exceeded $73,000. The average loan exceeded $40,000. Even with access to the "Bank of Mom and Dad" for a down payment, a median-income household in Toronto buying a median-income home would have to devote 56 percent of its income to mortgage payments.

Racial inequality is also baked into the wealth gap: Black Canadians and Indigenous people have home-ownership rates almost 28 percent and 23 percent lower than the national average, even in higher-income households. Home ownership has become a racist gated community because of decisions made at all three levels of government.

From the 1940s onwards, the federal government responded to bad rental conditions by subsidizing and promoting home ownership over renting, which it viewed as a temporary second-class option. This approach, in which governments provided land, loan guarantees, and set prices, worked at first. After 1.5 million homes were built between 1945 and 1960, home-ownership rates soared from 40 percent to 60 percent. Then results stalled. Over the next sixty years, home ownership slowly increased to a high of 69 percent in 2011, followed by a decade-long decline to 66.5 percent in 2021. Short of a Singapore-type policy intervention, in which governments build and allocate homes and strictly control prices, it's hard to imagine a scenario where home ownership would address the needs of all households.

Measures intended to spur home ownership (including capital gains tax exemptions for principal residences, low interest rates, and grants and tax-free savings accounts for first-time home buyers) often fuel speculation. Subsidizing speculation has led to the wealth gap. Between 1976 and 2016, price escalation increased net wealth in owner-occupied principal residences by $2.6 trillion, and then house prices doubled by 2023. One-twentieth of the wealth is owned by households headed by an adult under thirty-five (who make up 29 percent of adults). One-third of the wealth is owned by people sixty-five or over (21 percent of adults). But annual revenue from municipal property taxation decreased by $4.4 billion between 1976 and 2016, just as income tax rates have decreased and become more regressive. One generation benefited, at a huge cost to the next generations.

If you're a boomer who bought your first house in your twenties or thirties between 1965 and 1985, congratulations! You're sitting on huge unearned wealth that's blocking your child or grandchild from finding an affordable home near you. If you, my fellow boomer, recently voted for a mayor who promised no property tax increase, or if you opposed an affordable-housing development in your neighbourhood, shame on you. You're as bad as any REIT.

There's no magic-bullet fix. The current generation would need home prices to fall to a third of current prices (a quarter in Toronto, a fifth in Vancouver). If that happened overnight, two-thirds of households would lose value on their primary asset, and one-third would be paying off debt on an asset worth a fraction of its former value. That's what led to the collapse of economies during the Global Financial Crisis.

A softer alternative is holding home costs stable while tripling or quintupling incomes. This is the idea behind the CMHC's recommendation to vastly increase the number of market homes. However, even the CMHC's scenario of 5.8 million new homes by 2030 wouldn't make them affordable for median-income owners in big cities. Nor would it make a dent in homelessness or low-income housing needs. Canada's housing crisis won't be fixed through home ownership.

I'll go further. If home ownership remains the subsidized norm, no scenario will decrease homelessness, bring affordable housing into reach, and move Canada away from unsustainable sprawl. We need more non-market and market rentals and stronger tenant rights, which will require reversing at least some of the policy settings that resulted in windfall profits for owners.

This may harm the investment expectations of owners, especially those nearing retirement age. Are there ways they can convert some of their home to rental? Can younger households share the costs of owner-ship in ways that build community? Can the downside of reduced invest-ment profits lead, on the upside, to mixed-income, mixed-use apartments in mixed communities?

Flexible Home Sharing and Cohousing

Around the corner from where I grew up in Montreal, my friend Ursula has lived in the same three-storey home, originally a triplex, since just after her birth in 1963. She lived with her parents in the middle flat dur-ing her childhood. When she started university, she moved to the upper flat with roommates. When her father died, she and her mother lived in the upper flat and rented out the other two. After a few years, Ursula moved to the middle flat where she lived with roommates and then her husband. When their two children got older, they took over the upper flat, making it a duplex, and Ursula's mother moved to the ground floor. Ursula's mother, who is now in her nineties, continues to live there. She benefits from an accessible flat close to shopping, a library, and her bridge club. Ursula and her husband are considering converting the home back to a triplex so one of their adult children and their partner can live upstairs. This house may become that urban unicorn, a home passed down over generations.

Montreal's duplexes and triplexes assist this kind of flexibility. Across Canada, from the late nineteenth century to the 1960s, it was common for households to double up, have lodgers, or subdivide their homes as affordability mechanisms. In 1931, over one in four households in Toronto had a lodger or was doubled up. After the 1960s, the deconversion of secondary units and rooming houses predominated in most city centres, while conversions became illegal because of more stringent building and zoning codes. We tried to crush housing diversity. Stubborn diversity may be set for a return.

Cities have recently facilitated a new generation of subdivided homes and accessory dwelling units (ADUs), including garden suites and laneway apartments. Toronto offers a forgivable loan of $50,000 to help create new rental units. The loan can be converted to a grant over five years provided the rent stays below the market rate. Funding can be increased if the homes have two or more bedrooms or deep affordability. Portland, following slow take-up of its ADU scheme, offered easy subdivision of lots so owners could sell parcels. Dweller, a start-up in Portland, is prefabricating tiny homes that homeowners can put in their yards and rent out. They pay no upfront costs and keep 30 percent of the rental income. We can't duplex and triplex our way out of the housing crisis, but we can facilitate affordable rentals on existing properties.

Several start-ups are simplifying the process of renting out spare rooms, and others are promoting intergenerational co-living. Canada HomeShare started in Toronto in 2018 with one hundred placements but experienced a three-year hiatus during COVID-19. It matches older households in larger homes with students in need of housing. Students pay $400 to $600 a month to rent a room and are expected to provide five to seven hours a week of companionship and help around the home. The service includes a criminal record check and interviews with the senior landlord and lodger before it arranges tenancy contracts.

Other start-ups are helping people copurchase properties. GoCo Solutions works in Toronto with households who can't afford current prices but are looking for ways to help with childcare and senior care needs and alleviate loneliness. GoCo facilitates access to financing (always risky when there are two or more households engaged in a purchase) and the development of contracts. Husmates, a "dating app for copurchasers," brings together intergenerational families or two or more households who agree on the location, maintenance, dispute resolution, and exit strategies. In an age of higher divorce rates, there's nothing inherently riskier about purchasing with a friend or even a stranger rather than a spouse.

The cohousing movement: Multiple households work together on a lot or group of lots to create and develop co-owned homes. *Baugruppen* (building groups), as they're known in Germany, allow greater affordability, because several households work together to create multiunit homes that meet their needs. The homes usually include shared common space, such as a garden or children's play area, and other aspects of shared living, such as a laundry and communal meals and social activities.

The cohousing movement is distinct from the nonmarket cooperative movement. Canada has at least twenty cohousing communities that are members of a national cohousing association. Seniors' cohousing projects include Wolf Willow in Saskatchewan and Harbourside in British Columbia. In The Hague, in the Netherlands, sixty cohousing communities for seniors now combine shared facilities such as a communal room and visiting nurses with self-government and a commitment to mutual care.

Charles Montgomery is a member of one such community. Little Mountain Cohousing in Vancouver is a six-storey building that opened in 2021. It includes twenty-five homes, a roof garden, a common kitchen and dining room, and a children's playroom. The households have communal meals two to three times a week, and residents have arranged informal after-school care and other mutual aid. As Montgomery points out, this is, at best, a middle-income solution: the apartments cost $88 per square metre to construct, or about $880,000 per home. But the apartment building replaced three houses in an area where $5 million is the asking price.

Montgomery notes that regulations and financing are huge barriers to housing innovation: "It can take as little as four months to get permission to replace an old detached house with a luxury mini-mansion. But despite the high praise our project received from politicians and planners, it took us two and a half years for us to get permission to build. Each month of waiting cost us $55,000 in consultant fees and loan interest. If we had gained permission within a year, we would have saved a whopping $40,000 per apartment."

Cohousing and subdividing homes require relaxed zoning and building codes, grants or forgivable loans for affordable rental creation, and much faster financing and planning approvals. At best, cohousing will assist some median-income households. ADUs will only assist low-income households if income assistance or substantial grants are offered. And unless these options are on a community land trust, they will be subject to speculation, like any other market option.

Self-Built Housing, Tiny Homes, and Encampments

Along with flexible houses, self-built housing is another old DIY idea enjoying a resurgence. Historically, hundreds of thousands of homes across Canada were constructed by the families who lived in them. Entire neighbourhoods such as Earlscourt in Toronto in the 1910s and the Antigonish Movement's co-ops in Nova Scotia in the 1930s were developed through self-built housing. In the United States, one-third of all single-family homes in 1949 were constructed by owners. In Canada, the Veterans Land Act made cheap land, financing, and technical assistance available, including construction courses, model home kits, and on-site inspections. Collective self-built housing can promote a sense of community. But self-built housing is now being sold as a libertarian, "one weird trick" solution to the global housing crisis. Heaven forbid we solve the crisis by building publicly owned housing.

In the 1990s, ten thousand "Grow Homes" were constructed in Montreal and across Canada and the United States. Grow Homes are 168-square-metre townhouses with four-metre frontages. They were sold in partially finished states. The basement and second storey were later completed based on the household's future needs and means. The homes were less expensive (about one-quarter the cost of the average Montreal home in 1991) and more energy-efficient because of their replicable rowhouse design, smaller size, and prefabricated components. Nearly three-quarters of households who made further renovations did so without a professional builder. The model continues to be popular, particularly in Montreal. It's an entirely private-sector model that reveals how greater density and affordability can be facilitated with reformed zoning codes (the original homes required modifications to lot sizes and setbacks) and more relaxed building codes. Because of the high cost of land, this model could meet the needs of median-income first-time home buyers rather than the moderate-income households it was designed to assist.

The best-known organization associated with self-built homes is Habitat for Humanity. According to its website, Habitat works in seventy countries around the world, and there are fifty affiliates across Canada. Its model is simple: households who apply and are accepted purchase their home through a no-down-payment mortgage geared to their income and contribute at least five hundred volunteer hours to Habitat, either directly helping with construction or in their second-hand ReStore shops. Once they move in, homeowners pay 30 percent of their gross income as a monthly mortgage payment, which includes principal repayment and property tax. They're responsible for maintaining their own home. Habitat provides "homeowner education classes," ranging from financial literacy and budgeting to home repair and maintenance. Participants can sell their properties after the mortgage is repaid, but Habitat retains the right of first refusal on repurchasing homes for reuse by other households in need.

Habitat is a niche response and not, strictly speaking, self-build (the construction teams are led by professionals). It built 267 homes in 2019 and a total of 3,886 homes since it started in Canada in 1985. A 2012 study found that 50 to 90 percent of applicants are turned away, mostly because their incomes are inadequate to pay a monthly mortgage, even one that is subsidized. In 2019, a class-action lawsuit by fifty Edmonton households charged that Habitat for Humanity was requiring them to apply to a bank for half of their mortgage and pay interest as part of that loan, which they couldn't afford to do. The Edmonton affiliate claimed it was a victim of its own success: it had accumulated $27 million in debt after repurchasing some of the 2,500 homes it built in the city.

Having said that, Habitat is one of the few nonmarket developers with a Canada-wide mandate and the capacity to scale up. In June 2023, it announced a bold plan for 10,000 new homes over seven years in the Waterloo Region, northwest of Toronto. Habitat promised a Victory Houses–type program (70 percent ownership and 30 percent rental homes) based on free government land, cost-based production, and means-testing for households. They've embraced four- to six-storey

Dignity Village in Portland | Paul Dunn for *YES! Magazine*

buildings rather than Habitat's traditional townhouse model. Their target is middle-income households priced out of home ownership. Although they talk about moderate-income "nurses, teachers and personal support workers," their criteria target households earning between $67,266 and $102,610 or 80 to 120 percent of median income, higher than most salaries for nurses, teachers, and personal support workers. Habitat and Grow Homes, under current funding settings, don't help low-income households. Self-built ownership can't be the simple answer to progressively realizing the right to housing.

Several low-income-led self-build-housing initiatives, particularly in Latin America, have been inspired by development theorist John Turner's motto "Housing Is a Verb." In Alto Comedero, Argentina, the Tupac Amaru collective, led by Indigenous women, constructed 2,700 fifty-square-metre two-bedrooms around collective barbeques, playgrounds, sports fields, and a large swimming pool. Like the Antigonish Movement in Canada, their initiative was part of a larger self-help economic development in a neglected and stigmatized area. In 2011, the collective, which trained low-income people in construction, built the tiny homes for CAD$40,000 each – 33 percent cheaper than local public housing and four times the pace of private-sector builders.

In Portland, Dignity Village has been on government land since 2004. It began as a tent-based encampment. Now, sixty people live in **tiny homes.** Each tenant can only live in Dignity Village for two years. Water, sewage, and garbage collection are provided by the city. Self-built with the help of volunteers using donated materials, the homes have no toilets, so the city provides a toilet block and one propane-heated shower. It's not enough for sixty people. Because the site is isolated (a thirty-five-minute bus ride to most services), it took many years to arrange for on-site social services from an agency that could provide employment support, social security applications, housing searches, health-care access, mental health and addiction support, and ID and other document services.

Dignity Village is a self-governed and gated community. It has a democratically elected council of nine residents who are responsible for day-to-day decisions. All residents can vote on big decisions (like whether to evict a resident or enter into contracts with service providers) in town hall–style meetings. Unlike private landlords, the community does not bar people with criminal records from living there. Police call-outs are half as likely as they are in the city on average. But the community does have higher rates of eviction than many transitional housing programs.

Residents pay thirty-five dollars a month in rent for homes that range in size from 4.5 to 9 square metres. They must adhere to five rules: no violence, no theft, no alcohol or drugs within a one-block radius, no "constant" disruptive behaviour, and the performance of at least ten hours per week of village upkeep work. A 2010 evaluation reported significant cost savings compared to alternative programs. The annual operating budget is CAD$38,000, six dollars per individual per night, as compared to seventeen dollars per night in "warming centre" shelters and eighty-eight dollars per night in transition houses. Dignity Village has the same big issue as any transitional housing program: 70 percent of those forced to leave after two years return to homelessness because there are no affordable housing options. .

Allowing dozens of permanent tiny-home or mobile-home villages in every Canadian city might be one fast, relatively effective ad-hoc response to homelessness. The great advantage of the Dignity Village model is that it's self-built and self-managed, which may make it more empowering than a home in a four-storey building provided by an agency. Disadvantages include long waits for essential social services and inadequate water and sanitation services. But these are political barriers as much as they are faults of the concept. Another barrier is the visibility of self-built homes, especially if they have toilet and shower blocks, rather than more conventional buildings. Propane stoves are a fire and carbon monoxide risk, but detectors are cheap, and electrical hook-ups are possible. Six to ten tiny homes in a conventional lot still have less density than a four-storey building with common spaces downstairs, and the latter is certainly more suited to Canada's weather extremes. The biggest problem with Dignity Village and other tiny homes is that they're seen as transitional solutions. They must be considered permanent housing until there are better alternatives.

Tiny homes have been proposed across Canada, but so far only one initiative has begun to scale up, and it isn't self-built or self-managed. Homes for Heroes in Calgary was completed in 2019. It has twenty tiny homes, each 28 square metres, aimed at homeless veterans. Each self-contained home has a kitchen, bathroom, Murphy bed, basic cable, Wi-Fi, and telephone line. They cost roughly CAD$70,000 per unit and were supported by government grants and a $1.5 million corporate donation. The complex has on-site supports and a community garden. The courtyard model is convivial and cheaper than an apartment building, but the homes aren't as accessible as four-storey modular, and they house fewer people with less common space. The homes are transitional, with a maximum two-year stay. Another twenty homes were constructed in Edmonton, and more projects are planned for Kingston and Winnipeg.

Another potential model emerged in Toronto when Khaleel Seivwright, a carpenter, designed and built one hundred tiny shelters and dropped them off in Toronto's parks and ravines in 2021. The shelters, constructed for $1,000 each, are the size of a single-person tent – two metres by one metre – and not tall enough to stand in. They include a window for light and are stuffed with enough insulation to stay warm overnight in winter, particularly since body heat can assist in a structure that small. They have carbon monoxide and smoke detectors. For his work, which was entirely on "his dime and his time" along with donations, Seivwright was slapped with an injunction forbidding any further construction. The structures were removed from the approximately seventy-five encampments now active in Canada's largest and richest city and destroyed by city staff.

There's a strong rights-based argument for municipalities to stop wasting money tearing down "informal" tiny shelter communities in public spaces such as parks. A rights-based approach would accept that these communities are a strong visual reminder of the impact of the housing crisis that also provide a much safer and humane alternative to sleeping in inadequate shelter services. Encampments can – if provided with basic water, sanitation and garbage services, and heating and cooling – be a short-term alternative, so long as livable, sustainable permanent alternatives are built simultaneously. Tiny home clusters are a potentially inexpensive option, like mobile-home communities, and perhaps a better visual fit with single-storey homes in suburbs. They aren't the most efficient or humane way to end homelessness. Permanent homes with supports – Housing First – are still the best way.

The case studies visually symbolize an individualistic and privatized "self-help" alternative. But, they are shaped by government action and inaction as much as any other housing option. Habitat for Humanity relies on government land grants and charitable donations to provide middle-income households with affordable housing, and the self-build aspect is performative. Dignity Village and tiny shelters rely on city services and land, donated materials, and nonprofit supports. Grow Homes, like any form of permanent urban housing, rely on water, sewer, public transit, and other infrastructure as well as zoning and building permissions.

"Housing" is a verb, and governments need to fund and enable inexpensive alternatives, whether self-built or nonmarket. There's no "one weird trick" to enabling the right to housing without government action, including tiny homes and self-builds.

Single-Family Lot Conversions to Apartments

One of the advantages of zoning- and building-code transformation is that it would open the door to small-scale developers and rental-housing providers. One intriguing model is the apartment block common in Athens called a *polykatoikia* (pronounced "pol-i-kat-i-KEE-A" for those who wish to drop this term into casual conversation). They arose during a post–Second World War housing shortage, when the Greek government had no money to fund public housing and banks were reluctant to lend to developers. Developers purchased land from individual owners in return for a share of the constructed homes to live in or rent. The government offered tax concessions. Over three decades, about 35,000 apartment blocks were built. The number of flats varied from ten to twenty-four, with an average size of seventy-five square metres (two to three bedrooms). Most were built on single lots.

The polykatoikia's easily replicable "dumb box" design was quickly constructed around Athens, which has a six-storey height limit but no use-based zoning. This means homes on lower floors interspersed with roof-top decks or set-back penthouses, shops, doctor's offices, and even small industrial workshops. Despite being walk-ups, the most expensive flats are generally on the top floors, which have more sunlight and less noise. Workshops and cafés, along with generous balconies and a good climate, mean lively streets, day and night, a boon to neighbourhood life. The buildings' reliance on central heating and shared electricity led to problems during extreme austerity measures imposed after the Global Financial Crisis. Some tenants couldn't pay their share of energy costs. The aging concrete structures house owners and tenants who have lived in the buildings their entire lives. The predominance of this elderly "overhoused" population signals the need to renew buildings every fifty to seventy years. With these limitations in mind, this model suggests a way for aging empty nester homeowners in Canada to remain in their neighbourhoods while supplementing their retirement savings with rental income.

Recycle, Renovate, Convert

Economists often speak of the rent gap – the distance between the current return on land and the potential return on land in a market-based economy. New well-located condominiums found sites by demolishing or converting older rental apartments. How can we prevent the displacement of low-cost housing communities near jobs and services and develop new low-cost housing communities on scarce urban land coveted by powerful market redevelopers?

Three mechanisms have already been discussed:

- ending exclusionary zoning everywhere and subdividing existing homes
- setting nonmarket housing targets for cities and neighbourhoods
- establishing renter protections and rental-only or nonmarket-only zoning.

But we also need to consider the steep environmental costs of knockdown rebuilds. This housing sector is one of the biggest producers of waste, often toxic, in the case of asbestos insulation. France has led the way in developing high-quality, durable, low-impact materials and approaches to the circular economy – a framework that keeps materials and buildings in circulation for as long as possible to reduce waste and pollution.

In 2021, the Pritzker Prize, the highest award in architecture, went to a French firm led by Anne Lacaton and Jean-Philippe Vassal that rejected public-housing demolition and low-income "social cleansing." Instead, they prioritized renovation and the expansion of nonmarket housing while keeping residents in place. The Tour Bois-le-Prêtre in the north of Paris was in poor repair and needed an energy retrofit. The sixteen-storey postwar tower block had ninety-six homes. The design solution expanded existing flats with winter gardens or enclosed balconies and added new flats on the sides of the concrete structure. Most importantly, renovations proceeded in a careful, incremental way so that nobody had to move out, rents were not raised, and there was no "stock transfer" to a private developer. Nobody was "decanted," the new euphemism for those temporarily or permanently evicted from their homes.

These lessons haven't yet percolated to the Anglosphere, where the rhetoric of "social mix," the financialization of land, and contempt for nonmarket housing has destroyed many postwar public-housing projects. In London alone, fifty public-housing estates underwent "regeneration" from 2010 to 2020. Although the total number of homes doubled, London saw a net loss of 8,000 nonmarket rental homes. Some see this as economic realism. Rights advocates see it as social cleansing – replacing low-income tenants with high-income homeowners.

Regent Park in Toronto, Canada's oldest and largest public-housing project, was built between 1946 and 1960 and has a total of 3,200 homes. It replaced "slum housing" that was deemed too decrepit to preserve, although similar homes to the south and north were selling for millions by the turn of the twenty-first century. Regent Park residents were told they could move back into shiny new public homes, but only 23 percent did so. Originally, only 20 percent of Regent Park's residents could be on social assistance, but Toronto Community Housing showed a preference for people with disability, refugees, and women escaping domestic violence who would otherwise be homeless. Their low incomes, exacerbated by social assistance and public-housing subsidy austerity, meant the buildings deteriorated with no new capital investment in retrofits.

Fifty years after low-income people were evicted from "slum housing" to create Regent Park, another generation of low-income people were evicted on the same site. During both evictions, it was claimed the eviction would be good for poor people: lower-income tenants would interact with their higher-income neighbours, for example, and learn social norms about workforce participation. The largest local condominium developer, Daniels Corporation, led the public-private partnership. Two thousand public homes in Regent Park South were replaced, and five thousand condominiums were added, some with limited first-time sale "affordability." The development included no new nonmarket homes, and in some cases, the new homes were smaller. The three-to-five-year relocation process led only half of the residents to exercise their right to return. The project included a new school, health centre, arts centre with a café, supermarket, and bank, but the financialized model of re-development simply wasn't financially viable, even with a seventy-to-thirty market-nonmarket split. In late 2021, the project's net loss was

$1.58 billion, including contributions of $494 million from municipal, provincial, and federal governments. A shortfall of $182 million as of 2019 was paid for by the municipal government. Windfall profits from condominium sales went to the private developer; the risks, as is always the case with public-private partnerships, were borne by taxpayers.

At the very least, a ballot of residents should be required to approve a knockdown rebuild of their homes. They should have informed consent as to the right of return, and the length of time absent from their homes should be guaranteed. Given the environmental, economic, and social costs of knockdown rebuilds, governments need to step up to preserve nonmarket housing on government land.

Aaron Webster Co-op is an example of a knockdown rebuild redevelopment that maximized well-located affordable homes and minimized displacement. A four-storey with thirty-one units, the building was constructed in Vancouver in the late 1970s. Forty years later, it was starting to show its age. It had severe water damage, so renovation was not an option. The Community Land Trust relocated residents into a new building nearby then tore down and rebuilt the co-op as a six-storey, sixty-four-unit building on the same lot. Delays and shortfalls in rent subsidies meant residents couldn't move back until late 2023, but they could at least use the same local services in a similar home in the meantime.

Conversions from office or commercial use don't displace tenants. With a third of its office space vacant, Calgary is spending $1 billion over the next decade to convert 560,000 square metres of downtown office space into new uses. One of the first buildings to be converted is Sierra Place, the former head office of Dome Petroleum, vacant for three years before the city purchased it. The ten-storey building is being converted into seven three-bedroom units, fifty-four two-bedrooms, and thirty-one studio apartments, reflecting the need for larger rental homes downtown, as demonstrated in a housing needs assessment. Calgary's downtown is close to schools, parks, and social services, many in adjacent residential neighbourhoods with declining populations. Aside from six storeys of social housing, there will be four storeys of mixed uses, including a childcare centre and an emergency shelter with support services. For a change, low-income households in nonmarket housing are being seen as vital to the social mix in a declining area.

Similar initiatives are occurring throughout Canada. In London, Ontario, 138 supportive homes will be developed in two former hospital buildings. The City of Toronto is downsizing from fifty-five offices to fifteen and converting at least eight of those buildings into five hundred affordable homes. In Winnipeg, the former flagship store of the Hudson's Bay Company, valued at zero dollars because of its decrepitude, is being turned over to thirty-four Manitoba First Nations as an act of reconciliation. With $100 million committed, mostly from the federal government, the six-storey, 56,000-square-metre building will include affordable housing, assisted living, a healing centre, a daycare, a museum, and meeting spaces and a restaurant, incorporating the old store's Paddlewheel Restaurant.

I recently cowrote a report for the Alliance to End Homelessness Ottawa arguing for the conversion of underutilized federal properties, including office space, in that city, along with land owned by all three levels of government, to scale up nonmarket housing from about 150 to 1,000 homes a year. Although the City of Ottawa identified eighteen "shovel ready" sites near the new rapid transit system in 2018, progress on new nonmarket housing has been slow, and the risk of selling the land to private developers in return for vague promises of affordability or a new sports stadium is high.

Then there are shopping centres, which have become less viable in an era of shop-from-home e-tail. According to one shopping centre developer, "twenty years ago we were building malls, ten years ago we were expanding malls, five years ago we were closing malls." Now they're converting malls into mixed-use 15-minute communities.

Vancouver's Oakridge Centre, a popular 1950s-era mall, is being rebuilt as Oakridge Park – eleven hectares of land with more than three thousand condominiums, retail spaces, and amenities such as a community centre and library. Most of the capital for this high-priced housing is coming from a pension fund.

Square One in Mississauga, originally developed in the 1980s, will be the largest mixed-use development in Canada, with 1.7 million square metres of commercial and residential space across more than fifty hectares. It will include eighteen thousand new residential units around existing and new retail space and will connect to the Hurontario Light

Rail Transit line. Square One is among fourteen shopping centres with residential redevelopment proposals in Toronto and the suburbs of Mississauga and Brampton.

Mall redevelopments have less risk of NIMBY zoning battles, and they have pre-existing shops, transit lines, and services. The sixty-year-old Cloverdale Mall in Toronto, with thirteen hectares, is proposing ten residential towers ranging from seventeen to forty-eight storeys, 185,000 square feet of retail space, some 23,500 square feet of community amenities (including a daycare and community centre), and 1.5 hectares of parkland. Cloverdale is willing to retain older stores loved by residents, in contrast to Malvern Town Centre, where there is no promise to retain TAIBU Community Health Centre, an organization serving Black communities in the Greater Toronto Area. The private developers in all these cases are planning to build small condominiums for older, wealthy empty nesters who wish to downsize. They are not considering affordable rentals for larger households. There's land use mix but no social mix.

For environmental and social reasons, the federal government needs to prioritize the redevelopment of office buildings, shopping malls, hospitals, and other large-scale infrastructure into mixed-use communities that include residences. Rather than regulating minimalist, inclusionary zoning requirements, governments should purchase properties for large-scale nonmarket housing with affordable ownership options, either on leased government land or a community land trust. There's no reason why rental-only zoning or limited-equity ownership can't be applied to high-rise conversions, particularly those adjacent to rapid transit such as Oakridge. And there's every reason to incentivize affordability, accessibility, and energy efficiency in these conversions, whether they are owned or rented.

New Ways of Living Together

Canada has seen a gradual decrease of "traditional" families, both dual-parent and single-parent. Alternatives such as living alone, with roommates, or with extended family members have grown in popularity. But housing hasn't kept up with household needs.

Over 4.4 million people lived alone in 2021, up from 1.7 million in 1981. This number represents 15 percent of all adults aged fifteen and older in private households. But you need affordable housing to live alone. The fact that singles are most prevalent in Quebec (20 percent), which has the lowest rate of core housing need in Canada, and least prevalent in Nunavut (8 percent), which has the highest need, is no coincidence.

Households composed of roommates are the fastest-growing household type. From 2001 to 2021, the number of roommate households increased by 54 percent, although they're still only 4 percent of households. Another 7 percent of households are composed of multiple generations of a family, two or more families, or a family living with an additional person. These households have grown by 45 percent in the last twenty years, because of affordability issues and changing needs around care. Although these trends reflect temporary COVID-19 arrangements, there is a long-term trend toward new household forms.

In response to demographic changes, Singapore has developed three-generation flats to cater to multigeneration families who want to live under one roof. Each flat features four bedrooms and three bathrooms and has an internal floor area of about 115 square metres. The Proximity Housing Grant was also introduced in 2015 to help families buy a resale flat to live with or close to one another for mutual care and support. Following changes to the policy in 2018, families and singles can now receive grants of CAD$20,000 or $10,000 to purchase a resale flat within four kilometres of their parent's or child's home.

I began my discussion of cohousing with warnings about its affordability limitations in Canada. But in Europe, the far more advanced *baugruppen* model is a hotbed of social and environmental innovation. In Germany and Switzerland, housing developed by and for small groups of households makes up 5 percent of total housing. It's particularly popular in cities, making up 25 percent of all housing in Zurich, 20 percent in Dresden, and 14 percent in Hamburg. This housing model consciously addresses both affordability and developing communities of care.

The Munich baugruppe WagnisART took advantage of municipal subsidies, free land for nonmarket-housing construction, and demand-side subsidies. Equity capital is required to buy in but on a sliding scale based on income rather than home size: $6,400 to $48,000 for a small thirty-square-metre one-bedroom. In 2020, on the market side, rent was $570 for a one-bedroom. On the social housing side (two-thirds of units), it was $150, truly accessible for low-income households. This is close to the Singapore model, where there is limited-equity home ownership on a community land trust, which ensures affordability in perpetuity.

Zurich's Kalkbreite, which operates as a nonmarket mixed-use and mixed-income community, has eighty-two apartments of various types for up to 250 residents built above a tram depot. According to its website, in addition to apartments for families and shared flats intended for students aged sixteen to twenty-five, Kalkbreite also offers space for other alternative forms of living. These cluster apartments consist of ten small apartments (twenty-six to forty-five square metres), each with a bathroom and small kitchen for one or two people. Each cluster shares a kitchen/ living room and fibre-optic connection. The clusters have a paid chef. From Monday to Friday, dinner is offered to everyone at a moderate price, and residents decide whether they want to join the communal meal (by appointment) or plan their own meal. Other members of Kalkbreite can buy into the meal plan. Clusters are intended for seniors and young working-age singles or couples. They could also be used as a group home for people with disabilities.

Kalkbreite has nine "residential jokers" with built-in bathrooms but no kitchen. These rooms can be rented out for a limited period, depending on individual needs, ranging from six months to four years, depending on the situation. They can be rented out as short-stay rentals, or to students or temporary workers (like a consultant working on a project) who only require accommodations for a few months. The complex also includes an eleven-room guesthouse for visiting family members (who receive a discount) or tourists and seven rooms to aid working from home (meeting rooms, yoga studios, or club meetings) that can also be rented out.

Hamburg's Baugemeinschaft Sophienallee is a five-storey, sixteen-home project created to bring together seniors, young families, and single people in a building with a shared roof terrace, garden, and community rooms. It features a variety of unit sizes and a diversity of owners (seniors, young families, DINKs [dual income, no kids], singles). Construction costs were about twenty-three dollars per square metre, less than a quarter of the costs reported for Vancouver's Little Mountain Cohousing. To give another example: Berlin's 3Xgrün, a five-storey, thirteen-home wood building with prefabricated cross-laminated timber walls, was constructed in 2011 for sixteen dollars per square metre. Unlike Canada, these places have lower land costs, quicker and more flexible approvals processes, and building codes and construction systems that reflect years of successful experimentation in small-scale development.

This is the kind of housing Canada needs to pursue: affordable, energy-efficient, small-scale developments that provide tenure security without windfall profits for the few and misery for the many. The CMHC could do much more to secure financing for cohousing opportunities, particularly those on a community land trust with a long-term (at least forty-year and preferably perpetual) affordability covenant.

In the 1990s, Freiberg, a city of 250,000 people in the south of Germany, provided small lots at reduced prices for eleven thousand homes in the eco-neighbourhood of Vauban. The homes were all developed on the baugruppen model. The community, a former military base, is car-free, with a single multistorey parking garage. When I spoke to Wolf Daseking, Freiberg's chief planner, now retired, his only regret was that they didn't insist on a community land trust, which would have kept the homes affordable in perpetuity. Today, the only affordable options that remain are an army barracks transformed into a student co-op and a mobile home community.

Expanding Ownership Options

Self-building, subdividing, cohousing, limited-equity ownership, and conversions demonstrate new ways to live together and use scarce urban land. They exemplify triple-bottom-line sustainability. Inexpensive ownership options can be legalized through revised zoning and building codes, by encouraging community land trusts, and by guaranteeing financing for new forms of shared ownership. Ownership options that respect people's rights and engender caring will support a better future for younger generations and better "aging in place" for older generations.

A mobile home community and communal green space
near a student co-op in Vauban, Freiberg.

10

Who Should Pay?

If the goal of better housing policy is to prioritize public welfare over private profit in the efficient use of well-located land, then we as a nation need to tackle three destructive myths. The first is that piecemeal local negotiation over individual multifamily developments means good planning. Instead, we should be planning to scale up low-cost housing on a national level, using an industrial approach characterized by clear rules and rapid action. The second is that "growth should pay for growth." It is unjust to penalize new renters and buyers for the terrible policy decisions of previous generations. And the third is that property taxes, as they are currently applied, are an acceptable way to subsidize housing for low-income households. Instead, we should be relying on progressive wealth and income taxes to redress huge inequalities in wealth and prospects for a good life that are the result of generations of bad housing policy. If we're going to combat these myths, we need policy and taxation reforms, at the municipal, provincial, and federal levels.

The Hidden Costs of Delays

Here are the stages of housing development in simplified form:

1 Decide who you want to serve (number, size, cost, and tenure of homes, often known as a "program").

2 Find initial financing (such as a land-acquisition mortgage) to purchase a property (or in the case of government land, bid on a site).

3 Engage in preliminary studies such as environmental assessments (to see if there are any contaminants on site) and consultations with nearby residents (a good thing to do even if there is no need for a public hearing).

4 Develop a pro forma (expected expenses and revenues).

5 Develop a design (usually in consultation with an architect), which may result in changes to the pro forma.

6 Find more financing to develop or redevelop the property (this may entail preliminary approval for a mortgage and insurance).

7 Obtain planning approval and a building permit.

8 Find a builder.

9 Start construction.

10 Complete construction and find tenants or buyers.

Your site will be inspected by municipal staff before construction, during construction, and at the end of construction before occupancy. You may need to consult with architects, lawyers, electricians, plumbers, environmental engineers, surveyors, appraisers, and mortgage providers and funders (banks, credit unions, pension funds, governments, social investors). Even the most straightforward and small-scale projects are complicated.

See the appendix (Table 1) for a summary of the phases of development, approximate timelines, and main risks associated with building homes in Canada.

It's possible to move from program to move-in within a year, but systems would need to be radically different from the current norms. Anything that adds uncertainty – rezoning complicated by NIMBYism, rapid interest-rate increases, construction cost increases (both materials and labour), difficulty finding financing (because of expected low rates of return or insufficient assets), and frequent policy changes – endangers the viability of a project. Time is money: the more time it takes for approvals, the more risks of interest-rate changes or expensive holding costs, including "bridge financing" between huge initial outlays and revenues. When it comes to low-income housing, tenant incomes and low overheads (expected returns in relation to costs) increase the risks.

In most Canadian cities, ridiculously long approval times exacerbate housing inequalities. In 2021, the Expert Panel on the Future of Housing Supply and Affordability, established by the BC and Canadian governments, pointed out that chronic underzoning and site-by-site deal making allows local governments to treat development proposals as "hostage situations." It recommended linking federal infrastructure funding to rezoning and housing approvals, which is beginning to happen with Canada's Housing Accelerator Fund, introduced in 2023.

Approval times vary widely among municipalities. Every six-month delay in the approval process adds between $16,000 and $20,000 to the cost of a single high-rise home, about 1 percent of total costs per month. McKinsey estimates that simplified approvals processes (good technical support from staff, clear information, fast-tracking, as-of-right zoning) can reduce housing costs by 12 to 16 percent. Part of the problem is the range of technical studies required – up to sixty, depending on the municipality or project.

In Toronto's East End, an experienced nonmarket-housing developer purchased a site in 2019 to redevelop it as a mid-rise affordable co-op with thirty-three units. (The previous owner, a co-op operator, had attempted for three years to gain approvals to redevelop the site but could not line up the city permits and CMHC funding.) Applications for site-plan approval stretched over three years. The cost of the project increased by 30 percent as interest rates rose by 150 basis points. The organization struggled to line up funding from various sources, including the city's affordable-housing incentive program and the CMHC. Delays meant an extra $3 million in construction costs and the need for more equity to offset the interest-rate hikes. Delays threatened the project's viability.

There are signs of improvement. Several Canadian cities, including Edmonton (deemed the best city for development), have created a ninety-day benchmark for approvals. Edmonton's updates are transparent. Two more initiatives would be useful: preapproved prototype apartment-building templates and simplified processes for small infill developments on single lots.

Only half of the homes approved by municipalities actually get built. Land-value taxes and empty-home taxes might help, but builders blame high interest rates and construction and labour shortages for slowdowns since COVID. Across Canada, three in five builders surveyed by the Canadian Home Builders' Association said they built fewer units in 2023 than in 2022, and 23 percent said they're cancelling projects altogether. The Building Industry and Land Development Association recently estimated one hundred months – just over eight years – between land purchase and move-in in the Greater Toronto Area. Factory-built components might help with productivity issues, but Canada needs to jump-start both approvals and construction so projects can be completed in one year. And once again, the model for both factory-built efficiency and the kind of urgency needed to address those most affected by the housing crisis was found in the Rapid Housing Initiative, Canada's first supply-side initiative to end homelessness, in 2020.

The Costs of Ending Homelessness

A program to end homelessness would scale up the federal Rapid Housing Initiative (which focuses on low-cost supply) and combine it with Reaching Home: Canada's Homelessness Strategy (which coordinates local service provision and preventing homelessness). The goal would be to end chronic homelessness in a decade and attain functional zero homelessness in three decades. It would be based on the Housing First model of permanent homes without conditions and appropriate services (if necessary), better information sharing, by-name lists, eviction protection, and higher welfare rates.

Unlike in the United States, Canada does not require developers to make public the costs or rents of projects subsidized by any level of government. Most developers guard this information closely. On the condition of anonymity, a developer of supportive housing provided me with the costs for twenty-three projects developed between 2010 and 2023 in mid-sized Ontario cities, along with estimates for three projects not yet completed. Capital funding came in the form of grants or long-term low-rate financing from all levels of government, churches, social finance organizations, and individual donors. Most of the apartments are studios and one-bedrooms, with a smattering of two-plus-bedrooms. The average home size ranges from twenty-four to forty-two square metres. Most of the projects involve housing above redeveloped single-storey buildings such as churches and fire halls using free-leased land. The number of apartments per building varies widely, from thirteen to ninety-five, although the provider found a "sweet spot" at about forty homes. All buildings have elevators and some form of common space on the ground floor.

Supportive-housing developers, like all developers, have seen huge cost increases in recent years. Whereas projects in 2010 had hard costs of $131 per square metre or between $63,000 and $92,000 per unit (depending on size), costs during the pandemic ranged between $300 and $360 per square metre or between $200,000 and $270,000 per unit. Costs continued to increase in 2023 because of material and labour shortages and rising interest rates.

Keeping in mind the importance of meeting accessibility and energy-efficiency requirements and including common spaces and landscaping, the supportive-housing developer recommended a benchmark cost of $400,000 for a studio or one-bedroom apartment (in Ontario, British Columbia, or the North). The developer recommended waiving all municipal approval and development fees for deeply affordable housing, the continuation of GST waivers, and more factory-built construction efficiencies. Finally, given there are no guarantees of an ongoing grant-based program, the developer recommended a long-term financing approach: a forty-year, five-percent fixed-term mortgage guaranteed by the federal government but also available from social finance, mainstream banks, and investment funds.

Waiving GST (a measure introduced in late 2023 for all purpose-built rentals) and providing $400,000 financing per unit could be the basis of a viable and stable nonmarket housing program. This model is similar to the long-term financing offered by governments in Denmark, Finland, and France. It would reduce upfront costs from the Rapid Housing Initiative. It would require increasing loan guarantees to supportive-housing developers by $8 billion a year. This is considerably more than the deficit load for the Rental Construction Financing Initiative, but we'd be moving toward deep affordability, which the existing program doesn't do at all. Building 200,000 new supportive homes in a decade would cost four cents per Canadian taxpayer per month – a small price to pay to end chronic homelessness.

Unlike the Rapid Housing Initiative, an effective program to end homelessness would require matching funding from provinces or, failing that, the municipalities. The current welfare rate for single people – $375 per month for rent – does not cover operating and maintenance costs and mortgage payments, so additional rent subsidies are needed. High-needs residents require support services at a ten-to-one ratio. With the collaboration from all three levels of government, the program could even fund five on-site social workers with flex hours, including one overnight shift.

The provinces would need to pay for social supports, increase rent subsidies or welfare rates (which have stagnated for thirty years), waive PST (and land-transfer tax, if applicable), and provide free-leased land. Municipalities would need to approve proposals quickly with no public hearings, provide free-leased land, and waive application fees, development charges (parkland, schools, and so on), and property tax. For our developer in question, these needs would translate into about $7,000 annually for supports plus $5,000 a year in additional rent subsidies (or higher social assistance rates) per tenant. If the provinces refuse to come on board, then the federal government could provide funding directly to municipalities or regions, which would then be clawed back from health and social transfers.

For those not swayed by arguments centred on rights or morality, ending homelessness would mean huge cost savings for governments and taxpayers. Canada's data hasn't been updated since 2005, but that year a permanent supportive home cost up to $18,000 per year, including both the capital costs of housing and the operating subsidy necessary to make up for inadequate welfare income, as well as provision of services. That same year, municipalities paid up to $42,000 per bed (or mat on the floor) in an emergency shelter, while provincial governments paid up to $120,000 per bed for hospitalizations and incarceration. Finland reported a cost savings of $21,000 per person per year when it moved to a Housing First model. Those who sneer at the "truckloads of money" it would take to scale up low-income-housing don't seem to care about the

Home Truths

supertankers of cash feeding the pipeline from shelters to institutions to encampments.

While studio and one-bedroom apartments are suitable for single people and couples who require supportive housing, about 10 percent of very-low-income households, including Indigenous families, need two or more bedrooms. Buildings with larger apartments could be grouped around a green space and have ground floors with cafés or childcare centres and some support services. Modular housing prototypes could be adopted for long-term care and assisted-living homes, with the proviso that every type of home should allow for privacy (a room with a bed and a bathroom) and include common spaces such as meeting rooms, communal kitchens, or outdoor gardens.

A grants-based program to end homelessness by scaling up supportive housing by 200,000 homes in a decade would cost the federal government $8 billion a year. Another $1 billion per year should be added to shift local services away from emergency shelters toward permanent supportive housing. Provinces and territories would need to provide $3 billion per year in housing subsidies and social and health supports. Municipalities would need to provide free-leased land and waive development charges and property taxes.

Of this sum, $800 million a year of federal money should go to a "for Indigenous, by Indigenous" program to build 6,000 new homes a year and to provide homelessness prevention and health and social supports. The funding would be in the form of low-interest, long-term loans with matching expenditures from the provinces and territories. The additional funding would recognize the higher costs of construction in rural, remote, and northern communities and the backlog of need for larger supportive homes for women and children suffering the effects of intergenerational trauma caused by Canada's genocidal policies.

The Costs of a Low-Cost, Nonmarket Housing Program

To build 1.8 million nonmarket homes over a decade (180,000 homes a year), the federal government would need to return to strategies that worked from the 1960s to the 1980s and in other countries – free-leased land plus direct grants or long-term, low-rate guaranteed financing.

Because nonmarket housing doesn't require health and social service funding, or by-name lists, as is the case with addressing homelessness, the costs are broken down separately. The target would be providing permanent adequate homes for one-third of those in need over the next decade. The goal would be to gradually scale up to provide adequate, environmentally sustainable homes for all Canadians in three decades.

A 2019 Metro Vancouver study found that with free land, wood-frame construction, and no direct subsidies, the average nonmarket break-even rent could be as low as $1,273 per month for a one-bedroom, $1,641 for a two-bedroom, and $2,009 for a three-bedroom. The following could drive rents even lower: eliminating parking requirements; waiving municipal fees, HST, and property taxes; government-backed fifty-year mortgage financing at 5 percent; prefabricated modular housing; accelerated permitting processes; and economies of scale such as replicable designs. Working backwards from a goal of rents of $1,000 a month for a one-bedroom and no more than $1,600 for a three-bedroom, this model would be feasible at $600,000 per home, with 80 percent of the financing covered by either a federal or provincial long-term, low-rate mortgage.

Supportive and affordable nonmarket housing would depend on the Federal Lands Initiative, which identifies and leases suitable, well-located government land from all three levels of government. To give one example, Canada Post, a Crown corporation, owns or leases over three thousand post offices and more than five hundred depots and processing plants. There are more post offices in Canada than Tim Hortons doughnut shops, and their coverage is more extensive, from big cities to tiny northern communities. Many of these postal buildings are single-storey and need substantial renovation to accommodate electric vehicle docking stations, which are part of Canada Post's environmental sustainability plan. Many of these sites could be redeveloped with three to eleven storeys of "housing on top," forming a new generation of post offices as community hubs, with services like local banking and community-supported agriculture pick-ups.

The federal government should also encourage, as a condition of infrastructure funding, nonmarket housing on all well-located provincial, territorial, and municipal land, including housing on top of rapid transit stations, government liquor stores, health centres, libraries, fire halls, and recreation centres. The Housing Assessment Resource Tools project has mapped hundreds of such locations in a dozen municipalities.

An industrialized approach with larger sites and preapproved designs for prefabricated apartments (much like the Victory Houses model) would save money. An apprenticeship program to train a new generation of construction workers could be supplemented by a program to provide them with affordable housing (the Whistler model). In France, companies pay into a payroll tax that goes toward the government nonmarket finance fund. In turn, large companies obtain guaranteed housing allocations for some of their workers. Another model that works is providing young people who have experienced homelessness with construction training. Blue Door, an agency that provides emergency and transitional housing for homeless people in York Region, north of Toronto, has supported two hundred trainees since 2020. It covers enrolment fees, transport costs, and securing apprenticeships.

New builds are key, but so, too, are maintaining affordability and building up nonmarket assets through acquisitions. Larger apartment buildings or rooming houses at risk of losing affordability could be purchased with government-provided down payments and turned over to nonmarket providers to be financed by long-term, low-cost mortgages. Grants to support the initial costs of new builds and acquisitions should go to nonmarket providers with over one thousand homes or coalitions of smaller providers brought together under a land trust. Larger nonmarket entities could then offer competitive jobs to the next generation of housing developers and managers.

In government accounting, low-interest mortgages should not be considered the same as direct expenditures. The first advantage of long-term, low-rate financing is that homes remain affordable for the length of the financing. The second advantage is that it's an infrastructure investment, as opposed to the sunken cost of subsidizing higher-cost market rentals through demand-side supplements. The third advantage is that the cost of upfront grants would be daunting, even if the federal government were to invest 2 percent of its GDP in new, acquired, and renovated housing supply, or $34 billion annually. On the other hand, the federal government withdrew support for nonmarket housing in the late 1980s partly because of its long-term carrying costs. But critical infrastructure costs money. The federal government needs to stop shifting debt for collective rights such as housing, education, health care, and pensions onto individual households. It should develop a long-term, stable, revolving loan fund such as those in place in France, Denmark, and Finland, which could be purchased as a retirement investment, just like any bond.

In addition to waiving GST, the federal government needs to guarantee low-rate, long-term mortgages; promote the rapid expansion of nonmarket and affordable rentals through tax concessions (described below); and lease all well-located, appropriate government land at no cost. Funding for transit improvements should be linked to housing targets (an extension of the Housing Accelerator Fund).

Canada's annual GDP is about $1.7 trillion, and 14 percent – $238 billion – is poured into market real estate. This proportion is double the OECD average. In 2016, there was $1.5 trillion in retirement investment funds in Canada, much of it parked in real estate investment trusts (REITs). This overreliance on REITs for high returns has harmed low-income households. Canada's five largest banks alone hold $7 trillion in assets, much of it tied up in mortgages. The CMHC's current limit of mortgage-backed securities under the National Housing Act is $150 billion. Even at $600,000 per new home, and assuming 20 percent equity from non-market developer assets, guaranteeing financing for 200,000 homes a year (the total for supportive and nonmarket affordable housing) would be $96 billion a year in a revolving loan fund. This fund would require a 60-percent increase in mortgage-backed securities from the CMHC.

Yes, the numbers are big, but Canada has the money, and infrastructure is an expensive necessity.

The National Housing Strategy should require the provincial governments to identify and lease all well-located land at no cost to nonmarket providers, waive PST and land-transfer taxes, and either provide a guaranteed livable income or ongoing housing benefits to low-income tenants to bring their rents to 30 percent of household income. This may well require a total commitment from the provinces and territories of $3 billion a year.

Municipal government should provide free-lease government land, expedited approvals using new building-code rules and as-of-right zoning with no minimum parking requirements, and waive development and application fees and property taxes for incorporated nonprofit housing providers. (Property taxes are currently waived for many nonprofit providers such as colleges and universities, faith communities, and some public housing, and the provincial government must approve the waivers.)

These are the types of funding arrangements that we'd need to hit a 20 percent target for nonmarket housing within three decades.

Retrofitting Homes for Access and Energy Efficiency

A federal retrofit program should promote energy efficiency and accessibility without causing homes to become unaffordable. It would need a ten-year target; a focus on homes in the North that are low cost and in poor repair; and a substantial "for Indigenous, by Indigenous" component (at least 10 percent of total costs).

Like any form of infrastructure, homes need consistent operating funds and retrofits every twenty to thirty years. Over 1 million mostly low- and moderate-income households live in high-rises that are between forty and seventy years old. High-rises are the largest single source of private-market housing affordable to these households. Since 2015, Canada has lost 180,000 nonmarket units because of the end of subsidies for low-income households. In Toronto and Mississauga, the proportion of low-income families in apartment towers increased from 34 percent in 1981 to 43 percent in 2006, and the percentage of units housing more than one person per room doubled. Half of all apartment towers contain 50 percent or more residents born outside of Canada, and the same proportion have 20 percent or more of residents under the age of nineteen. Residents can't afford energy retrofits. Canada needs to increase low incomes to support essential upgrades on homes or subsidize rents for low-income households.

Germany shows a way forward.

The Kreditanstalt für Wiederaufbau (KfW) was created to facilitate postwar reconstruction under the Marshall Plan. Today, it finances new builds and retrofits that meet the government's climate-change goals. It takes a systems approach: it provides expert advice, direct installations, and a combination of loans and grants for retrofits. The bank loans up to CAD$155,000 per home for retrofits, of which 30 percent can be transferred into a grant if energy performance standards are met. The range of eligible improvements includes insulating walls and roofs, replacing windows, and replacing gas and oil boilers with solar thermal, heat pumps, and local district heaters. Between 2006 and 2009, it awarded $75 billion in loans and grants to rehabilitate 9 million units, which triggered $150 billion in investments. Over $2.8 billion in heating costs have been saved yearly, equalling 1.2 metric tons of carbon dioxide per year. From 2006 to 2011, 894,000 jobs were created and 5.7 megatonnes of greenhouse gas emissions were eliminated.

To some extent, Canada's Green Municipal Fund echoes this approach. For two decades, it provided low-interest loans to local governments to improve the energy efficiency of their assets, including housing. The initial endowment was $1.65 billion, and the fund approved $137.4 million in loans and $74.6 million in grants in 2020–21. Germany has a little over twice the population of Canada; even adjusting for population, it invests over one thousand times as much in housing retrofits.

The Tower Renewal Partnership – an alliance of architects, charitable foundations, and researchers based in the Greater Toronto and Hamilton Area – worked with the CMHC to devise triple-bottom-line solutions to retrofit still-viable apartments. Through mortgage refinancing, renovation tax credits, a capital gains tax incentive for sales to nonmarket owners, and portfolio-scale approaches, several complementary goals could be attained: reducing greenhouse gas emissions by 60 percent or more, improving resilience and well-being, and mitigating negative impacts on tenants. The Toronto Community Housing Corporation recently received $1.34 billion from the federal government for asset renewal and retrofits. This approach may need to be extended to privately owned rental apartments to avoid wide-scale renoviction. Alternatively, a bold acquisitions program could acquire many of these buildings and pass them on to nonmarket providers.

In either case, the annual cost, mostly borne by the federal government, would be around $9 billion annually. Transfers to lower levels of government should be conditional on their ability to meet approval targets and provide free land, exemptions, rent supplements, and basic income increases.

Making Federal Taxation Fairer

The OECD uses three separate categories – new housing, subsidies, and retrofitting – to calculate housing spending. Singapore spends a remarkable 7 percent of its GDP on nonmarket housing. The French government spends 1 percent on nonmarket housing, split equally between supply, retrofit, and subsidy. In Canada, 0.7 percent goes to nonmarket housing, a total of $14.7 billion.

After three decades of virtually no investment in housing infrastructure, a baseline of 1.5 percent of Canada's GDP ($25 billion annually, adjusted for inflation) might realize the right to housing. The federal government would spend $19 billion annually on direct infrastructure (acquiring land and energy and accessibility retrofits). The provincial government would spend (via welfare or subsidies) $6 billion on health and social services. Taxation incentives and long-term mortgages would not be included in the sum.

This is a higher price tag than the National Housing Strategy (which started at $40 billion over ten years but ballooned to $89 billion). But the spending has a focused target. The federal government should also strive to decrease the wealth gap, increase investment in new homes, and dampen speculation in old homes. Interest rate increases aren't lowering house prices, and they're making rentals scarcer.

Canada is far from tenure neutrality. In 2010, the Federation of Rental-housing Providers of Ontario reported that 94 percent ($17 billion) of housing-related subsidies, mostly from the federal government, went to homeowners. The total cost of subsidizing nonmarket housing that year totalled $2 billion. Two key federal tax measures subsidize the wealthiest homeowners at the expense of renters. First, the government justified the principal residence exemption for capital gains tax on the grounds that homes are a basic need. But no such exemption was offered to renters. Between 2015 and 2022, the exemption led to $55 billion in lost revenue – four times the amount spent on the National Housing Strategy.

The second tax measure is the nontaxation of imputed rents. Landlords pay tax on rent revenue. Homeowners don't pay tax on the value of having a home to live in. Landlords can deduct mortgage payments, repairs, utilities, and legal and professional fees from their profits, but they pay tax on their profits and pass that cost on to renters. The Netherlands, Switzerland, and Denmark tax imputed rents – that is, the amount owners would be paying if they rented their homes.

The federal government offers many other deductions and tax credits, but the capital gains tax exemptions on resales alone (and REITs, which exist to maximize returns from renters, are also exempt from capital gains tax) cost $10.4 billion a year in 2022. Ninety percent of the value of this tax break went to the 10 percent of households earning the highest incomes.

What would happen if the capital gains tax were charged on the sale of principal residences over a set amount, let's say $2 million? There would certainly be a lot of paperwork: there were 446,000 home sales in 2019 alone. Seniors who expected to downsize and "cash out" might be dissuaded from doing so, creating a stickier ownership market and disadvantaging seniors who have property but little income.

Polling by Generation Squeeze suggests that messaging matters. Only 48 percent of Canadians are aware of the principal residence exemption. Those who knew about it felt the capital gains tax exemption was either "a great deal" or a "fair amount" to blame for rising home prices. The same proportion agreed that "municipal zoning processes keep developers from building the right supply." Seventy percent felt "investors," especially "foreign investors," were to blame. The message that appealed to potential voters? "The rise in housing wealth inequality is unfair to retirees in the Prairies and Atlantic Canada. They pay taxes on their pension income just like the retiree does in Vancouver or Toronto. But they didn't gain hundreds of thousands, if not millions, of dollars in home equity. Many retirees in Vancouver or Toronto did. By failing to tax the wealth gained by owners in Vancouver and Toronto, we expect retirees in the Prairies and Atlantic Canada to pay more than their fair share of taxes."

Canadian regionalism might make the difference if any political party wanted to take on this "third rail" taxation issue.

Another possibility is a wealth tax. The Canadian Centre for Policy Alternatives has proposed a surtax on the 0.5 percent of households with over $10 million in net wealth. These households would pay 1 percent on wealth over $10 million, 2 percent on wealth over $50 million, and

3 percent on wealth over $100 million. The result – an estimated $32 billion in the first year and $409 billion over a decade. This money could pay for a greatly expanded supportive- and nonmarket-housing programs, including energy and access retrofits.

The government could make permanent the elimination of sales taxes on the construction of rental housing, recognizing it as an essential good. Tax incentives from the 1950s and 1960s could be brought back for nonmarket and market developers, particularly if they promoted affordability, energy efficiency, and accessibility. Capital gains tax and recaptured depreciation (due upon the sale of an existing purpose-built rental-housing project) could be deferred, provided the proceeds are reinvested in new purpose-built market rental affordable to low- and moderate-income households. Increasing the capital cost allowance on newly constructed purpose-built rental buildings would also provide strong incentives to create new purpose-built affordable rental housing. Finally, and perhaps most controversially, if a sale is to a nonprofit market provider or land trust through an acquisition fund, capital gains tax could be waived for private owners of multipurpose rentals. This initiative would fuel the construction of nonmarket homes and protect the affordability of purpose-built rental housing. It would also reward large investors who have been active in renovictions, so perhaps the tax break could be linked to reinvestment in new purpose-built rental housing.

Making Provincial Taxation Fairer

The provinces, like the federal government, rely heavily on income tax, which is progressive, and sales taxes, which is regressive. The federal government and several provinces withdrew sales tax from rental construction in September 2023. That's a good start.

The provincial government could also encourage direct and indirect investment in the construction of nonmarket and affordable housing by taxing speculative investment. For instance, the provinces could heavily tax nonprimary-residence home transfers, which would affect small- and large-scale speculators, especially those buying to evict tenants and resell. A Singapore tax on properties sold within three years, implemented in 1996, enabled it to fund social housing and subsidize home ownership for lower-income households. In 2021, the government taxed the sale of second (20 percent) and third (30 percent) properties.

Provincial governments can take action to make property assessments fairer and more transparent. British Columbia's property-assessment system is accessible to the public, so anyone can find out who owns what property. It's updated annually. In contrast, Ontario and Alberta have privatized, opaque systems that are updated less frequently. The *Toronto Star* found that 69 percent of the lowest-value homes were overassessed while 47 percent of the highest-value homes were underassessed. As of 2023, all properties were still being assessed based on 2016 sales prices, but home prices had more than doubled. The reporters had to review tens of thousands of properties one by one using a single City Hall computer. The private company that Ontario sold its public assessment system to in 2002 (for which municipalities pay $200 million a year) refused to make its data available.

In 2022, Housing Assessment Resource Tools had to pay the Ontario assessment company $40,000 to find government-owned land that might be suitable for nonmarket housing. We could only display the information publicly for a year. Alberta's private assessment company won't let us display similar information. Making provincial assessment systems publicly owned would improve accountability.

Provincial governments can also help municipalities reform regressive tax systems. Higher taxation rates on commercial or multiunit properties punish renters and small businesses.

Flat-rate property taxes could be replaced by a graduated system, where higher-value homes are taxed at a higher rate. Finland, Denmark, and Germany are among the countries that do this. In 2018, the BC government introduced four new taxes as part of its affordable-housing agenda. The first, the luxury homes tax, was levied on owned homes that sell for more than $2 million, not on apartment buildings. The second was an additional 5 percent on property-transfer taxes for homes above $3 million. The third was a higher property-transfer tax rate for overseas buyers. The fourth was a tax on foreign owners who don't occupy their properties and Canadians with vacant properties. These increases had polling support in the 72 to 75 percent range.

A 2022 analysis from the Canadian Centre for Policy Alternatives found these taxes had some positive impacts. For instance, the luxury home tax brought in $487 million over four years, even though it applied to only the top 1.4 percent of homes. But the revenues didn't go back into affordable-housing programs. The property-transfer tax brought in about $349 million. A Singapore-type property-transfer tax (aimed at non-principal homes or foreign buyers at higher rates) might be more lucrative. Neither tax was intended to dampen demand for luxury homes or price inflation, and they didn't. The tax is the equivalent of one high-end restaurant bill, with alcohol, for four people.

The foreign buyers' tax was intended to cool down demand, associated with international money laundering. The share of foreign purchases fell 2.5 percent in 2018, 2.0 percent in 2019, and 1.3 percent in 2020. In parts of the province where the tax wasn't levied, the foreign share fell by a similar amount. But the tax did bring in considerable revenue: $519 million over four years. Again, the revenues should have flowed into affordable-housing programs rather than general revenues.

Finally, the vacant homes tax brought more rental properties into the market, but not enough to lower rents. The CMHC's data suggest 11,118 condo units were added to Metro Vancouver's rental market in 2019 and another 7,137 in 2020. About 5,000 were conversions to rental and the remainder were new condos. In 2021, 2,550 more condos were added, but these were almost all new condos. The year 2020 was characterized by diminished demand from students and temporary residents during COVID-19, so these factors must be considered alongside tax changes. The tax applied to only 0.1 percent of properties and raised $80 million in 2020–21. But it costs about $10 million per year to administer since it's more complicated than a simple addition to a property tax or property transfer tax.

France uses a payroll tax to fund nonmarket housing. The tax has the additional value of taxing suburban "freeloaders" who use inner-city office space. Payroll taxes are certainly less visible than property taxes and could be an additional funding source for nonmarket housing.

Increased property taxes for luxury properties over $1 to 2 million could cross-subsidize property taxes being waived for nonmarket housing and deferred for lower-income residents. But there's a basic problem with property taxes. They punish improvements to a property while rewarding those who sit on their wealth. If you add another unit to your home, you will (once assessments catch up) pay more property tax. If you do nothing to that empty lot while that new apartment building next door pays development charges on a new community centre, congratulations, you just got increased property values for when you sell.

There is a tax that's progressive and effective in driving environmentally and socially sustainable outcomes. Land value taxes recognize that value is determined by location in relation to jobs, goods, and services. Each time a new transit station, library, or playground is built, it increases land values, whether land is vacant, has a single-family home, or has an apartment building on it. While people from around the region may benefit from a transit line, the primary beneficiaries are those who own homes and businesses close to a station, who obtain what tax wonks call a "windfall gain." The fairest way to fund those improvements is through a land value tax that rewards developments that use urban land efficiently.

Land value taxes have a long history in western Canada. By 1914, approximately two-thirds of the cities in British Columbia, all of Alberta, and one-fourth of Saskatchewan taxed land solely; the remainder taxed the land value at a higher rate than the property value. But NIMBY homeowners' associations complained that their backyards were being threatened by land taxes. By the 1960s, NIMBYs were in the political ascendancy, and tenants and unions were unable to stop the tide.

A watered-down version of land value taxation is tax increment funding, which designates a proportion of increased property taxes to local improvements. The City of Toronto proposed such a tax for new transit lines but recognized it would only cover 5 to 10 percent of costs. Tax increment funding is used in cities such as Portland and New York City. But it's not enough to make significant changes to city revenues.

The OECD recommends land value taxes to encourage development in urban areas with good infrastructure, particularly when combined with a "use value" tax, which would apply lower rates to areas zoned for farmland, forests, or other environmental uses. Studies have shown that land value taxation leads to higher rates of development and higher densities. Land value taxes have been put to particularly good use in

Singapore, reflecting the value of high-density development in the city. The Danes also use a land value approach: they tax properties at one one-thousandth of their land value rather than at the value of the building itself. This means residents of well-located single-family homes pay higher taxes than renters in apartment buildings, which rewards intensification. Land value rates can be combined with property rates – it doesn't need to be one or the other.

Improving municipal property taxation is possible, but it will depend on support from the provinces and political courage at the municipal level.

Making Municipal and Regional Taxation Fairer

Canada and the United States are much more reliant on property taxes for municipal revenue than European cities, which often receive a share of income, sales, or fuel taxes. Property taxes have the great disadvantage of being highly visible because they're charged in lump sums to homeowners (but hidden in rents). Sales and income taxes, in contrast, are automatically added to bills or automatically deducted from paycheques.

Perhaps because of that visibility, cities manage property taxes poorly. Big cities with climbing housing prices tend to have decreasing rates, infrequent assessment updates, and an opaque process that underestimates the value of expensive properties. Toronto and Vancouver have some of the lowest property taxes in Canada. Social service budgets get cut, while police budgets increase. (Police budgets are set by police service boards, which have less accountability than city councils.)

The most regressive taxes benefit existing residents but punish new developments and renters and owners who live in new homes. Development charges are a feature of English-language industrialized countries, intended to keep property taxes low and bribe established homeowners into supporting development. Development charges include a wide variety of fees charged to proposed projects: application fees, permit fees, educational levies, parkland fees, and community-benefit charges. In Ontario, development charges appeared after the Second World War when suburban municipalities were recovering from bankruptcies during the Depression. Developers paid for the installation of roads, sewers, and water in a subdivision; in turn, the local authority allowed suburban sprawl. By the 1980s, urban development charges had become a rapidly growing source of revenue in US cities. Wealthy homeowners led tax revolts as part of the neoliberal wave taking over political discourse. The approach was explicitly exclusionary: "Existing taxpayers ... see little reason for paving the way for newcomers," as one 1987 US study put it. Development charges were seen as a "fee for residency." Canada tends to adopt terrible ideas from south of the border. This was one of them.

The radically regressive nature of development charges was understood by urban economists, if not by leftist activists, some of whom continue to advocate for charges such as inclusionary zoning to "make developers pay." Developers are now expected to pay not only for roads or community centres in specific suburban developments, but also for transit, community services, and water and sewer maintenance and upgrades. The benefits accrue to the surrounding established homeowners.

Development charge regimes vary widely in Canadian cities. In St. John's, high-rise development charges (including parkland, education, community amenities, and so on) were $22 per square metre as of 2022. In Vancouver, they were $1,640 per square metre, or $123,000 for a seventy-five-square metre apartment. Development charges in the Greater Toronto Area increased by an average of 30 to 36 percent between 2020 and 2022, and charges for apartments per square metre are twice as high as charges for detached homes. The CMHC has estimated that municipal charges now account for 15 percent of the total construction cost on a high-rise rental project in Toronto.

Developers pass these charges on to the household buying or renting the new home. The increased cost of new homes drives up local prices, promoting gentrification and tenant displacement.

Inclusionary zoning, a subset of development charges, likewise originated in the neoliberal era in the United States. Inclusionary zoning works in two ways. It forces market developers to build a small proportion of lower-cost "below market" new housing (the costs are passed on to new buyers or renters). Or it uses free or low-cost land, tax incentives, density bonuses, or other subsidies to bribe market developers to build this housing. Both strategies rest on a booming housing market and a theory of trickle-down benefits that doesn't hold water.

Inclusionary zoning produces minimal benefits with poor efficiencies. After fifty years of inclusionary zoning in Massachusetts, only one-fifth of municipalities achieved their goal of having 10 percent of new housing affordable to the lowest-income 40 percent of households. California's low-income housing requirements have gone unmet in most communities, and project-by-project negotiations have been blamed for increasing the difficulty of building adequate supply in high-land-cost areas such as San Francisco. Inclusionary zoning requirements in Montreal have been ignored by developers, who prefer to pay additional development charges.

Inclusionary zoning does little to address the need for nonmarket, low-cost housing. What's worse, the idea of trickle-down housing is used as a rationale to give government land to developers. A target-based system focused on directly creating or acquiring nonmarket housing would be more efficient and fairer in terms of who pays for what.

Development charges give unearned gains to neighbouring home-owners. Community infrastructure improves, home values increase, but no capital gains taxes are levied. In contrast, new renters "receive no such capital gains. Their higher rents are, in effect, an uncompensated burden that stems from the private financing of infrastructure to serve new residents." In other words, newcomer renters pay a regressive tax for the privilege of living in the same neighbourhood as homeowners.

In 2018, Ontario municipalities collected $2.23 billion in development charges and $21.8 billion in property tax. In 2022, Ontario limited development charges for "affordable and attainable" housing. Most municipalities could easily raise their "lost" revenue by updating assessments, increasing property tax rates, or introducing a wealth tax. Some argue that higher development charges on land that was previously agricultural or undeveloped would better reflect the environmental and economic costs of this growth. But if municipalities directly paid for infrastructure in new areas, they might be better motivated to stop sprawl.

Municipalities say they need other sources of income to be less reliant on development charges. Finnish cities are funded through sales and corporate and property taxes. But they provide social services that in Canada are the responsibility of the provinces. One thing is certain: development charges and the notion of "growth paying for growth" are antithetical to building well-located housing. These charges need to be reduced, and in the case of nonmarket housing, eliminated.

It's unfair for municipalities to shoulder the costs of nonmarket and affordable housing and homelessness. But it's equally unfair for municipalities to punish new housing, which is part of the solution to inadequate housing. The federal and provincial governments should adequately fund affordable housing to stop cities from pushing the burden onto anyone who needs a new home. They should do a better job of funding critical infrastructure, but they should definitely link that funding to municipalities supporting "smart growth," including much more housing near transit and other infrastructure.

A Fairer Tax and Policy System

The price tag for a scaled-up nonmarket-housing program isn't shocking. The revenues are easily available. But they require taxation and policy reforms across all three levels of government in Canada that rely on evidence-based policy of how to most productively increase housing on well-located land for the greater public good.

1 Income redistribution services, including emergency shelters and nonmarket housing, should be funded from progressive taxation sources (income or wealth taxes) rather than regressive sources (current property taxes or development charges). The provincial government, not municipalities, should be responsible for all costs related to emergency shelters and health or social supports related to housing (including long-term care). The federal government should fund nonmarket- and supportive-housing infrastructure and essential infrastructure upgrades. A progressive property tax, supplemented by a land value tax, could overcome reliance on development charges.

2 Get rid of taxes (development charges, regressive property taxes, inclusionary zoning) that punish newcomers, particularly newcomers who rent.

3 Cities should be able to charge nonresidents who use services. An employee-based personal income tax (or payroll tax) could tax

commuters who use urban services, offsetting property tax exemptions for nonmarket housing. Road usage and parking should be taxed heavily.

4 The federal government needs consistent, predictable taxation benefits and exemptions for purpose-built rentals, buildings with regulated affordable rents, and buildings that are energy efficient and accessible.

11

What Can We Do?

Canada is in a housing crisis. But that crisis is fixable. There have been better times and worse times, and there are better and worse countries. All levels of government can make better, evidence-based housing decisions – if voters demand it.

The situation in Canada is getting worse. Supply is not keeping up with population growth and change. There were more new homes built in the early 1970s than today. Purpose-built rental construction, market and nonmarket, has declined the most in the past fifty years, and it's the type of housing we need the most. Housing speculation is harming our economy. Sprawl in search of affordability is harming our environment. Homelessness is harming our society. As a nation, we must stop supporting speculation and start supporting the right kind of home building.

Prices and rents have escalated in the past two generations. In the 1970s, first-time home ownership was affordable to moderate-income households in the second income quintile; now first-time home ownership in Canada's largest cities is only available to those in the highest income quintile. Renting is now unaffordable to moderate-income households in most cities. Homelessness has increased exponentially since the 1990s, driven by the absence of rental homes affordable to low-income households.

As a nation, we need to return to using income categories to understand and gauge housing affordability. We must start with the question,

Who can afford what housing where? We must set targets to prioritize the needs of those who need affordable housing the most.

Learning from What's Worked Elsewhere

No country has found the magic bullet. Singapore has one of the highest rates of home ownership in the world (close to 90 percent) and the highest rate of public housing (80 percent). But there are stresses. A median home now costs 4.5 times the median income. This is about half of Canada's median multiple, but it still raises alarm bells about affordability. Singapore limits eligibility for public housing to heterosexual couples over twenty-one or single people over thirty. This means that 2SLGBTQ+ couples lose out and more adult children live with their parents because they don't want to rush into a relationship to obtain housing. Noncitizens, including asylum seekers and temporary foreign workers, are also ineligible for public housing. And rentals are as unaffordable as they are in Canada.

We can reject Singapore's homophobia and xenophobia but embrace its lessons about scaling up housing quickly, setting price and size targets, and focusing on good neighbourhood design.

Japan's housing model, characterized by high building rates but rapid depreciation, has led to extremely high vacancy rates and some of the least expensive housing in the world: 11 percent of household income. About 60 percent of households own, and 40 percent rent. A diminishing stock of public housing represents 7 percent of homes. Japan has the lowest rate of homelessness in the world: 4,000 people in a country of 123 million. Unlike Canada, it has a declining population and deeply entrenched xenophobic resistance to global migration and multicultural change. Yet Japan's permissive approach to building walkable, transit-friendly, socially diverse communities is worth emulating.

Xenophobia is hardly limited to Asian countries such as Singapore and Japan. Canada, Austria, France, Denmark, Finland, and Sweden have seen a rising tide of anti-immigrant rhetoric, in part because immigrants (rather than bad policy) are blamed for stressing the housing supply. However, statistics show that many countries are doing better than Canada when it comes to housing policy.

Canada has seen some of the highest price increases in the world (although New Zealand is almost as bad). Housing is responsible for an unusually large proportion of our GDP, and our mortgage debt is extremely high, two indicators that we spend too much as a nation on speculation and not enough on production. Our carbon dioxide emissions are high compared to other northern countries, and commuting times are also high.

Each of the five "exemplar" countries has at least one impressive outcome. (See the appendix for data illustrating these points.)

- Austria spends a lot less of its GDP on housing because nonmarket-housing costs a society less than market housing.
- Germany has more affordable-housing options, including rental homes, near jobs.
- France has seen low price increases and a low proportion of its GDP tied up in housing debt. Less reliance on fossil fuels and strict environmental construction standards play a part in its low carbon dioxide emissions. It, like Germany, is better at building homes close to jobs.
- Finland has seen ownership price decreases and has low carbon dioxide emissions, partly because of decarbonization and reliance on electricity and district heating. Its commuting times are among the lowest in the world.
- Denmark has a high ratio of mortgage debt, but its carbon dioxide emissions are half those of Canada, and it has much shorter commute times.

But what about equity? What is the situation of renters in these countries?

Let's look at renter households in the lowest income quintile.

Canada isn't the worst place to be a low-income tenant. Finland, for all its commitment to Housing First, has a higher proportion of low-income households in unaffordable housing than Canada. But it's addressing its shortfalls by scaling up nonmarket housing and renovating homes for energy efficiency. Germany has the best outcomes for low-income renters. Maybe its emphasis on purpose-built rentals and low barriers to ownership entry through baugruppen cohousing has paid off. Austria's reliance on nonmarket-housing construction (based on the Vienna model) has led to good outcomes for low-income renters. France still has far too many low-income renters under stress, but its emphasis on equalizing the proportion of nonmarket housing in every community means service workers are more likely to live in Paris than service workers in Toronto or Vancouver. As for Denmark, its low-income outcomes aren't much better than Canada's, but it's hard to beat its commitment to energy retrofits.

Let's compare how much these countries spend on nonmarket housing. We already know Canada spends the most on market housing. The OECD measures three components of nonmarket and affordable-housing spending: new nonmarket housing, demand-side subsidies, and energy retrofits.

France, Finland, and Germany commit 1 percent of their GDPs to nonmarket housing. France has a higher proportion in construction and acquisitions, Finland more in housing subsidies (mostly to nonmarket-housing providers). In recent years, Germany has greatly increased its spending on nonmarket housing, after divesting itself of most social-housing stock after reunification in 1999. Austria, with its long-term and relatively stable commitment to nonmarket housing, spends less than most countries. Canada is the only OECD country, other than Switzerland, that doesn't provide data.

I want to focus on Germany, where citizen power has transformed housing. How does it maintain good outcomes for low-income tenants even as it extends a hand in the global refugee crisis? How has it managed to shift from divesting itself of nonmarket housing to radically rebuilding and reacquiring low-cost options?

Affordable Housing and Citizen Activism in Germany

Germany, unsurprisingly, ended the Second World War with a much greater housing crisis than any of the countries I've discussed, except for Japan. At least one in five German homes was destroyed during the war.

East Germany, hardest hit by wartime bombing, pursued a communist path: universal, low-cost, state-provided public housing, but without the design innovation or community-development element of Sweden's Million Programme. West Germany also had high rates of postwar public housing, characterized by both state-subsidized supply and demand-side housing subsidies. In West Germany, public housing was seen as an emergency postwar measure rather than a long-term investment, and affordability covenants were strictly time-limited, from five to thirty years.

The neoliberal abandonment of nonmarket-housing stock in the 1990s was rapid and comprehensive. In West Germany after reunification, nonmarket housing declined from 20 percent of total stock in 1991, to 6 percent in 2005, to 3 percent in 2020. In the meantime, East German public housing was downloaded from the federal responsibility to the municipalities. Municipal housing companies were expected to operate without federal subsidies – a familiar tale in Canada. By the early 2000s, 500,000 public homes had been sold to international housing investment firms. These firms allowed the stock to deteriorate and rents to rise. Eventually, tenants had to move so properties could be redeveloped, at which point they were sold to new investment companies. By 2013, 19 percent of multitenant housing was owned by large-scale financialized actors intent on high returns – a situation similar to Canada's today. In Berlin, Vonovia owns 160,000 nonmarket homes that it's trying to convert into condominiums.

Berlin and Hamburg, Germany's two largest cities, have the taxation and regulation powers of states. After rents rose 33 percent between 2013 and 2019, the Berlin government voted to freeze rents and return some back to 2013 levels. The Supreme Court overturned the decision two years later, but in 2023, the federal government limited rent increases to 6 percent over three years, and only to the point of parity with rents in an area.

Local activism led to federal action. In 2021, a Berlin referendum to expropriate 240,000 homes from large investors won by 60 percent. The state government ordered a lengthy review of the referendum, but the expert panel decided Berlin could go ahead. The details of compensation are still unclear (e.g., should investors get current market value or what they initially paid?), as are plans to maintain and keep the buildings affordable. But this victory is a testament to the strength of tenant activism.

Like Canada and Sweden, Germany is experiencing an overall housing supply shortage because governments under the sway of liberalism abandoned rental housing supply policies. Approved but uncompleted homes doubled from 320,000 to 693,000 between 2008 and 2018. In 2021, the new left-of-centre government supported purpose-built rentals through tax relief for private market construction of affordable homes. The federal government also offered financial incentives to states and municipalities to build nonmarket housing, along with favourable financing to cooperatives (including private-market baugruppen). Municipalities were allowed to pre-emptively purchase affordable rentals at risk of being lost.

YIMBY activism led the way in the big cities. Hamburg, a city of 1.8 million in a metropolitan area of 5 million, has been using targets, finance, and a partnership approach to address population needs since the centre-left Social Democrats won power in 2011. In the first year of the first agreement, 6,000 new homes were approved – 3,500 private rentals, 1,100 municipal public housing, and 900 other nonmarket homes, including cooperatives. All large developments included public spaces. In return, Hamburg pledged to reduce development approval times to three months, coordinate subsidy delivery, and amend regulations that would stop affordable-housing construction in inner cities.

Recent population growth has included refugees: 40,000 in 2016 alone, most of them very-low-income. Annual housing-needs assessments helped increase and improve housing supply targets to 16,000 a year: one-third nonmarket with subsidized construction costs, one-third regulated rental, and one-third market ownership. This rule of thirds is strongly reminiscent of the Curtis Report's recommendations for Canada in 1944. Hamburg has met these targets every year since 2016. In the words of the mayor, ample rental stock is the "best rent cap."

Scale is integral to Hamburg's approach. Mitte Altona, adjacent to two commuter rail stations, is a redevelopment of a twenty-six-hectare rail maintenance site. It has 2,500 residential units (one-third nonmarket),

Mitte
Altona

shops, and community services. Federal funding helped the city purchase the site. When I visited the half-built site in May 2022, I was struck by the way the eight-hectare park, which had playing fields and schools, anchored the development. Homecare services help older residents in scattered homes. Streets have wide sidewalks and bike paths, and very few cars. It's strongly reminiscent of St. Lawrence in Toronto, down to its reliance on cooperative housing societies to create a sense of community. Near the east end sits the former Holsten Brewery, the future site for 1,500 low-cost residential units and light industry.

In 2022, construction began on Oberbillwerder, which is adjacent to a suburban rail station northeast of the central city. When finished, the site will have 7,000 apartments around a square-kilometre meadow. Slated to accommodate 16,000 residents and up to 7,000 jobs, Oberbillwerder is even more compact than its neighbouring development, Neuallermöhe, identical in size but with 3,800 apartments. Less space means fewer cars. Car-free bicycle and pedestrian paths will link the community to the city centre, and only half of the residents will be offered a space in eleven parking garages around the perimeter.

In Hamburg, mixed-use, mixed-income, sustainable communities have been developed through consistent targets, partnerships with market and nonmarket developers, control over land, and large-scale neighbourhood planning. Voters responded by returning the Social Democrat–Green coalition to power.

Federal Game Changers

Canada has much to learn from Germany, particularly its partnership approach. We have a National Housing Council made up of individual advocates rather than sectors. The council produces reports that critique the National Housing Strategy that are then ignored by the federal government. Canada needs a powerful sector-based council to help steer decisions at all levels of government. The council should represent nonmarket and market developers, finance providers, provincial and local governments, and advocates. It would brainstorm solutions, and the federal government would enact them using a "partnership accord" approach.

Here are lessons from the past and from international good practices:

1 Use one common definition of affordable housing, linked to income categories, to calculate housing needs for everyone, not just "private" households.

2 Create a long-term thirty-year strategy (updated every five years and informed by a strengthened National Housing Council) to progressively realize the right to adequate housing.

3 Set and monitor provincial and municipal targets and subtargets during twice-yearly meetings between federal, provincial, Indigenous, and municipal ministers. These meetings can inform spring budgets and fall economic statements and conditions on the transfer of social, health, and infrastructure funding.

4 Ensure that "for Indigenous, by Indigenous" strategies receive adequate support, including giving National Indigenous Collaborative Housing Inc. (NICHI) say over funds.

5 Ensure every household has adequate income to afford housing – moving from ad-hoc rent supplements to a guaranteed annual income or provincial welfare increases linked to federal transfer payments.

6 Legalize apartments everywhere through infrastructure funding agreements with municipalities linked to zoning- and building-code reform and meeting targets.

7 Improve tenure neutrality and dial back speculation through wealth taxes, regulation of investment funds, and restrictions on principal residence exemptions on capital gains tax.

8 End homelessness with a Housing First approach that includes accurate annual statistics and a federal-provincial-territorial supportive-housing program.

9 Rapidly increase funding for low-cost nonmarket housing (at least 1 percent of GDP and using all suitable government land).

10 Increase affordable market rental housing for moderate- and median-income households through taxation mechanisms linked to affordability, access, and the environment.

11 Protect renters by attaching conditions to financing for nonmarket-housing construction.

Home Truths

Provincial Game Changers

The provinces and territories should focus on the social welfare functions they abandoned in a harmful era of austerity politics.

1 Ensure that all individuals and households have adequate income to pay for housing by increasing welfare and the minimum wage or administering a federally set guaranteed minimum income.
2 Ensure adequate social and health supports to end homelessness and provide supportive housing to all those who need it, including youth in care and aging out of care, seniors, people with disabilities (including addictions), and survivors of violence. The target should be 0.5 percent of GDP spending.
3 Ensure that tenants are protected from evictions (including from rent increases), and fund eviction prevention through law clinics and rent banks.
4 Regulate and enforce restrictions on short-term rentals in any market with a vacancy rate of less than 8 percent.
5 Make information about property ownership (including annual data on land ownership and property assessments) public.
6 Lease all suitable transit-oriented government land (including land held by transit agencies and school boards) to nonmarket housing.
7 Allow municipalities to have landlord registries and to enact property tax reform (including property-tax exemptions for nonprofit-housing providers and land value taxes).
8 Ensure that building and zoning codes are harmonized, to enable well-located low-cost housing.

Municipal Game Changers

Municipalities and regions must move from a culture of "making new-comers pay for development" to encouraging new nonmarket and market housing.

1 Legalize well-located multiunit apartments everywhere through radical zoning- and building-code reform.

2 Commit to by-name lists and a coordinated response to permanently housing the homeless rather than relying on emergency shelters.

3 Commit to having an equal distribution of nonmarket housing across the city – ideally, 20 percent nonmarket housing in every neighbourhood.

4 Help nonmarket-housing providers scale up by prioritizing nonmarket development on government land, coordinating grants and financing from other levels of government, and waiving property taxes.

5 Commit to development decisions within forty-five days (with an as-of-right system of delegated approvals that doesn't require public hearings).

6 Shift from development charges to progressive property taxes, particularly land value taxes.

7 Ban short-term rentals in communities where the rental vacancy rate is lower than 8 percent, and institute a landlord registry to help ensure tenant rights, including fair rents and rapid repairs.

Becoming a Houser

Options for Homes, a nonprofit housing developer in Toronto, sells buttons that say "I'm a Houser." Perhaps because the slogan's close to that affectionate Canadian insult "hoser," these buttons sell like hotcakes. Canada is in a housing crisis, but many places in Canada and around the world give housers reason to hope.

"I'm a Houser" button. | Courtesy of Leah Blunden.

A colleague challenged me recently to say one good thing about Canada's most populous cities and provinces. I didn't hesitate. Toronto is now using income-related definitions of affordability. After three decades of failed trickle-down development on city-owned land, it's slowly and painfully starting to directly support nonmarket housing. Montreal is aiming for 20 percent nonmarket housing and 20 percent family-friendly apartments in livable 15-minute cities. Vancouver is using government land to reach targets based on income, tenure, and household size. Calgary is taking a comprehensive approach, bringing together government land, accelerated approvals, and financing coordination. Edmonton is leading the way in equity-based zoning and speeding up approvals. Ottawa has an excellent public-housing provider and under-utilized government land.

At the provincial level, Ontario has housing targets for municipalities, although they fall short of diagnosing who needs what housing where, and at what price. Quebec still has some of the best outcomes, in part because of its history of good zoning, good housing policy, and tenant activism. Alberta still has its Housing First policy. And British Columbia is the best province in terms of having nonmarket- and market-housing targets linked to zoning- and building-code reform.

There are many points of light across the country.

British Columbia's recent improvements aren't an accident. In 2017, the Co-operative Housing Federation of BC, in collaboration with the BC Non-Profit Housing Association, Vancity Credit Union, LandlordBC, and other members of the Rental Housing Coalition, released "An Affordable Housing Plan for BC" just prior to an election. The NDP won a minority government, backed by the Green Party. This plan became the basis for Homes for BC, a ten-year action plan with a target of 114,000 homes for low- and moderate-income households (nonmarket and market). The plan has subtargets for Indigenous and student housing, supportive housing to address homelessness, and transitional housing for women and children fleeing violence. The province has a strong alignment between YIMBY and nonmarket advocacy, something that is not always true across the rest of the country.

Although the province codesigned its policies, information on completions isn't transparent and housing completions have trailed projections. Still, between 2018 and 2021, almost 2,000 "rapid response to homelessness" homes were completed, as were 1,500 nonmarket homes and 5,700 student homes. These outcomes are greater than in the rest of Canada combined, except for Quebec. And British Columbia has now turned to enabling affordable housing at the municipal level. The province is way ahead of the federal government's Housing Accelerator Fund in setting municipal targets and linking zoning- and building-code change to funding.

British Columbia's progress also comes from resolving First Nation treaty claims. Senáḵw, at the head of False Creek in central Vancouver, is part of the unceded territory of the Sḵwx̱wú7mesh Úxwumixw (the Squamish Nation). The land was the site for a seasonal fishing village, which became a permanent village in the nineteenth century. In 1868, the federal government established Kitsilano Indian Reserve No. 6, a parcel of land of approximately fifteen hectares. Over the decades to come, it was annexed until the residents were finally given a small payment and barged off the land. A decades-long court battle launched in the late 1970s led to four hectares of Kitsilano Reserve lands being returned in 2003.

On this tiny site, a quarter the size of St. Lawrence in Toronto, 6,800 new rental and condominium homes are being developed in eleven towers of up to fifty-six storeys. The Nation has entered into a partnership with Westbank, a private market developer. Both parties will share the profits equally, but the Nation will provide the land under a long-term lease, and Westbank will secure the financing to cover $3 billion in construction costs. Because the land is owned by a sovereign Nation, it's not constrained by height limits set by their NIMBY neighbours in Kitsilano, who filed an injunction to block water and sewer connections to the site while piously intoning Indigenous land acknowledgments. Aside from below-market homes reserved for Sḵwx̱wú7mesh households, the project is market-based, with projected revenues of between $16 million and $20 million over the next century, which will help fund long-term economic development for the Nation's 20,000 members. In other words, some settlers are finally going to pay the rent.

Senáḵw will be accessible and environmentally sustainable, with limited on-site parking and provisions for surprisingly extensive green spaces between buildings. The project is negotiating with the federal government for greater affordability for more units. It's also an example of upzoning for reparations – control over profits flows to the descendants of those most directly excluded from housing wealth. Purpose-built rental housing in central Vancouver should be welcomed with open arms, not lawsuits from racist neighbours.

Meanwhile, in July 2023, ACORN Canada (the Association of Community Organizations for Reform Now), which has more than 160,000 members in twenty neighbourhood chapters, organized protests in nine cities to call on the federal government to give the right of first refusal on apartment-building purchases to land trusts, co-ops, tenants, and nonmarket providers. They also called for a national acquisition fund to give these entities the financial backing to purchase the buildings. From Vancouver to Halifax, tenants have showcased buildings where recent evictions and large rent increases threaten them with homelessness. A new generation of tenant activism is making its mark.

In Ottawa, the Starts with Home campaign, launched by the Alliance to End Homelessness Ottawa, is endorsed by 155 organizations, including the Ottawa Board of Trade, ACORN, the Ottawa Coalition to End Violence Against Women, and the Ottawa Tourism Board. It calls for nonmarket housing on government land, tenant protection against evictions, landlord licensing, and creation of an acquisition strategy for at-risk affordable housing.

Across Canada, coalitions are demanding housing rights. The Black Community Housing Advisory Table stepped up to provide emergency shelter to about three hundred African refugee claimants after they were left sleeping on Toronto streets in mid-summer 2023 due to jurisdictional squabbles. The Right to Housing Coalition eked out a homelessness strategy from the Manitoba government in 2023. The Women's National Housing and Homelessness Network led a human rights claim to the Office of the Federal Housing Advocate in 2022, providing evidence of systemic housing discrimination against women and girls. Make Housing Affordable!, a group in Ottawa led by young renters, has called for an end to exclusionary zoning, density bonuses, and more partnerships with nonmarket-housing developers.

During the 2021 federal election, Vote Housing, a coalition of homelessness and nonmarket-housing advocates, commissioned a national poll. Over a third of people said they'd either experienced homelessness or knew someone who had. Eighty percent of Canadians said they'd vote for a political party proposing to end homelessness and build affordable housing. A separate 2022 poll found that affordable housing was the top national issue for voters.

What can you do? Canada is a democracy, and advocacy groups and coalitions can have a huge impact. The first step is to stay informed. Social media as an accurate news source waxes and wanes – support local, independent investigative journalism from outlets such as *The Tyee*, *The Local*, and *The Narwhal*. Homelesshub.ca is a good source for recent news and research, as is the Canadian Housing Evidence Collaborative. Join a group and follow their social media feeds. Disagree without attacking people. One of the most distressing aspects of social media is rights-based activists and YIMBYs attacking each other rather than attacking terrible political decisions together. My experience from thirty-five years of advocacy politics is that a small group of people can have a large impact. Engage with political leaders as fellow human beings. Talk with them, not at them.

Federally, the National Right to Housing Network brings together local groups that work on the right to housing. The Canadian Housing and Renewal Association advocates for nonmarket housing, and the Co-operative Housing Federation of Canada represents nonmarket co-ops. Many provinces have organizations that represent community or cooperative housing providers who organize election-based campaigns. The Canadian Alliance to End Homelessness, which brings together providers and advocates, has taken the lead on Vote Housing campaigns. National Indigenous Collaborative Housing Inc. (NICHI), the newest national nonmarket-housing organization, upholds and advances housing as a human right for Indigenous peoples. There are national organizations for community land trusts, cohousing, and other innovative housing solutions. The National Pensioners Federation is working on seniors' housing, and the Pan-Canadian Voice for Women's Housing and the Women's National Housing and Homelessness Network are feminist organizations that advocate together – the former from a provider perspective, the latter from a research perspective.

The Canadian Centre for Housing Rights helps organize local housing rights coalitions. Almost every large city has a YIMBY organization with a name such as More Neighbours or Abundant Housing, and they're beginning to coalesce nationally. There are provincial coalitions such as the Alliance for a Liveable Ontario that bring together environmental sustainability and housing advocacy.

Go to city council meetings and advocate for more housing. Supports tenants fighting against unfair rent increases and evictions. Speak to councillors and political candidates about the need for more affordable housing. Speak out at provincial and federal budget consultations. If you have a room or two to spare, consider finding a tenant.

Consider where you're going to live when you get older. Consider where the next generation will live – and six generations after that. Consider the needs of people who aren't directly related to you, especially those who have faced and continue to face systemic discrimination in housing. We all need safe and secure homes in which we can care and be cared for, in which we can live in dignity. The Curtis Report was right: the rule of thirds is a target that can provide adequate homes for all, particularly if it's embedded in forward-thinking infrastructure strategies that combine equity with environmental sustainability.

Canada has the wealth and ingenuity to switch paths to fix its housing crisis. We have the legal framework in the National Housing Strategy Act to do the right thing. All we need is the political will to move forward. You have a role in shaping that collective will.

Acknowledgments

Unlike my previous book, *Clara at the Door with a Revolver,* which was written in a solitary and somewhat obsessive state before and during COVID-19, *Home Truths* sprang from conversations that span decades. My early interest in housing was piqued by my mother, Sheila Whitzman, a real estate agent who hated her local zoning bylaws with such passion I think of her as the ur-YIMBY. Cynthia Davis drew me into Les Voisin(e)s de Devonshire, a neighbourhood group advocating for nonmarket housing on the site of a former school in Montreal. During my master's degree in Toronto, I fell in with some wonderful feminist housing activists at Women Plan Toronto, particularly the late Regula Modlich and my longtime consulting partner Deborah Hierlihy. Professor Richard Harris was an inspiration throughout my academic life as a historical researcher who cares deeply about contemporary relevance. Similarly, Caroline Andrew and Fran Klodawsky taught me much about the intersections of gender, housing, and violence prevention.

At the University of Melbourne, I had the privilege of working with a terrific team of researchers in Transforming Housing. I want to particularly thank Rebecca Clements, Andrew Martel, Matt Palm, Kate Raynor, and Sasha Sheko for putting up with uncertain funding and problematic faculty politics. The Robs – McGauran and Pradolin – showed me what good development practice was all about, while Catherine Brown taught me about social finance. Kimbra White helped me think deeply about deliberative "big tents."

Since my return to Canada, I've been exceptionally lucky in being surrounded by smart and energetic housers, and I'm sure I'll forget a few in these acknowledgments. First and foremost, thanks to the team at the Housing Assessment Resource Tools project at the University of British Columbia: Alexandra Flynn and Penny Gurstein, the lead researchers; Craig Jones, number cruncher and project director extraordinaire; and Martine August, Joe Daniels, Morika di Angelis, Andres Penalosa, Cameron Power, Andrew Rigsby, Sam Roberts, Mikayla Tinsley, and so many others. I continue to benefit from the wisdom of nonmarket development leaders such as Thom Armstrong, Jill Atkey, Margaret Pfoh (the three BC Musketeers), Ray Sullivan, and Courtney Lockhart, and rights advocates such as Khulud Baig, Michele Biss, Kaite Burkholder Harris, Leilani Farha, Marie-Josée Houle, Emily Paradis, Bruce Porter, Sahar Raza, and Kaitlyn Schwann.

Once again, UBC/On Point Press has provided excellent guidance and support: James McNevin as acquisitions editor; Katrina Petrik and Carmen Tiampo in production; Laraine Coates and Kerry Kilmartin in marketing; and especially Lesley Erickson, who edited both the Clara and Home books and who was right about everything, even the things I hated.

I rely on family and friends to keep me sane while writing, and I want to particularly thank Mary Fairhurst Breen for online Scrabble and book-writing chat; Karen Ocana, Jeffrey Kastner, Ursula Mueller, Michael Judson, and Nancy Breitman for great excuses to visit Montreal; Jennifer Ramsay for a Toronto home away from home and being my Wordle buddy; Jo-Anne Guimond for long walks in Ottawa; and my Or Haneshamah Synagogue, Iron North gym, and Hintonburg Read Whatever You Want Book Club gangs for providing a life outside writing. My children – Simon Hunt, Molly Hunt, and Lewis Wiegand – remind me why I want to be a good ancestor. My husband, David Hunt, does line editing, handholding, and cheerleading for all my books and continues to be the smartest and wisest man I know.

Appendix

Table 1: The timeline and risks of multiunit development

Phase of development	Primary activities	Timeline	Risks
Predevelopment and entitlement approval	Locate/control site Planning Predevelopment loan Environmental assessment Preliminary design Financial feasibility Municipal planning approval Construction financing	0.5 to 5+ years Depends on size and complexity	Anything that adds time, e.g., environmental issues; NIMBYism; need for variances, rezoning, or official plan amendments Interest rate increases Public policy changes Inability to secure financing Construction cost increases
Development and construction	Acquire site Detailed drawings Building permits Select contractor Construction Marketing Mortgage financing	0.5 to 5 years Or 0.5 to 2 years after presales if ownership property (e.g., condo) Depends on size and complexity	Market or economy changes Public policy changes Cost over-runs, e.g., due to strikes, bad weather, etc. Interest-rate increases before mortgage financing is locked in Can't secure long-term financing Financers risk loan default
Occupancy and management	Marketing Property management Paying expenses Maintenance and repair Paying off debt	Maximum would be the life of the building	Marketing risk Tenant credit risk High vacancy Excessive damage Interest-rate increases

Source: Jill Black, "The Financing and Economics of Affordable Housing Development: Incentives and Disincentives to Private-Sector Participation," Cities Centre, University of Toronto, Research Paper 224, September 2012.

Table 2: Housing tenure and outcomes, Canada versus five European countries

	Own/own with mortgage/ rent (%)	House price increase 2010–20 (%)	Housing as percent of GDP, 2022	Mortgage debt as percent of GDP, 2022 or most recent	Housing carbon dioxide emissions (tonnes/capita)	Average commuting time (minutes)
Canada	**30/39/31**	**79**	**14.0**	**75**	**1.80**	**30.3**
Austria	30/20/50	67	5.2	50	1.2	29.4
Germany	26/18/56	57	7.8	39	1.80	27.1
France	23/16/61	13	6.0	65	0.75	22.7
Finland	33/31/36	-4	7.4	64	0.86	21.0
Denmark	15/36/49	26	6.0	82	0.90	23.1

Source: Data compiled from OECD, "Affordable Housing Database," 2021, https://www.oecd.org/housing/data/affordable-housing-database/.

Table 3: Low-income households and nonmarket housing, Canada versus five European countries

	Population, 2023 (millions)	Low-income, cost-overburdened tenants, 2020 (%)[a]	Nonmarket stock, 2020 (%)	Number new nonmarket, 2020	Canadian equivalent	Number deep renovations, 2020	Canadian equivalent
Canada	38.8	34.5	4	~1,500[b]	1,500	33,509	33,509
Austria	9.0	19.4	24	17,000	73,300	7,400	31,309
Germany	83.3	15.5	13	25,565[c]	11,907	79,700	37,123
France	64.8	29.2	16	76,076[d]	45,600	111,000	66,500
Finland	5.5	44.6	11	9,000	63,500	n/a	n/a
Denmark	5.9	33.3	21	2,700	17,800	39,900	262,400

Source: Data compiled from OECD, "Affordable Housing Database," 2021, https://www.oecd.org/housing/data/affordable-housing-database/.

Notes:

a Expressed as 40 percent of net post-tax income, not 30 percent of pretax income.

b The CMHC does not provide data on home completions by tenure or affordability range. The only National Housing Strategy program affordable to low-income households (the Rapid Housing Initiative) reported 3,713 completed homes between October 2020 and June 2023. The Rental Construction Financing Initiative completed 9,003 units. None were affordable. The National Housing Co-investment Fund completed 10,229 units. One-third were nonmarket, and many were unaffordable to low-income people. Both were launched in 2018, so these outcomes were averaged over five years.

c Represents 2019 data. Germany only reports new social rental (3 percent of stock), not municipal public (5 percent) or cooperative (5 percent) that have "aged out" of the thirty-year operating agreements associated with mortgages but continue to have housing charges based on cost, not market rent.

d Represents 2019 data. France reported new builds (42,030) and acquisitions (33,996) separately.

Table 4: Percentage of GDP spent on nonmarket housing, Canada versus five European countries

	Demand-side subsidies	Builds	Retrofits	Total
Canada				0.10[a]
Austria	0.09	0.25	0.14	0.48
Germany	0.73	0.06	0.16	0.95
France	0.69	0.20	0.11	1.00
Finland	0.88	0.05	n/a	0.93
Denmark	0.72	0.03	0.03	0.78

Source: Data compiled from OECD, "Affordable Housing Database," 2023, https://www.oecd.org/housing/data/affordable-housing-database/, and Housing Europe, *The State of Housing in Europe 2021*, 2021.

Note:

a In 2019, the Parliamentary Budget Office provided this proportion based on all federal affordable-housing expenditures, including grants and financing to unaffordable market housing under the Rental Construction Financing Initiative. Provinces and municipalities contribute at least an equal sum for permanent nonmarket housing and demand-side housing supplements. The fact that expenditures are not broken down by tenure or investment type (like in almost every other country) contributes to Canada's housing crisis.

Notes

Introduction

3 **"an event or series of events":** Ricardo Tranjan, *The Tenant Class* (Toronto: Between the Lines, 2023), 2.

4 **40,000 people in emergency shelters:** Infrastructure Canada, *Everyone Counts 2020–2022: Results from the Third Nationally Coordinated Point-in-Time Counts of Homelessness in Canada,* 2023.

4 **evictions, 2016–21:** Silas Xuereb and Craig Jones, *Estimating No-Fault Evictions in Canada: Understanding BC's Disproportionate Eviction Rate in the 2021 Canadian Housing Survey* (Vancouver: UBC Housing Research Collaborative, 2023).

4 **Low-income renters living on minimum wage:** David Macdonald and Ricardo Tranjan, *Rental Wages in Canada* 2022 (Ottawa: Canadian Centre for Policy Alternatives, 2023); **Quebec has lost affordable rentals:** Steve Pomeroy, *Updating Analysis on Erosion of Lower Rent Stock from 2021 Census* (Hamilton, ON: Canadian Housing Evidence Collaborative, 2022).

4 **average house price doubled:** Parliamentary Budget Office, *House Price Assessment: A Borrowing Capacity Perspective,* 2022; **wages increased by only 7 percent:** Statistics Canada, "Average Earnings, 1998 to 2021," Quality of Employment in Canada (cat. no. 14280001), May 30, 2022.

4 **2.5 times the median household income:** Urban Reform Institute, *Demographia International Housing Affordability,* 2022; **Vancouver ... a fifth of what they are now:** Cheryl Chan, "Minimum Income to Buy a Home in Vancouver Rises to $246,100," *Vancouver Sun,* September 18, 2023.

4 **income categories:** https://hart.ubc.ca/housing-needs-assessment-tool/.

6 **home-ownership rates/stark intergenerational wealth divide:** Statistics Canada, "To Buy or to Rent: The Housing Market Continues to Be Reshaped

by Several Factors as Canadians Search for an Affordable Place to Call Home," *The Daily*, September 21, 2022.

6   **avocado toast:** Miriam Quick, "The Avocado Toast Index: How Many Breakfasts to Buy a House?," *BBC News*, May 30, 2017.

6   **trouble paying their bills:** Financial Consumer Agency of Canada, *FCAC Report: The Financial Well-Being of Canadian Homeowners with Mortgages*, June 2023.

7   **highest levels of household debt:** Bank of Canada, *Financial System Review – 2022*; World Economic Forum, "Canada's Household Debt Levels Are the Highest in the World," December 7, 2017; and Organisation for Economic Co-operation and Development, *OECD Economic Surveys: Canada 2023*, March 2023.

11 **a basic moral test:** https://www.gensqueeze.ca/.

12 **Canada's nonmarket housing:** Canada Mortgage and Housing Corporation, "Results of the Social and Affordable Housing Survey – Rental Structures," November 30, 2021, https://www.cmhc-schl.gc.ca/blog/2021/results-social -affordable-housing-survey-rental-structures.

Chapter 1: What Is a Home?

14 **when it's fixed:** https://fixed.africa/.

14 **Jamii:** https://www.jamii.ca/.

15 **rather than for speculative profit:** David Hulchanski, "Planning New Urban Neighbourhoods: Lessons from Toronto's St. Lawrence Neighbourhood," in *Directions for New Urban Neighbourhoods: Learning from St. Lawrence*, ed. David Gordon (Toronto: Ryerson Polytechnic Institute, 1989), s. 3-1.

15 **Eleanor's story:** personal communication, June 2022, recounted with permission of family.

17 **Residential School:** Angela Sterritt and Courtney Dickson, "'This Is Heavy Truth': Tk'emlúps te Secwépemc Chief Says More to Be Done to Identify Unmarked Graves," *CBC News*, July 15, 2021.

17 **Kikékyelc: A Place of Belonging:** https://lmofcs.ca/kik%C3%A9kyelc -a-place-of-belonging/.

17 **Silas, Melissa, and Colleen's stories:** personal communications, July 2022, recounted with permission.

19 **What rooming-house residents needed:** Walter Firey, *Land Use in Central Boston* (Cambridge, MA: Harvard University Press, 1948).

19 **converted into single-family homes or torn down:** Melissa Goldstein, *Fixing the Leaky Bucket: A Comprehensive Policy and Program Framework to Preserve Toronto's Supply of Deeply Affordable Housing* (Toronto: Parkdale Neighbourhood Land Trust, 2020).

19 **"for Indigenous, by Indigenous" housing strategy:** Canadian Housing and Renewal Association, Indigenous Housing Caucus Working Group, *A For Indigenous By Indigenous National Housing Strategy*, May 2018.

20 **Universal Declaration of Human Rights:** Kafui Attoh, "What Kind of Right Is the Right to the City?," *Progress in Human Geography* 35, 5 (2011): 669–85.

21 **elements of adequate housing:** UN Committee on Economic, Social and Cultural Rights, "General Comment No. 4: The Right to Adequate Housing (Art. 11(1) of the Covenant)" (doc. no. E/1992/23), December 13, 1991; UN OHCHR/UN-Habitat, "The Right to Adequate Housing," Fact Sheet 21/rev.1, 2009.

22 **core housing need** and **homelessness:** Canada Mortgage and Housing Corporation, "The National Housing Strategy Glossary of Common Terms," May 17, 2022.

23 **forced evictions:** Canadian Centre for Housing Rights, "Proportionality: A Legal Framework to Make Eviction a Last Resort in Canada," July 13, 2023.

23 **"Under human rights law, relocation":** Canadian Human Rights Commission, "A Focus on the Housing and Homelessness Crisis," 2022.

23 **basic-needs approach:** CMHC, "Defining the Affordability of Housing in Canada," *Research Insight*, January 2019.

24 **"Accessibility refers to":** CMHC, "National Housing Strategy Glossary."

24 **Statistics Canada has mapped access:** Alessandro Alasia, Nick Newstead, Joseph Kuchar, and Marian Radalescu, *Measuring Proximity to Services and Amenities: An Experimental Set of Indicators for Neighbourhoods and Localities* (cat. no. 18-001-X) (Ottawa: Statistics Canada, 2021).

25 **Canadian Indigenous scholars:** Jesse Thistle, *Definition of Indigenous Homelessness in Canada* (Toronto: Homelessness Hub, 2017), 6.

25 **home is characterized by positive qualities:** Witold Rybczynski, *Home: A Short History of an Idea* (New York: Viking, 1986); bell hooks, "Homeplace: A Site of Resistance," in *Yearning: Race, Gender and Cultural Politics* (Boston: South End Press, 1990), 41–49; and Matthew McCrae, "The Story of Africville," Canadian Human Right Museum, February 23, 2017.

26 **two books shaped my thinking:** Dolores Hayden, *Redesigning the American Dream: The Future of Housing, Work, and Family Life* (New York: Norton and Company, 1986); and Clare Cooper Marcus and Wendy Sarkissian, *Housing as If People Mattered: Site Design Guidelines for Medium-Density Family Housing* (Berkeley: University of California Press, 1986).

27 **an infrastructure of care:** Emma Power and Kathleen Mee, "Housing: An Infrastructure of Care," *Housing Studies* 35, 3 (2020): 484–505.

28 **5 percent of Canadians lived alone:** Statistics Canada, "The Shift to Smaller Households over the Past Century," *Canadian Megatrends*, May 17, 2018; Statistics Canada, "Home Alone: More Persons Living Solo Than Ever Before, but Roomies the Fastest Growing Household Type," *The Daily*, July 13, 2022; and Government of Canada, *Action for Seniors Report*, 2014.

28 **highest rate of death in long-term care:** Centre for Equality Rights in Accommodation, *Older Persons Living in Long-Term Care Homes and the Right to Adequate Housing in Canada*, April 2022, 5.

Chapter 2: How Did We Get in This Mess?

In this chapter, I draw on three key works on Canadian housing policy history: John Bacher, *Keeping to the Marketplace: The Evolution of Canadian Housing Policy* (Montreal/Kingston: McGill-Queen's University Press, 1993); Greg Suttor, *Still Renovating: A History of Canadian Social Housing Policy* (Montreal/Kingston: McGill-Queen's University Press, 2016); and H. Peter Oberlander and George Fallick, *Housing a Nation: The Evolution of Canadian Housing Policy* (Ottawa: CMHC, 1992).

30 **including larger apartments:** Canadian Alliance to End Homelessness, Smart Prosperity Institute, and REALPAC, *The National Housing Accord: A Multisector Approach to Ending Canada's Rental Housing Crisis*, August 2023, 11.

31 **downloaded responsibility for housing programs:** Jen St. Denis, "Why Can't We Build Like It's the 1970s?," *The Tyee*, April 22, 2022.

32 **and many more were lost:** Steve Pomeroy, Nicholas Gazzard, and Allan Gaudreault, *Promising Practices in Affordable Housing: Evolution and Innovation in BC and Quebec*, 2019, http://www.focus-consult.com/wp-content/uploads/Evolution-and-Innovation-in-BC-and-QC-FINALx-1.pdf.

32 **"relationships to land, water":** Jesse Thistle, *Definition of Indigenous Homelessness in Canada* (Toronto: Homelessness Hub, 2017), 6.

32 **Housing policy in Turtle Island:** Edward Mills and Harold D. Kalman, "Architectural History of Indigenous Peoples in Canada," *Canadian Encyclopedia*, September 30, 2007.

33 **In Montreal, rents ... Toronto in 1914:** Bacher, *Keeping to the Marketplace*, 39–42.

33 **In his 1911 "slum report":** Carolyn Whitzman, *Suburb, Slum, Urban Village: Transformations in Toronto's Parkdale Neighbourhood, 1875–2002* (Vancouver: UBC Press, 2008), 111–12.

33 **boarding and doubling up:** Peter Baskerville, "Familiar Strangers: Urban Families with Boarders, Canada, 1901," *Social Science History* 25, 3 (2001): 321–46; and Richard Harris, "The Flexible House: The Housing Backlog and the Persistence of Lodging," *Social Science History* 18, 1 (1994): 31–53.

33 **"There is no apparent prospect":** Michael Dennis and Susan A. Fish, *Low-Income Housing: Programs in Search of a Policy* (Ottawa: Ministry of State for Urban Affairs, 1972), 2.

34 **Curtis Report:** Advisory Committee on Reconstruction, *Housing and Community Planning: Final Report of Subcommittee* (Ottawa: Dominion of Canada, 1944).

35 **establishment of the CMHC:** Jill Wade, "Wartime Housing Limited, 1941–1947: Canadian Housing Policy at the Crossroads," *Urban History Review* 15, 1

(1986): 40–59; and Danielle Bochove, "How Wartime Victory Houses Shaped Modern Toronto," *Bloomberg CityLab*, March 24, 2021.

36 **Victory House sold for $19,000:** Shawn Micallef, "Bought for $19,000, Sold for More Than $2 Million, This Don Mills Home Is a Reminder of When Canada Helped Canadians House Themselves," *Toronto Star*, March 13, 2021.

36 **purpose-built rentals through tax incentives:** Oberlander and Fallick, *Housing a Nation*.

37 **"at no level of government":** Dennis and Fish, *Low-Income Housing*, 13–14.

38 **capital gains tax of 50 percent:** Paul Kershaw, "Policy Forum: Revisiting the Principal Residence Exemption and Public Support for Reducing the Home Ownership Tax Shelter," *Canadian Tax Journal* 70, 4 (2022): 827–42.

38 **"to bring home ownership within":** CMHC, quoted in Oberlander and Fallick, *Housing a Nation*, 112.

39 **average life expectancy:** Statistics Canada, "Life Expectancy, 1920–1922 to 2009–2011," *The Daily*, May 17, 2018; and Aaron O'Neill, "Life Expectancy at Birth in Canada from 2011 to 2021, by Gender," *Statista*, February 5, 2024.

39 **lasting impact on housing supply:** Oberlander and Fallick, *Housing a Nation*, 120.

39 **deinstitutionalization of about 400,000 people:** CMHC, *Housing in Canada 1945 to 1986: An Overview and Lessons Learned*, 1987.

39 **Multi-Unit Residential Buildings (MURB) program:** Oberlander and Fallick, *Housing a Nation*.

40 **over 50 percent of renters ... property speculation:** Oberlander and Fallick, *Housing a Nation*, 117.

40 **1986 City of Toronto report:** Phillipa Campsie, *A Brief History of Rooming Houses in Toronto* (Toronto: University of Toronto Centre for Urban Studies, 1994).

41 **1970s onwards ... 73,000 older, larger, and more affordable purpose-built apartments:** Matti Siemiatycki and Karen Chapple, "Perspective on the Rental Housing Roundtable," independent report for City of Toronto's 2023 Housing Action Plan, March 2023, 7.

42 **target of 30,000 nonmarket homes per year:** Oberlander and Fallick, *Housing a Nation*, 136.

42 **neoliberalism took hold:** Manuel Aalbers, "The Great Moderation, the Great Excess and the Global Housing Crisis," *International Journal of Housing Policy* 15, 1 (2015): 43–60.

43 **sales tax burden on new rental construction:** Siemiatycki and Chapple, "Perspective on the Rental Housing Roundtable."

43 **the National Housing Strategy (NHS) adopted:** Government of Canada, *Canada's National Housing Strategy: A Place to Call Home* (cat. no. Em12-54/ 2018E-PDF) (Gatineau, QC: Employment and Social Development Canada, 2018); and Government of Canada, "A Stronger and More Resilient Canada: Speech from the Throne 2020," September 23, 2020, https://www.

canada.ca/en/privy-council/campaigns/speech-throne/2020/speech-from-the
-throne.html.

44 **seven federal government evaluations:** Ben Segel-Brown, *Federal Program Spending on Housing Affordability* (Ottawa: Office of the Parliamentary Budget Officer [PBO], 2019); Ben Segel-Brown, *Federal Program Spending on Housing Affordability in 2021* (Ottawa: PBO, 2021); Carleigh Busby, *Federal Program Spending on Housing in 2022* (Ottawa: PBO, 2023); Auditor General of Canada, *Chronic Homelessness, 2022*; National Housing Council, *Analysis of Affordable Housing Supply Created by Unilateral National Housing Strategy Programs, 2022*; and House of Commons, *Housing Accelerator Fund: Report of the Standing Committee on Human Resources, Skills and Social Development and the Status of Persons with Disabilities* (two reports: October 2022 and June 2023; chair: Robert J. Morrissey).

45 **recently created national standards for long-term care:** Health Canada, "Statement by Ministers Duclos and Khera on Long-Term Care Standards," January 31, 2023.

Chapter 3: Who's in Charge?

46 **Sweden's Million Programme:** Thomas Hall and Sonia Viden, "The Million Homes Programme: A Review of the Great Swedish Planning Project," *Planning Perspectives* 20, 3 (2005): 301–28.

47 **homes were in poor condition:** Marie Urfels, "From State Support to Market and Financialization Measures in Crisis Times: A Comparative Literature Review of German and Swedish Systems," University of Malmo, SBV Working Papers Series 22:1, 2022.

49 **state-supported prefabrication:** Erik Stenberg, *Structural Systems of the Million Home Era* (Stockholm: KTH School of Architecture, 2013); Rod Sweet, "Why Sweden Beats the World Hands Down on Prefab Housing," *Global Construction Review*, May 28, 2015; and Terner Center for Housing Innovation, UC Berkeley, *Housing in Sweden: An Overview*, November 2017.

51 **41 percent of housing in Sweden is still nonmarket:** Housing Europe, *The State of Housing in Europe 2021*.

51 **Canada has three levels of government:** Gabriel Eidelman, Tomas Hachard, and Enid Slack, eds., *The Municipal Role in Housing*, Who Does What Series (Toronto: Institute on Municipal Finance and Governance, Urban Policy Lab, University of Toronto, 2022).

53 **"politicians can't be trusted":** Angus Reid Institute, "Trust in Government: Canadians Wary of Politicians and Their Intentions," June 24, 2019.·

53 **Canada's tax revenues:** Library of Parliament, "Personal Income Taxes in Canada: Revenue, Rates and Rationale," *Hillnotes*, October 18, 2021.

53 **Incomes are highly unequal:** David Macdonald, *Canada's New Gilded Age: CEO Pay in 2022* (Ottawa: Canadian Centre for Policy Alternatives, 2024).

54 **"marginal effective" corporate tax rate:** Department of Finance, Canada, "Marginal Effective Tax Rates," Canada.ca, July 18, 2019.

54 **capital locked up in housing:** David Williams, "OECD Predicts Canada Will Be the Worst Performing Advanced Economy over the Next Decade," Business Council of BC, Economic Perspectives, December 14, 2019.

55 **Canada's social spending:** PressProgress, "Canada's Social Spending Is Still among the Lowest in the Industrialized World," March 16, 2019.

55 **household debt is greater than our annual GDP:** World Economic Forum, "Canada's Household Debt Levels Are the Highest in the World," December 7, 2017; Statistics Canada, "Gross Domestic Product by Industry, December 2022," *The Daily*, February 28, 2023.

55 **"shaky palace":** Matthew Edel, Elliot Sclar, and Daniel Luria, *Shaky Palaces: Homeownership and Social Mobility in Boston's Suburbanization* (New York: Columbia University Press, 1984).

56 **"competition of ideas":** C. Wyplosz, H. Sinn, A. Venables, D. Neven, P. Seabright, V. Grilli, J. Edwards, J. Danthine, J. Crémer, and D. Beggs, eds., *Making Sense of Subsidiarity: How Much Centralization for Europe?* (Paris: Centre for European Policy and Research, 1993).

56 **Ontario's Financial Accountability Office:** Financial Accountability Office of Ontario, "Comparing Ontario's Fiscal Position with Other Provinces: 2017–18," press release, February 14, 2019.

57 **welfare rates:** Jennefer Laidley and Mohy Tabbara, *Welfare in Canada 2022* (Toronto: Maytree Foundation, 2023).

57 **Ontario was the best province for nonmarket housing:** Greg Suttor, *Still Renovating: A History of Canadian Social Housing Policy* (Montreal/Kingston: McGill-Queen's University Press, 2016), 52.

58 **Ontario ... saw costs soar:** Suttor, *Still Renovating*, 152.

58 **77 percent of nonmarket-housing funding:** Eidelman, Hachard, and Slack, *The Municipal Role in Housing*, 3.

58 **British Columbia went in the opposite direction:** Steve Pomeroy, Nicholas Gazzard, and Allan Gaudreault, *Promising Practices in Affordable Housing: Evolution and Innovation in BC and Quebec*, 2019, http://www.focus-consult.com/wp-content/uploads/Evolution-and-Innovation-in-BC-and-QC-FINALx-1.pdf.

59 **Quebec financing:** Pomeroy, Gazzard, and Gaudreault, *Promising Practices*, 25.

60 **Alberta Housing First program:** Damian Collins and Madeleine Stout, "Does Housing First Policy Seek to Fulfil the Right to Housing? The Case of Alberta, Canada," *Housing Studies* 36, 3 (2020): 336–58.

60 **Recent audits of provincial and territorial:** Office of the Auditor General of Canada, *Yukon Housing: Independent Auditor's Report*, 2022; Financial Accountability Office of Ontario, *Housing and Homelessness Programs in Ontario*, 2022; and Canada–British Columbia Expert Panel on the Future of

Housing Supply and Affordability, *Opening Doors: Unlocking Housing Supply for Affordability*, June 2021.

60 **Groucho Marx:** *A Night at the Opera* (Beverly Hills, CA: MGM, 1935), https://www.youtube.com/watch?v=aswouE3H6AA.

61 **75 percent of GDP:** Tomas Hachard, "It Takes Three: Making Space for Cities in Canadian Federalism," *IMFG Perspectives* 31, 2020.

61 **property taxes have many sound principles:** Enid Slack and Richard Bird, "How to Reform the Property Tax: Lessons from around the World," *IMFG Papers on Municipal Finance and Governance* 21, 2015; and David Thompson, Greg Flanagan, Diana Gibson, Laleah Sinclair, and Andy Thompson, *Funding a Fairer Future: Progressive Revenue Sources for Canada's Cities and Towns* (Ottawa: Canadian Union of Public Employees, 2014).

61 **double the tax rate for older multitenant buildings:** City of Toronto, Property Tax Rates and Fees, 2023.

61 **Montreal manages 55,000 ... Toronto's 60,000:** Eidelman, Hachard, and Slack, *The Municipal Role in Housing*.

62 **Tillsonburg:** Mike Moffatt, "Ontarians on the Move, 2021 Edition. #9," *Medium* (blog), March 29, 2021.

Chapter 4: Who Needs What Homes Where, at What Cost?

63 **3.5 million additional homes:** CMHC, *Canada's Housing Supply Shortages: Estimating What Is Needed to Solve Canada's Housing Affordability Crisis by 2030*, June 2022.

63 **1.3 million vacant homes:** Jens von Bergmann and Nathanael Lauster, "Running on Empties: Putting Canadian Empty Homes Data into Context," *Mountain Doodles* (blog), August 19, 2019, doodles.mountainmath.ca.

64 **Vancouver's Empty Homes Tax:** Howard Chai, "Amount of Vacant Homes in Vancouver Down 36 Percent Due to Empty Homes Tax," *Storeys*, December 5, 2022.

64 **128,000 apartments and homes:** Jennifer Combes, Danielle Kerrigan, and David Wachsmuth, "Short-Term Rentals in Canada," *Canadian Journal of Urban Research* 29, 1 (2020): 119–34.

64 **large by international standards:** Lindsay Wilson, "How Big Is a House? Average House Size by Country – 2023," *Shrink That Footprint* (blog), January 4, 2024.

64 **overhoused:** CANCEA Research, "The Missing Middle," TREB Market Year in Review and Outlook Report, 2018; and Rachelle Younglai, "Unable to Downsize, More Seniors Are Living in Larger Homes with Empty Bedrooms," *Globe and Mail*, July 5, 2023.

65 **United Kingdom bedroom taxes:** Shelter, "How to Deal with the Bedroom Tax," 2023, https://england.shelter.org.uk.

65 **Singapore needs assessment:** Singapore Housing and Development Board, *50,000 Up: Homes for the People* (Singapore: National Library Board of Singapore, 1965).

66 **Singapore met those targets:** Belinda Yuen, "Squatters No More: Singapore Social Housing," *Global Urban Development Magazine* 3 (2007): 1–22; Abbas Jha, "'But What about Singapore?' Lessons from the Best Public Housing Program in the World," *World Bank Blog*, January 31, 2018; and Adam Majendie, "Why Singapore Has One of the Highest Home Ownership Rates," *Bloomberg CityLab*, July 8, 2020.

66 **green space has positive impacts:** McMaster University, "Trees in the City: The Roots of Health and Wellbeing," *McMaster Optimal Aging Portal* (blog), February 24, 2021.

67 **comparison of housing needs assessments:** Matthew Palm and Carolyn Whitzman, "Housing Need Assessments in San Francisco, Vancouver, and Melbourne: Normative Science or Neoliberal Alchemy?," *Housing Studies* 35, 5 (2020): 771–94.

68 **net loss of affordable-housing stock:** Steve Pomeroy, *Updating Analysis on Erosion of Lower Rent Stock from 2021 Census* (Hamilton, ON: Canadian Housing Evidence Collaborative, 2022).

68 **four in five households:** Statistics Canada, "To Buy or to Rent: The Housing Market Continues to Be Reshaped by Several Factors as Canadians Search for an Affordable Place to Call Home," *The Daily*, September 21, 2022.

69 **437,180 immigrants:** Statistics Canada, "Canada's Population Estimates: Record-High Population Growth in 2022," *The Daily*, March 22, 2023.

69 **net out-migration from Ontario:** Marc Desormeaux, "A Sudden Move: Understanding Interprovincial Migration Out of Ontario," *Provincial Pulse*, March 17, 2022.

70 **intraprovincial migration:** Mike Moffatt, "Ontarians on the Move, 2022 Edition. #2," *Medium* (blog), January 14, 2022.

70 **suppressed local demand:** Mike Moffatt, *Baby Needs a New Home: Projecting Ontario's Growing Number of Families and Their Housing Needs* (Ottawa: Smart Prosperity Institute, 2021); and Jens von Bergmann and Nathanael Lauster, "Still Short: Suppressed Households in 2021," *Mountain Doodles* (blog), October 3, 2022.

70 **suppressed household formation:** Mike Moffatt, Alison Dudu, and Maryam Hosseini, *Ontario's Need for 1.5 Million More Homes* (Ottawa: Smart Prosperity Institute, 2022).

70 **focused on the "low" and "moderate":** Pomeroy, *Updating Analysis*; and Greg Suttor, *Still Renovating: A History of Canadian Social Housing Policy* (Montreal/Kingston: McGill-Queen's University Press, 2016).

71 **HART project:** HART, "Housing Needs Assessment Tool," https://hart.ubc.ca/housing-needs-assessment-tool/.

71 **private households ... purpose-built rental stock:** Statistics Canada, "2021 Census of Population: Profile Table," November 15, 2023; and Roger Lewis, *A Profile of Purpose-Built Rental Housing in Canada* (Ottawa: CMHC, 2016).

72 **National Occupancy Standard:** Alina McKay, "National Occupancy Standards: Use and Misuse," BC Society of Transition Houses, 2021.

72 **Blended stepfamilies:** Mireille Vézina, "2011 General Social Survey: Overview of Families in Canada – Being a Parent in a Stepfamily: A Profile," Statistics Canada Analytical Paper (cat. no. 89-650-X – No. 002), 2012.

72 **Working from home:** Derek Messacar, René Morrisette, and Zechuan Deng, "Inequality in the Feasibility of Working from Home during and after COVID-19," Statistics Canada, June 8, 2020.

72 **Indigenous families:** Cathryn Rodrigues, Rita Henderson, Katelyn Lucas, Sean Bristowe, Kaylee Ramage, and Katrina Milaney, *Understanding Homelessness for Urban Indigenous Families: How Can We Envision Gendered and Culturally Safe Responses* (Toronto: Canadian Conservatory on Homelessness, 2020).

72 **a vicious circle:** McKay, "National Occupancy Standards"; and Margaret Little, "Between the Abuser and the Street: An Intersectional Analysis of Housing Challenges for Abused Women," *Canadian Review of Social Policy* 72–73 (2015): 35–64.

73 **Vancouver expects:** City of Vancouver, *Family Room: Housing Mix Policy for Rezoning Projects*, 2016.

73 **"housing continuum":** CMHC, "The Wheelhouse: A New Way of Looking at Housing Needs," *Housing Observer*, August 7, 2019.

73 **"put home ownership in reach":** Prime Minister of Canada, "Making Housing More Affordable for Canadians," press release, April 8, 2022.

73 **Kelowna's wheelhouse model:** City of Kelowna, *Our Homes Today and Tomorrow: A Housing Needs Assessment*, 2017.

74 **GBA+:** British Columbia's Office of the Human Rights Commissioner, *Disaggregated Demographic Data Collection in British Columbia: The Grandmother Perspective*, September 2020.

74 **targeted for a third of funding:** CMHC, "Serving Women and Their Children through the National Housing Strategy," July 29, 2021.

75 **Women and children fleeting domestic violence:** Andrea Gunraj and Jessica Howard, "Why Is the COVID-19 Pandemic Linked to More Gender-Based Violence?," Canadian Women's Federation, April 9, 2021; Maire Sinha, "Measuring Violence against Women: Statistical Trends," *Juristat*, February 25, 2013; Kaitlyn Schwan, Alicia Versteegh, Melissa Perri, Rachel Caplan, Khulud Baig, Erin Dej, Jesse Jenkinson, Hannah Brais, Faith Eiboff, and Tina Pahlevan Chaleshtari, *The State of Women's Housing Need and Homelessness in Canada: Key Findings*, ed. Arlene Hache, Alex Nelson, Eva Kratovchvil, and Jayne Malenfant (Toronto: Canadian Observatory on Homelessness Press, 2020).

75 **Female heads of households and single mothers:** Jeremiah Prentice and Elena Simonova, "Housing Conditions of Female-Led Households," Socio Economic Analysis: Housing Needs and Conditions, March 2019; Schwan et al., *The State of Women's Housing Need*.

76 **Seniors:** Canadian Institute for Health Information, "Seniors in Transition: Exploring Pathways across the Care Continuum," accessed February 2024; Rohan Kembhavi, "Canadian Seniors: A Demographic Profile," Elections Canada, Research Note, November 2012; and Statistics Canada, "One in Ten Canadian Households Living in Core Housing Need in 2018," *The Daily*, November 2, 2020.

76 **Young adults:** Statistics Canada, "One in Ten Canadian Households"; and Schwan et al., *The State of Women's Housing Need*.

76 **Indigenous peoples:** Indigenous Services Canada, *Annual Report to Parliament*, 2020; Statistics Canada, "Housing Conditions among First Nations People, Métis and Inuit in Canada from the 2021 Census," *Census in Brief*, September 21, 2022; Rodrigues et al., *Understanding Homelessness*; "Meeting Canada's Obligations to Affordable Housing and Supports for People with Disabilities to Live *Independently* in the Community," submission to UN Special Rapporteur on the Right to Housing, May 15, 2017; Schwan et al., *The State of Women's Housing Need*; Canadian Housing and Renewal Association, *Indigenous Housing Caucus Day: Highlights Report 2018*, April 2018; Aboriginal Housing Management Association, *British Columbia Urban Rural and Northern Indigenous Housing Strategy*, January 2020; and National Housing Council, *Report and Recommendations to the Minister of Housing and Diversity and Inclusion on Urban, Rural, and Northern Indigenous Housing*, March 2022.

77 **Racialized people:** CMHC, "The National Housing Strategy Glossary of Common Terms," May 17, 2022; Statistics Canada, "The Canadian Census: A Rich Portrait of the Country's Religious and Ethnocultural Diversity," *The Daily*, November 26, 2022; Statistics Canada, "One in Ten Canadian Households"; Centre for Equality Rights in Accommodation, *Addressing the Evictions and Arrears Crisis: Proposal for a Federal Government Residential Tenant Support Benefit*, February 2022; and Scott Leon, Abinaya Balasubramaniam, and Brenda Roche, *"Fighting to Keep Your Home in a Community": Understanding Evictions through Service Provider and Community Leader Perspectives in North York Communities* (Toronto: Wellesley Institute, 2023).

77 **Recent immigrants, especially refugees:** Statistics Canada, "Immigrants Make Up the Largest Share of the Population in Over 150 Years and Continue to Shape Who We Are as Canadians," *The Daily*, October 25, 2022; and Teresa Wright, "Growing Number of Newcomers, Refugees Ending Up Homeless in Canada," *CBC News*, August 9, 2019.

78 **2SLGBTQ+ people:** Statistics Canada, "Socioeconomic Profile of the Lesbian, Gay and Bisexual Population, 2015 to 2018," *The Daily*, March 3, 2021; CMHC, "LGBTQ2S+ Housing Needs and Challenges," *Housing Observer*, June 15, 2022; and Marco Redden, Jacqueline Gahagan, Hannah Kia, Aine M. Humble, Arne Stinchcombe, Eli Manning, Joch Ecker, Brian de Vries, Liesl L. Gambold,

Brent Oliver, and Ren Thomas, "Housing as a Determinant of Health for Older LGBT Canadians: Focus Group Findings from a National Housing Study," *Housing and Society* 50, 1 (2022): 113–37.

78 **People with physical disabilities:** CMHC, "Housing Conditions of Persons with Disabilities," *Research Insight*, May 2018; "Meeting Canada's Obligations to Affordable Housing"; Ministry for Seniors and Accessibility, *Listening to Ontarians with Disabilities: Report of the Third Review of the Accessibility for Ontarians with Disabilities Act, 2005*, January 2019; and Emma Woolley, "What Are the Housing Needs of People with Mobility Issues?," *Homeless Hub*, September 16, 2016.

79 **People with intellectual or cognitive disabilities:** "Meeting Canada's Obligations to Affordable Housing."

79 **People with psychosocial disabilities:** "Meeting Canada's Obligations to Affordable Housing."

79 **Veterans:** Built for Zero Canada, "Functional Zero Homelessness Question and Answer Document," February 2021; and Veterans Affairs Canada, "Facts and Figures Summary," March 2021.

79 **people who have been incarcerated:** John Howard Society of Toronto, *Homeless and Jailed: Jailed and Homeless*, August 2010.

80 **Spillover suburbs and ex-urban areas/Declining and peripheral areas:** Statistics Canada, "Canada's Fastest Growing and Decreasing Municipalities from 2016 to 2021," *Census in Brief*, February 9, 2022; and HART, "Housing Needs Assessment Tool."

81 **Northern and Indigenous communities:** National Housing Council, *Reports and Recommendations*; Canadian Housing and Renewal Association, *Indigenous Housing Caucus Day*; Office of the Federal Housing Advocate, "Budget 2023 Fails to Address Canada's Housing Emergency," press release, March 31, 2023; and National Indigenous Collaborative Housing Incorporated (NICHI), https://nichi.ca/.

Chapter 5: Can Canada End Homelessness?

85 **Functional zero homelessness:** Built for Zero Canada, "Functional Zero Homelessness Question and Answer Document," February 2021.

85 **Housing First:** Homeless Hub, "Housing First," https://www.homelesshub.ca/.

85 **goal to end homelessness:** Mika Ronkainen and Elina Eskelä, *Helsinki's Housing Policy: A Historical Overview and the Current Situation* (Helsinki: City of Helsinki Central Administration, 2022).

86 **"Name on the Door":** Jon Henley, "'It's a Miracle': Helsinki's Radical Solution to Homelessness," *The Guardian*, June 3, 2019.

87 **cost-benefit analyses:** Marybeth Shinn and Jill Khadduri, "How Finland Ended Homelessness," *Cityscape: A Journal of Policy Development and Research* 22, 2 (2020): 75–80.

87 **Helsinki has a target:** Ronkainen and Eskelä, *Helsinki's Housing Policy*.

87 **ARA's annual standardized count:** personal communication with Linden Jarmo, Director, ARA, June 12, 2023.

88 **shelter costs of no more than $420:** HART, "Housing Needs Assessment Tool," https://hart.ubc.ca/housing-needs-assessment-tool/.

88 **CERB bump:** Statistics Canada, "To Buy or to Rent: The Housing Market Continues to Be Reshaped by Several Factors as Canadians Search for an Affordable Place to Call Home," *The Daily,* September 21, 2022; and Jennefer Laidley and Mohy Tabbara, *Welfare in Canada 2022* (Toronto: Maytree Foundation, 2023).

88 **guaranteed livable income:** Senate of Canada, "Why a Guaranteed Livable Income? Our Perspective," 2020.

90 **At Home/Chez Soi:** Mental Health Commission of Canada, *National Final Report: Cross-Site at Home/Chez Soi Project,* 2014; Damian Collins and Madeleine Stout, "Does Housing First Policy Seek to Fulfil the Right to Housing? The Case of Alberta, Canada," *Housing Studies* 36, 3 (2020): 336–58; and Carolyn Whitzman and Marie-Eve Desroches, *Women's Housing: Balancing "Scaling-Up" and "Caring" in Montreal, Gatineau, and Ottawa* (Ottawa: Institute of Feminist and Gender Studies, University of Ottawa, 2020).

91 **by-name lists:** Built for Zero Canada/Canadian Alliance to End Homelessness, "By-Name Lists," 2023, https://bfzcanada.ca/by-name-lists/; Statistics Canada, "Municipalities in Canada with the Largest and Fastest-Growing Populations Between 2011 and 2016," *Census in Brief,* February 8, 2017.

92 **veterans:** Built for Zero Canada, "Functional Zero Homelessness."

92 **Medicine Hat:** Leif Gregerson, "How a Small Canadian City Took on Chronic Homelessness," *Next City,* August 11, 2022; and Province of Alberta, "Vacancy Rates by Municipality," January 1, 2023, https://open.alberta.ca/opendata/vacancy-rates-by-municipality.

92 **upgrading inadequate single-room occupancy hotels:** City of Vancouver/Housing Vancouver, *Single Room Occupancy (SRO) Revitalization Action Plan,* 2017.

93 **Six thousand single-occupancy hotel units:** BC Housing, "SRO Renewal Initiative Series: Public Private Partnerships," April 2018; and Pivot Legal Society, "Strathcona Camp Residents Issue a Human Rights Report Card to Province and City on Decampment Process," press release, April 29, 2021.

93 **temporary modular housing:** City of Vancouver, "Temporary Modular Housing," https://vancouver.ca/people-programs/temporary-modular-housing.aspx; CMHC, "A Temporary Building Leaves a Lasting Impression," September 29, 2021; CMHC, "Building Housing Quickly When It Matters Most," *Housing Observer,* June 30, 2020; and Elizabeth McSheffrey, "'Shame': Vancouver Modular Housing Residents Protest Planned Removal Next Month," *Global News,* June 20, 2023.

94 **Happy City:** National Housing Strategy, CMHC, Happy City, and Reos Partners, *Recommendations and Roadmap for Social Wellbeing in Modular*

Housing: Design and Programming Recommendations to Nurture Health and Social Support for Vulnerable People, 2022.

95 **McCurdy Place:** Katie DeRosa, "Social Service Agencies Running Modular Housing Sites in B.C. Decry Lack of Resources," *Vancouver Sun,* December 29, 2022.

95 **Rapid Housing Initiative:** Steve Pomeroy, *Review and Options to Strengthen the National Housing Strategy* (Ottawa: Office of the Federal Housing Advocate, 2021); and Canadian Housing and Renewal Association, *Blueprint for Housing,* 2022.

98 **Rapid Housing Initiative in London, Ontario:** Abe Oudshoorn, Amy Van Berkum, Steven Rolfe, Carrie Anne Marshall, Andrea Krywucky, Miranda Crockett, Susana Caxaj, Natasha Thuemler, Jason Gilliland, Sarah McLean, Vanisa Ezukuse, Yinka Ariba, and Deanna Befus, *Indwell: Making Supportive Housing Work for Canada's Most Vulnerable – Final Report* (London, ON: Centre for Research on Health Equity and Social Inclusion, Western University, 2022).

99 **grey wave:** Martine August, "The Coronavirus Exposes the Perils of Profit in Seniors' Housing," *The Conversation,* July 26, 2020.

99 **financialized market firms:** Martine August, *The Financialization of Housing in Canada: A Summary Report for the Office of the Federal Housing Advocate,* 2022.

100 **Hogewyck:** Sarah Tranum, "Dementia Villages and Co-housing: How Canada Can Rethink Long-Term Care," *The Conversation,* January 23, 2022.

100 **Together by the Sea:** Erin Haluschak, "Providence on Track, Budget for Transformation of the Views in Comox Next Year," *Comox Valley News,* May 1, 2023.

102 **Canadian Senate:** Senate of Canada, "Why a Guaranteed Livable Income?"

Chapter 6: Why Start with Nonmarket Housing?

103 **3 million very-low- and low-income households:** Carolyn Whitzman, *A Human Rights-Based Calculation of Canada's Housing Shortages* (Ottawa: Canada Human Rights Commission, 2023).

103 **subsidies are less efficient than direct support:** Julie Lawson, Lawrence Troy, and Ryan van den Neiuwelant, "Social Housing as Infrastructure and the Role of Mission Driven Financing," *Housing Studies* 39, 2 (2022): 398–418.

104 **Vienna:** City of Vienna, *Residential Construction in Vienna 1920–2020* (Vienna: Holzhauzen, 2018); Wolfgang Forster, "80 Years of Social Housing in Vienna," City of Vienna, 2002; Nicholas Falk and Jonah Rudlin, *Learning from International Examples of Affordable Housing* (London: Shelter/The URBED Trust, 2018); and Michael Eliason, *Unlocking Livable, Resilient, Decarbonized Housing with Point Access Blocks,* report prepared for City of Vancouver, 2021.

107 **Austria, with 23 percent nonmarket housing:** OECD, "PH4.1: Public Spending on Support to Social Rental Housing," 2020.

108 **Vienna's Housing First model:** City of Vienna, *Residential Construction*; and Carla Weinzierl, Florian Wukovitsch, and Andreas Novy, "Housing First in Vienna: A Socially Innovative Initiative to Foster Social Cohesion," *Journal of Housing and the Built Environment* 31 (2016): 409–22.

108 **Viennese who lived in market housing:** Francesca Mari, "Imagine a Renters' Paradise: It Might Look Like Vienna," *New York Times Magazine*, May 23, 2023.

108 **Toronto/Vancouver average rents:** Rent Panda, "Canadian Monthly Rental Report: October 2022," 2023.

108 **"epicentre of Europe's housing woes":** Jack Sidders, Ainoa Goyeneche, and Maron Eder, "Vienna Becomes Epicenter of Europe's Housing Woes," *Bloomberg News,* May 19, 2023.

110 **needs-based target for Canada:** HART, "Housing Needs Assessment Tool," https://hart.ubc.ca/housing-needs-assessment-tool/; and Whitzman, *A Human Rights-Based Calculation*.

111 **Both the Canadian Housing and Renewal Association and Scotiabank:** Canadian Housing and Renewal Association, *Blueprint for Housing,* 2022; Rebekah Young, "Canadian Housing Affordability Hurts," *Scotiabank Global Economics,* 2023.

111 **expected return on investment:** Real Estate Institute of BC, "The Real Estate Development Process," July 2021; and BuyProperly.ai, "How to Calculate ROI in Real Estate to Maximize Your Profit."

111 **long-term payoffs:** Greg Suttor, Chidom Otogwu, and Nick Falvo, *The Co-op Difference: Comparing Co-op and Market Rents in Five Canadian Cities* (Ottawa: Cooperative Housing Federation of Canada, 2022).

112 **fragmented system:** Steve Pomeroy, *Discussion Paper: Envisioning a Modernized Social and Affordable Housing Sector in Canada* (Ottawa: Centre for Urban Research and Education, Carleton University, 2017).

112 **McKinsey report:** Jonathan Woetzel, Sangeeth Ram, Jan Mischke, Nicklas Garemo, and Shirish Sankhe, *A Blueprint for Addressing the Global Affordable Housing Challenge* (McKinsey Global Institute, October 2014).

112 **France's targets:** Yonah Freemark, "Mandating Access to Affordable Housing, City by City: Is France's Fair-Share SRU Law a Model for U.S. Metropolitan Areas?," Lincoln Institute, September 2021; Arthur Acolin, "The Public Sector Plays an Important Role in Supporting French Renters," *Brookings Institute* (blog), April 20, 2021; and Alan Durning, "Yes, Other Places Do Housing Better: Case 3, Paris," *Sightlines,* July 21, 2021.

113 **In Austria, approximately 40 percent:** Falk and Rudlin, *Learning from International Examples*.

113 **Community land trusts:** Replan, *Community Land Trusts: A Solution to Vancouver's Affordable Housing Crisis* (Vancouver: False Creek South Residents Association, 2017).

114 **Denmark's National Building Fund:** Michelle Norris and Julie Lawson, "Tools to Tame the Financialisation of Housing," *New Political Economy* 28, 3 (2023): 363–79.

114 **Half of all nonmarket housing in Canada:** Statistics Canada, "Canada's Population Estimates: Record-High Population Growth in 2022," *The Daily*, March 22, 2023.

114 **Whistler Housing Authority:** Alison Taylor, "Whistler Housing Authority Comes of Age with 1,900-Unit Legacy," *Pique*, November 23, 2011; Marc Lee, *Getting Serious about Affordable Housing: Towards a Plan for Metro Vancouver* (Vancouver: Canadian Centre for Policy Alternatives, 2016); Justin McElroy, "Whistler's Affordable Housing Model Is Below-Market and Free of Speculation: Why Isn't It Used Elsewhere?," *CBC News*, January 24, 2019; and HART, "Housing Needs Assessment Tool."

116 **Centretown Citizens Ottawa Corporation:** Centretown Citizens Ottawa Corporation, "Our Story," https://ccochousing.org/; and Fran Klodawsky and Caroline Andrew, "Acting Locally: What Is the Progressive Potential?," *Studies in Political Economy* 59, 1 (1999): 149–71.

117 **Beaver Barracks:** World Habitat Awards, "CCOC Beaver Barracks Development: Finalist 2013"; and Housing Partnership Canada, "Canadian Mixed-Model Development," research bulletin, August 2020.

118 **cooperative housing originated in the Antigonish Movement:** Coady Institute, St. Francis Xavier University, "Masters of Their Own Destiny: The Coady Story in Canada and across the World"; and Co-operative Housing Federation of Canada, "History of Co-op Housing."

118 **Nonmarket student housing:** H. Peter Oberlander and George Fallick, *Housing a Nation: The Evolution of Canadian Housing Policy* (Ottawa: CMHC, 1992).

119 **Les Artistes du Ruisseau:** https://coopruisseau.ca/.

119 **Co-operative Housing Federation of BC:** https://www.chf.bc.ca/community-land-trust/.

119 **Compass Housing NS:** "Compass Nova Scotia Making Waves Towards Sustainability and Growth," *Co-operative Housing Federation of Canada* (blog), January 8, 2020.

Chapter 7: Can Housing Become Abundant Again?

122 **unaffordable, overcrowded, insecure, and inaccessible:** Centre for Urban Growth and Renewal/United Way Toronto, *Strong Neighbourhoods and Complete Communities: A New Approach to Zoning for Apartment Neighbourhoods*, May 2012.

123 **Zoning:** Julie Lawson and Hannu Ruonavaara, *Land Policy for Affordable and Inclusive Housing: An International Review*, SmartLand, 2020, https://smartland.fi/wp-content/uploads/Land-policy-for-affordable-and-inclusive-housing-an-international-review.pdf; Andrew Whittemore, "Exclusionary Zoning: Origins, Open Suburbs, and Contemporary Debates," *Journal of the American Planning Association* 87, 2 (2021): 167–80; and City of Edmonton, "Zoning Bylaw Renewal: Principles and Approach," 2019.

124 **In Toronto, 64 percent ... Montreal is an outlier:** Sun Yang, "A Visual Guide to Detached House Zones in 5 Canadian Cities," *DataLabTO*, 2019.

124 **prioritize housing cars:** Jeffrey Spivak, "People Over Parking," *Planning Magazine*, October 2018; and Michael Eliason, *Unlocking Livable, Resilient, Decarbonized Housing with Point Access Blocks*, report prepared for City of Vancouver, 2021.

125 **Parking provisions are unjust:** Martin Turcotte, "Life in Metropolitan Areas: Dependence on Cars in Urban Neighbourhoods," *Statistics Canada, Canadian Social Trends*, 2008; and Don Pittis, "Waiting for the Economic Impact as More Canadians Consider Going Car-Free," *CBC News*, May 13, 2019.

127 **Shanghai's 15-minute city strategy:** Min Weng, Ning Ding, Jing Li, Xianfeng Jin, He Xiao, Zhiming He, and Shiliang Su, "The 15-Minute Walkable Neighborhoods: Measurement, Social Inequalities and Implications for Building Healthy Communities in Urban China," *Journal of Transport and Health* 13 (2019): 259–73.

127 **population density:** University College London, The INEQ-CITIES Atlas, Barcelona, https://www.ucl.ac.uk/ineq-cities/atlas/cities/barcelona; Jeffrey Spivak, "Why Are European Cities So Dense?," *Bloomberg City Lab*, October 27, 2018; and Statistics Canada, "Canada's Large Urban Centres Continue to Grow and Spread," *The Daily*, February 9, 2022.

127 **Transit-oriented development:** Canadian Urban Transit Association, *Housing Is on the Line: How Public Transit Can Help Tackle Canada's Housing Crisis*, October 2023.

128 **Ottawa versus Japan:** Ottawa.ca, zoning definitions; "Land Use Zones under the City Planning Law in Japan," *Plaza Zone* (blog), July 13, 2022; Simval84, "Japanese Zoning," *Urban kchoze* (blog), April 6, 2014; and National Collaborating Centre for Healthy Public Policy, "Traffic Lane Width of 3.0 m in Urban Environments," March 2014.

129 **Japan's big six rail companies:** Roger Rudick, "SPUR Talk: The Japanese Model for Station Development," *Streetsblog SF*, November 1, 2018.

129 **no overnight on-street parking:** Paul Barter, "Japan's Proof-of-Parking Rule Has an Essential Twin Policy," *Reinventing Parking* (blog), June 4, 2014.

129 **The City of Tokyo has 13.5 million:** Tokyo Metropolitan Government, "Tokyo's History, Geography, and Population"; Alan Durning, "Yes, Other Countries Do Housing Better, Case Study 1: Japan," *Sightline* (blog), March 29, 2021; CMHC, "Canada Mortgage and Housing Corporation, Housing Starts, under Construction and Completions, All Areas, Quarterly," October 18, 2023.

130 **This was not always the case:** Durning, "Yes, Other Countries"; Eiji Oizumi, "Property Finance in Japan: Expansion and Collapse of the Bubble Economy," *Environment and Planning A* 26, 2 (1994): 199–213; Shun-ichi Watanabe, "Toshi keikaku vs machizukuri: Emerging Paradigm of Civil Society in Japan, 1950–1980," in *Living Cities in Japan: Citizens' Movements, Machizukuri and Local Environments*, ed. André Sorensen and Carolin Funck (New York: Routledge, 1994), 39–55.

131 **Auckland:** Ryan Greenaway-McGrevy and James Allan Jones, "Can Zoning Reform Change Urban Development Patterns? Evidence from Auckland," University of Auckland Economic Policy Centre, Working Paper No. 012, December 2023; and Matthew Maltman, "A Response to Murray and Helm on Auckland's Upzoning," *One Final Effort* (blog), June 5, 2023.

132 **Minneapolis:** Richard Kahlenberg, "How Minneapolis Ended Single-Family Zoning," The Century Foundation, report, October 24, 2019; Matthew Maltman, "A Detailed Look at the Outcomes of Minneapolis' Housing Reforms," *One Final Effort* (blog), April 17, 2023; and Benjamin Demers, "Measuring the Early Impact of Eliminating Single-Family Zoning on Minneapolis Property Values," *Journal of the American Planning Association* (blog), August 9, 2021.

133 **Austin:** Jared Brey, "Waiving Regulations for Affordable Housing Shows Results in Austin," *Next City*, September 22, 2020; and Austin Sanders, "Council Poised to Pass Three Housing Supply-Friendly Items," *Austin Chronicle*, June 9, 2023.

133 **Portland:** Michael Anderson, "Portland Just Passed the Best Low-Density Zoning Reform in US History," *Sightline*, August 11, 2020.

134 **Cambridge:** Andrew Gibbs, "What Can We Expect from Cambridge's New Affordable Housing Overlay?," *Harvard University Joint Center for Housing Studies* (blog), June 30, 2021.

134 **In Canada, changes have not been as radical:** "Edmonton City Council Votes to Remove Minimum Parking Requirements," *CBC News*, July 23, 2020; "Burnaby Credits New Policies for 'Historic Surge' in Cheaper Nonmarket Rentals," *Burnaby Now*, December 4, 2021; and City of Victoria, "Fast Lane for Affordable Housing Approvals," press release, April 14, 2022.

135 **Housing Accelerator Fund:** CMHC, *Housing Accelerator Fund: Pre-application Reference Material*, 2023.

135 **Urbanarium:** Urbanarium, "The Missing Middle Competition," https:// urbanarium.org/; and City of Edmonton, "'Missing Middle' Infill Design Competition," https://www.edmonton.ca/.

137 **Exclusionary zoning is policed through NIMBYism:** Tim Iglesias, "Managing Local Opposition to Affordable Housing: A New Approach to NIMBY," *Journal of Affordable Housing* 12, 1 (2002): 78–121; Michael Dear, "Understanding and Overcoming the NIMBY Syndrome," *Journal of the American Planning Association* 58, 3 (1992): 288–300; and GHK, *The Legal Basis of NIMBY: Final Report*, Advocacy Centre for Tenants in Ontario, November 2007.

137 **underlying psychological themes to NIMBY:** Nicholas Boys Smith and Keiran Toms, *From NIMBY to YIMBY: How to Win Votes by Building More Homes*, CREATEstreets, 2018; Max Holleran, *Yes to the City: Millennials and the Fight for Affordable Housing* (Princeton: Princeton University Press, 2022); Goss Gilroy Management Consultants, *Understanding Social Inclusion and NIMBYism in Providing Affordable Housing*, report for CMHC, March 15, 2019; and Aaron Moore and Michael McGregor, "The Representativeness of

Neighbourhood Associations in Toronto and Vancouver," *Urban Studies* 58, 13 (2021): 2782–97.

138 **The impacts of NIMBYism:** Jen St. Denis, "Social Housing Was Proposed for Kitsilano: Here's What Happened Next," *The Tyee*, July 12, 2002; Justin McElroy, "BC Government Using Legislation to Push through Supportive Housing Project Held Up by Lawsuit," *CBC News*, April 18, 2023; and Charlie Carey, "Kitsilano Residents Association Goes to Court Against Senakw Development," *CityNews*, October 6, 2022.

138 **"hostage situations":** Canada–British Columbia Expert Panel on the Future of Housing Supply and Affordability, *Opening Doors: Unlocking Housing Supply for Affordability*, June 2021.

139 **A US survey:** Corianne Payton Scally and J. Rosie Tighe, "Democracy in Action? NIMBY as Impediment to Equitable Affordable Housing Siting," *Housing Studies* 30, 5 (2015): 749–69.

139 **A Canadian review:** Jeannie Wynne-Edwards, *Overcoming Community Opposition to Homelessness Sheltering Projects under the National Homelessness Initiative*, CMHC, September 2003.

139 **third-party rights:** DLA Piper, "Third Party Objections," https://www. dlapiperrealworld.com/.

139 **Infill Roadmap:** City of Edmonton, *Infill Roadmap 2018: Welcoming More People and New Homes into Edmonton's Older Neighbourhoods*, June 2018.

140 **"duplex or triplex" our way out:** Michael Eliason, "A Triplex Bill Is Fine, But We Need Housing Action on a Truly Massive Scale," *The Urbanist*, January 29, 2020.

140 **667,000 homes changed hands:** Tara Deschamps, "Canadian Home Sales Set New Record in 2021, Topping Previous High by 20 Percent: CREA," *Global News*, January 3, 2022.

141 **"big dumb box":** Michael Eliason, "In Praise of Dumb Boxes," *The Urbanist*, August 22, 2018.

141 **stupid form-based zoning:** Conrad Speckart, "The Second Egress: Building a Code Change," *Second Guess* (blog), December 11, 2023.

141 **windows only on one wall:** Stephen Smith, "Why We Can't Build Family-Sized Apartments in North America," *Center for Building in North America* (blog), May 4, 2023; and Michael Eliason, *Unlocking Livable, Resilient, Decarbonized Housing with Point Access Blocks*, report prepared for City of Vancouver, 2021.

Chapter 8: How Can Renters Have the Same Rights as Owners?

144 **35 percent of "private" households:** Statistics Canada, "To Buy or to Rent: The Housing Market Continues to Be Reshaped by Several Factors as Canadians Search for an Affordable Place to Call Home," *The Daily*, September 21, 2022. The proportion would be higher if students, people in congregate housing, and homeless people were included.

144 **financialization:** Duncan Maclennan, David Graham, and Jinqiao Long, "Calming the Moose on the Loose: Rebuilding Canadian Housing Policies," Canadian Housing Evidence Collaborative, 2023; and Michelle Norris and Julie Lawson, "Tools to Tame the Financialisation of Housing," *New Political Economy* 28, 3 (2023): 363–79.

146 **Herongate:** Heatherington Land Trust, "Herongate: Stop the Destruction," April 18, 2019; Ricardo Tranjan, *The Tenant Class* (Toronto: Between the Lines, 2023), 52.

146 **PSP Investments:** Shareholder Association for Research and Education (SHARE), "Investors for Affordable Cities: Responsible Investment and Affordable Renting Housing in Canada," discussion paper, 2021.

147 **"building repositioning":** Neal Rockwell, "A Public Pension Fund Is Canada's Newest Mega-Landlord," *The Breach*, March 30, 2022.

147 **REITs ... now own 200,000 homes:** Martine August, *The Financialization of Housing in Canada: A Summary Report for the Office of the Federal Housing Advocate,* 2022. https://www.homelesshub.ca/sites/default/files/attachments/august-financialization-summary-report-ofha-en.pdf.

147 **May 2017 rent strike:** SHARE, "Investors."

148 **Legal Aid Ontario:** Alyshah Hasham, "Legal Aid Ontario Facing Up to $70 Million Funding Drop Amid COVID-19 'Perfect Storm,'" *Toronto Star,* July 13, 2020.

148 **Disallowing large investment firms:** SHARE, "Investors."

148 **United Nations Sustainable Development Goal:** https://sdgs.un.org/goals.

148 **Evictions:** Silas Xuereb and Craig Jones, *Estimating No-Fault Evictions in Canada: Understanding BC's Disproportionate Eviction Rate in the 2021 Canadian Housing Survey* (Vancouver: UBC Housing Research Collaborative, 2023); and Canadian Centre for Housing Rights, "Proportionality: A Legal Framework to Make Eviction a Last Resort in Canada," July 13, 2023.

149 **the number of rented condominiums:** Matti Siemiatycki and Karen Chapple, "Perspective on the Rental Housing Roundtable," independent report for City of Toronto's 2023 Housing Action Plan, March 2023.

149 **nonmarket landlords perform better:** Xuereb and Jones, *Estimating No-Fault Evictions*.

150 **Denmark:** OECD, "Social Housing: A Key Part of Past and Future Housing Policy," Employment, Labour and Social Affairs Policy Briefs, 2020; and Norris and Lawson, "Tools to Tame."

151 **Ørestad:** Nicholas Falk and Jonah Rudlin, *Learning from International Examples of Affordable Housing,* Shelter/The URBED Trust, July 2018.

151 **market rents are decided:** "Combating Rental Market Financialization in Denmark," Housing2030.org; and Rent Hero, "Why Is a Large Part of the Housing Market in Denmark Rent-Controlled?," https://renthero.dk/how-is-the-legal-rent-that-a-landlord-can-charge-calculated-for-rent-controlled-housing-in-denmark.

151 **transparent and available online:** Kateryna Shubina, "Gross Rental Yields in Denmark," *Global Property Guide,* December 12, 2023; and Kateryna Shubina, "Rental Returns in Toronto Are Moderate to Good," *Global Property Guide,* January 11, 2023.

152 **Blackstone:** Hettie O'Brien, "The Blackstone Rebellion: How One Country Took on the World's Biggest Commercial Landlord," *Guardian,* September 29, 2022; "Combating Rental Market Financialization in Denmark," Housing2030.org; and Bethany Millar-Powell, Bert Brys, Pierce O'Reilly, Yannic Rehm, and Alastair Thomas, "Measuring Effective Taxation of Housing: Building the Foundations for Policy Reform," OECD Taxation Working Papers No. 56, 2022.

153 **concentration of poor and racialized people:** O'Brien, "The Blackstone Rebellion."

154 **Canada lost half a million homes:** Steve Pomeroy, *Updating Analysis on Erosion of Lower Rent Stock from 2021 Census* (Hamilton, ON: Canadian Housing Evidence Collaborative, 2022).

154 **Rent regulations:** Canadian Centre for Housing Rights, "A Look at Rent Control Policies across Canada," July 14, 2022; and Advocacy Centre for Tenants in Ontario, "Vacancy Decontrol: What Is It, and Why Does It Matter?," September 30, 2021.

156 **45,000 purpose-built rental construction starts:** Philip Mendonça-Vieira, "Actually, Rent Control Is Great: Revisiting Ontario's Experience, the Supply of Housing, and Security of Tenure," *Okayfail.com* (blog), September 26, 2018.

156 **COVID-19:** CMHC, "Covid-19: Understanding Mortgage Payment Deferral," March 24, 2020; City of Ottawa, "Partial Property Tax Deferral Program," 2023; Victoria Gibson, "More Than 6,000 Ontario Tenants Could Face Eviction for Nonpayment of Rent during COVID-19, New Figures Show," *Toronto Star,* July 25, 2020; and on Massachusetts, Mendonça-Vieira, "Actually, Rent Control Is Great."

157 **Ontario Rental Housing Protection Act:** Allison Smith, Deanna Chorney, and Keir Mathews-Hunter, "Preserving What We Have: Insights on Rental Housing Demolition, Conversion and Replacement in Toronto," paper presented at the Ontario Professional Planners Institute conference, 2020; and John Michael McGrath, "First Impressions: What the Latest Housing Bill Will Mean for Ontario's Renters and Rural Areas," *TVO,* April 6, 2023.

157 **BC government allowed municipalities:** Zena Olijnyk, "Upholding New Westminster's 'Renoviction' Bylaw Inspires Confidence for Others to Do Same: Advocates," *Canadian Lawyer Magazine,* May 7, 2021.

158 **France versus Canada:** Arthur Acolin, "The Public Sector Plays an Important Role in Supporting French Renters," *Brookings Institute* (blog), April 20, 2021; and Ben Segel-Brown, *Federal Program Spending on Housing Affordability in 2021,* Parliamentary Budget Officer, 2021.

158 **as a renter in Denmark:** Mario Scian, "Buying a House in Denmark as Expat (2024): All You Need to Know," *Medium,* February 22, 2018.

159 **short-term rental definition:** City of Toronto, "Short-Term Rentals," https://www.toronto.ca/community-people/housing-shelter/short-term-rentals/; and "History of Short-Term Rentals," *Keycafe blog*, 2023.

159 **short-term rentals in Canada:** Jennifer Combes, Danielle Kerrigan, and David Wachsmuth, "Short-Term Rentals in Canada," *Canadian Journal of Urban Research* 29, 1 (2020): 119–34.

159 **law regulating short-term rentals:** Shane Dingman, "Toronto Embarks on Short-Term Rental Crackdown," *Globe and Mail,* January 6, 2021; and Maryse Zeidler, "Vancouver Landlord Investigated for Short-Term Vacation Rental Leases," *CBC News,* April 25, 2021.

160 **low-income housing tax credits:** US Government Accountability Office, *Low-Income Housing Tax Credit: Improved Data and Oversight Would Strengthen Cost Assessment and Fraud Risk Management,* September 2018; and Canadian Housing and Renewal Association (CHRA), *Blueprint for Housing,* 2022.

160 **licensing landlords:** City of Vancouver, "Strengthening the Conditions of Landlord Licensing in Vancouver," press release, March 23, 2022; Mary Baxter, "The Case for – and Against – Rental Licensing in Ontario," *TVO,* March 17, 2021; Ainslie MacLennan, "Montreal Launches Rental Price Registry, Certification of Landlords," *CBC News,* February 15, 2022; and Theresa McManus, "New Westminster to Fine or Revoke Licences of Buildings That Renovict Tenants," *New Westminster Record,* February 5, 2019.

161 **tenants complain:** Kerry Gold, "Renters Push for More Regulation as Number of Mom-and-Pop Landlords Continues to Grow," *Storeys,* June 28, 2023.

161 **1 million older high-rise rental homes:** Tower Renewal Partnership, *Tower Renewal Enabling Complete Communities,* April 2020.

162 **an acquisitions component:** Federation of Canadian Municipalities, "COVID-19 and Housing: Critical Need, Urgent Opportunity," September 2020; and CHRA, *Blueprint.*

162 **Milton-Parc:** Joshua Hawley and Dmitri Roussopoulos, "Introduction," in *Villages in Cities: Community Land Ownership, Co-operative Housing, and the Milton-Parc Story,* ed. Joshua Hawley and Dmitri Roussopoulos (Montreal: Black Rose Books, 2019), 8–17.

162 **less expensive than continually tearing down encampments ... Quebec acquisitions:** Joseph Daniels and Martine August, *Acquisitions for Affordable Housing: Creating Non-market Supply and Preserving Affordability,* UBC Housing Assessment Resource Tools (HART) project, 2023.

163 **tripartite collaboration:** Tower Renewal Partnership, *Tower Renewal Enabling Complete Communities.*

Chapter 9: Is There a Future for Affordable Home Ownership?

165 **Canada has 15 million private homes:** Statistics Canada, "Census Profile, 2021 Census of Population," February 9, 2022; Statistics Canada, "To Buy or to Rent: The Housing Market Continues to Be Reshaped by Several Factors

as Canadians Search for an Affordable Place to Call Home," *The Daily*,
September 21, 2022; Statistics Canada, "Canada's Population Estimates:
Record-High Population Growth in 2022," *The Daily*, March 22, 2023.

166 **widening wealth gap:** Beata Caranci, Francis Fong, and Mekdes Gebreselassie,
"Digging Beneath the Surface: Is Housing Perpetuating a Wealth Divide in
Canada?," TD Economics, October 5, 2022.

166 **home-ownership rates:** Alex Pollack, "Long-Term Home Ownership Trends:
The United States, England, and Canada," American Enterprise Institute,
March 26, 2014; and Statistics Canada, "To Buy or to Rent."

167 **One generation benefited:** Paul Kershaw, "Policy Forum: A Tax Shift – The
Case for Rebalancing the Tax Treatment of Earnings and Housing Wealth,"
Canadian Tax Journal 66, 3 (2018): 585–604.

168 **Ursula's story:** personal communication January 5, 2024, recounted with
permission.

168 **affordability mechanisms:** Richard Harris, "The Flexible House: The
Housing Backlog and the Persistence of Lodging," *Social Science History* 18, 1
(1994): 354; and Richard Harris and Kathleen Kinsella, "Secondary Suites: A
Survey of Evidence and Municipal Policy," *Canadian Geographer* 61, 4 (2017):
493–509.

169 **a new generation of subdivided homes:** City of Toronto, "Garden Suites";
Christian Britschgi, "Portland Legalized 'Missing Middle' Housing: Now It's
Trying to Make It Easy to Build," *Reason*, June 13, 2022; Dweller.com, "Fulfilling
the Promise of ADUs."

169 **Canada HomeShare, GoCo, and Husmates:** Sparrow McGowan, "With
Rentals Scarce, a Program That Houses Students with Seniors Is Growing
Fast," *University Affairs*, September 13, 2022; and Howard Akler, "'This Will Be
the Way People Buy Houses': Through Co-owning, a Toronto Mom, Her
Donor and His Partner Made a Modern Family," *Toronto Star*, May 13, 2023.

170 **The cohousing movement:** Canadian Cohousing Network, "About Us";
Katja Rusinovic, Marianne van Bochove, and Jolien Van de Sande, "Senior
Co-housing in the Netherlands: Benefits and Drawbacks for Its Residents,"
International Journal of Environmental Research on Public Health 16, 19 (2019):
3776.

170 **Baugruppen:** Manuel Lutz, "Lived Solidarity: Housing Co-operatives,"
Assemble Papers, November 20, 2019.

170 **Little Mountain Cohousing:** Charles Montgomery, "We Built a Home to
Solve Some of the Greatest Challenges of Our Times," *Vancouver Sun*,
December 8, 2021.

171 **Self-built housing:** Richard Harris, "Slipping through the Cracks: The Origins
of Aided Self-Help Housing, 1918–53," *Housing Studies* 14, 3 (1999): 281–309;
Helena Obremski and Claudia Carter, "Can Self-Build Housing Improve
Social Sustainability within Low-Income Groups?," *Town Planning Review* 90,
2 (2019): 167–93.

171 **"one weird trick":** Owen Hatherley, "France's Alternative to Gentrification," *Tribune Magazine*, March 2021.

171 **Grow Homes:** World Habitat Awards, "The Grow Home, Montreal, Winner 1999"; and Avi Friedman, "Preferences of First-Time Buyers of Affordable Housing: Evidence from Grow Homes in Montreal, Canada," *Canadian Journal of Urban Research* 9, 1 (2000): 1–22.

172 **Habitat is a niche response:** Dakshana Bascaramurty, "Habitat for Humanity: A Better Life, with Some Strings Attached," *Globe and Mail*, September 29, 2012; and Hamdi Issawi, "'We Followed Their Rules': Families Claim Habitat for Humanity's Mortgage Changes May Have Dashed Dreams of Home Ownership," *Toronto Star*, December 19, 2019; Liz Monteiro, "Ambitious Plan Promises 10,000 New Homes for Families in Waterloo Region, at Half the Cost They Sell for Now," *Waterloo Region Record*, June 21, 2023; and Rachelle Younglai, "As Home Prices Soar, Habitat for Humanity Helps Higher-Income Canadians Buy Properties," *Globe and Mail*, July 23, 2023.

173 **Latin America:** Justin McGuirk, *Radical Cities: Across Latin America in Search of a New Architecture* (London: Verso, 2014).

174 **Dignity Village:** Anson Wong, Jerry Chen, Renee Dicipulo, Danielle Weiss, David Sleet, and Louis Hugo Francescutti, "Combatting Homelessness in Canada: Applying Lessons Learned from Six Tiny Villages to the Edmonton Bridge Healing Program," *International Journal of Environmental Research and Public Health* 17, 17 (2020): 6279; and Marcus Harrison Green, "In Portland, Once Unwelcome Tent City Becomes 'Dignity Village,'" *The Tyee*, February 1, 2016.

175 **Homes for Heroes:** Wong et al., "Combatting Homelessness."

175 **Khaleel Seivwright:** Catherine Porter, "The Carpenter Who Built Tiny Homes for Toronto's Homeless," *New York Times*, April 16, 2021.

176 **stop wasting money tearing down:** Kaitlin Schwan and Julieta Perucca, *Realizing the Right to Housing in Canadian Municipalities: Where Do We Go from Here?* The Shift, 2022.

177 **polykatoikia:** Feargus O'Sullivan, "Behind the Accidentally Resilient Design of Athens Apartments," *Bloomberg News*, July 15, 2020; Anastasia Koutoumanou, "Recording the Use and Ownership Patterns of Apartments in the Athenian Apartment Block (Polykatoikia)," *Athens Social Atlas*, December 2018; and CoHab Athens, "Polykatoikia."

178 **circular economy:** Ralph Horne, Louise Dorignon, Julie Lawson, Hazel Easthope, Stefanie Dühr, Trivess Moore, Emma Baker, Tony Dalton, Hal Pawson, and Peter Fairbrother, *Informing a Strategy for Circular Economy Housing in Australia*, Australian Housing and Research Institute report, June 2023; and Hatherley, "France's Alternative to Gentrification."

179 **"regeneration":** London Assembly, Housing Committee, *Knock It Down or Do It Up? The Challenge of Estate Regeneration*, February 2015.

179 **Regent Park:** Sean Purdy, "'Ripped Off' by the System: Housing Policy, Poverty, and Territorial Somatization in Regent Park Housing Project, 1951–1991,"

Labour/Le Travail, 52 (2003): 45–108; Martine August, "Challenging the Rhetoric of Stigmatization: The Benefits of Concentrated Poverty in Toronto's Regent Park," *Environment and Planning A*, 46, 6 (2014): 1317–33; Laura Johnson and Robert Johnson, *Regent Park Redux: Reinventing Public Housing in Canada* (New York: Routledge, 2017); and Shauna Brail and John Lorinc, "Rebuilding Public Housing in Regent Park: The Shifting Dynamics of Financialized Redevelopment Models," *Journal of Planning Education and Research*, July 4, 2023.

180 **Aaron Webster Co-op:** Christopher Cheung, "The Secret to Real Affordability? Trust in Land," *The Tyee*, October 23, 2023.

180 **Sierra Place:** "Conversion of Empty Calgary Office Tower to Affordable Housing Set to Begin," *CBC News*, June 6, 2021; and Meghan Potkins, "$30M Office Tower Conversion Will Open 82 Affordable Housing Units Next Fall," *Calgary Herald*, January 26, 2022.

181 **Similar initiatives are occurring throughout Canada:** Vanessa Balintec, "Toronto's Turning Some of Its Offices into Housing: Advocates Say It's a 'Model' for Other Governments," *CBC News*, April 9, 2022; Ian Austen, "A Winnipeg Landmark Rich in Symbolism Comes under Indigenous Control," *New York Times*, April 30, 2022; and Carolyn Whitzman and Melissa Goldstein, *Our City Starts with Home: Scaling Up Non-profit Housing in Ottawa*, Alliance to End Homelessness Ottawa, report to City Council, April 2023.

181 **shopping centres:** Sheila Reid, "Canada Sees the Rise of Mall Cities," *Globe and Mail*, June 5, 2023; and Clarrie Feinstein, "Developers Are Turning 14 GTA Malls into Tiny Cities, with Cloverdale Leading the Way: Is This the Solution to Toronto's Housing Crisis?," *Toronto Star*, July 8, 2023.

182 **decrease of "traditional" families:** Statistics Canada, "Home Alone: More Persons Living Solo Than Ever Before, but Roomies the Fastest Growing Household Type," *The Daily*, July 13, 2022.

183 **Singapore:** Nicholas Falk and Jonah Rudlin, *Learning from International Examples of Affordable Housing*, Shelter/The URBED Trust, July 2018.

183 **baugruppen:** Anne-Lise Charroy, "Baugruppen: A Preview of a New Kind of Urban Housing," *Dynamic Cities Project* (blog), February 2022.

183 **WagnisART:** Manuel Lutz, "Living Labs for Housing: Co-operatives Reinvented," *Assemble Papers*, March 16, 2020.

185 **Vauban, Freiberg:** Iabal Hamiduddin and Nick Gallent, "Self-Build Communities: The Rationale and Experiences of Group-Build (Baugruppen) Housing Development in Germany," *Housing Studies* 31, 4 (2015): 365–83; Falk and Rudlin, *Learning from International Examples*; and Wolf Daseking, personal communication, May 15, 2022.

Chapter 10: Who Should Pay?

187 **stages of housing development:** The Real Estate Institute of BC website, "The Real Estate Development Process."

189 **"hostage situations":** Canada–British Columbia Expert Panel on the Future of Housing Supply and Affordability, *Opening Doors: Unlocking Housing Supply for Affordability,* June 2021.

189 **approval times:** Altus Group Economic Consulting, *CHBA National Municipal Benchmarking Study,* 2nd ed., Canadian Home Builders Association, October 2022; and Jonathan Woetzel, Sangeeth Ram, Jan Mischke, Nicklas Garemo, and Shirish Sankhe, *A Blueprint for Addressing the Global Affordable Housing Challenge,* McKinsey Global Institute, October 2014..

189 **purchased a site in 2019:** Matti Siemiatycki and Karen Chapple, "Perspective on the Rental Housing Roundtable," independent report for City of Toronto's 2023 Housing Action Plan, March 2023..

190 **Only half of the homes approved:** Regional Planning Commissioners of Ontario, "Regional Planning Commissioners Of Ontario Issue Inventory of Ontario's Unbuilt Housing Supply," press release, March 7, 2023; Canadian Home Builders' Association, "Housing Supply Outlook Dim as Builders Continue to Feel the Effects of Interest Rate Hikes," press release, November 2, 2023; Building Industry and Land Development Association, Federation of Rental-housing Providers of Ontario, Urbanation, and Finnegan Marshall, *Purpose-Built Rental Housing in the Greater Toronto Area,* February 2023.

190 **a developer of supportive housing:** personal communications with an Ontario-based supportive housing developer, January 30, 2024.

192 **High-needs residents require:** Abe Oudshoorn, Amy Van Berkum, Steven Rolfe, Carrie Anne Marshall, Andrea Krywucky, Miranda Crockett, Susana Caxaj, Natasha Thuemler, Jason Gilliland, Sarah McLean, Vanisa Ezukuse, Yinka Ariba, and Deanna Befus, *Indwell: Making Supportive Housing Work for Canada's Most Vulnerable,* final report, December 2022.

192 **ending homelessness would mean huge cost savings:** Steve Pomeroy, "The Cost of Homelessness: Analysis of Alternate Responses in Four Canadian Cities," National Secretariat on Homelessness, March 2005; and Marybeth Shinn and Jill Khadduri, "How Finland Ended Homelessness," *Cityscape: A Journal of Policy Development and Research* 22, 2 (2020): 75–80.

194 **A 2019 Metro Vancouver study:** Marc Lee, "How to Build Affordable Rental Housing in Vancouver," Canadian Centre for Policy Alternatives, March 2023.

194 **Canada Post:** Canada Post, 2020 *Sustainability Report,* 2021; and Delivering Community Power, "About."

195 **France payroll tax:** Arthur Acolin, "The Public Sector Plays an Important Role in Supporting French Renters," *Brookings Institute* (blog), April 20, 2021; "Construct: Skills Training for People Facing Homelessness," *Blue Door* (blog), January 19, 2023.

195 **acquisitions:** Federation of Canadian Municipalities, "COVID-19 and Housing: Critical Need, Urgent Opportunity," September 2020; and Joseph Daniels and Martine August, *Acquisitions for Affordable Housing: Creating*

Non-market Supply and Preserving Affordability, UBC Housing Assessment Resource Tools (HART) project, 2023.

196 **$1.5 trillion in retirement investment funds:** Guillaume Bédard-Pagé, Annick Demers, Eric Tuer, and Miville Tremblay, "Large Canadian Public Pension Funds: A Financial System Perspective, Bank of Canada, Financial System Review, June 2016; "Largest Banks in Canada in 2023, by Total Assets," *Statista* (blog), January 11, 2024; and CMHC, "Securitization Business Supplement: Third Quarter," September 30, 2023.

197 **high-rises:** Tower Renewal Partnership, *Tower Renewal Enabling Complete Communities*, April 2020; and Green Municipal Fund, *Inspiring Innovation: Annual Report, 2021–2022*.

197 **Kreditanstalt für Wiederaufbau:** Tower Renewal Partnership, *German Retrofit Financing*, 2017.

199 **to calculate housing spending:** Frank Clayton, *Government Subsidies to Homeowners versus Renters in Ontario and Canada*, Federation of Rental-housing Providers of Ontario, August 2010; and John Lorinc, "The Principal Residence Exemption Isn't Fair to Renters and Should Be Reconsidered," *Globe and Mail*, May 26, 2022.

199 **Canada's GDP:** Statistics Canada, "Housing Economic Account, 1961 to 2021," *The Daily*, January 15, 2023.

199 **imputed rents:** Bethany Millar-Powell, Bert Brys, Pierce O'Reilly, Yannic Rehm, and Alastair Thomas, "Measuring Effective Taxation of Housing: Building the Foundations for Policy Reform," OECD Taxation Working Papers No. 56, 2022

200 **Ninety percent of the value:** Paul Kershaw, "Policy Forum: Revisiting the Principal Residence Exemption and Public Support for Reducing the Home Ownership Tax Shelter," *Canadian Tax Journal* 70, 4 (2022): 827–42.

200 **Polling by Generation Squeeze:** Kershaw, "Policy Forum," quoting Research Co. for Generation Squeeze, "Poll: Majority of Canadians Support a Price on Housing Inequity," February 2022.

200 **wealth tax:** Alex Hemingway, "Why Canada Still Needs a Wealth Tax – And What It Could Fund," *Policynote*, May 9, 2023.

201 **Tax incentives:** Canadian Alliance to End Homelessness, Smart Prosperity Institute, and REALPAC, *The National Housing Accord: A Multi-sector Approach to Ending Canada's Rental Housing Crisis*, August 2023.

201 **A Singapore tax:** Gerjian Wijburg, "The Definancialization of Housing: Towards a Research Agenda," *Housing Studies* 36, 8 (2021): 1256–93; and Sumanthi Bala, "Singapore Hikes Property Tax in Latest Round of Cooling Measures," *CNBC*, April 27, 2023.

202 *Toronto Star*: Andrew Bailey, Kenyon Wallace, and Diana Zlomislic, "Star Investigation Finds Troubling Trend Hitting Toronto's Cheapest Homes While Mansions Catch a Break," *Toronto Star*, July 8, 2023; and Andrew Bailey, Kenyon Wallace, and Diana Zlomislic, "Toronto Property Assessments Are

Shielded from Public Scrutiny: This Is How We Discovered Many of Us Were Overtaxed," *Toronto Star*, July 8, 2023.

202 **BC government introduced four new taxes/2022 analysis:** Marc Lee, "BC's Property Tax Increases: What Has Been the Impact of the 2018 Changes?," *Policynote*, March 8, 2022.

204 **land value taxes:** Mark Cameron, "Ontario 360: Land-Value Taxation – Transition Briefing," Ontario 360, 2018; Christopher England, "Land Value Taxation in Vancouver: Rent-Seeking and the Tax Revolt," *American Journal of Economics and Sociology* 77, 1 (2018): 59–94; and Julie Lawson and Hannu Ruonavaara, *Land Policy for Affordable and Inclusive Housing: An International Review*, Turku University Smartland Institute, 2020; and OECD, *Rethinking Urban Sprawl: Moving Towards Sustainable Cities*, June 2018.

205 **property taxes for municipal revenue:** Enid Slack and Richard Bird, "How to Reform the Property Tax: Lessons from around the World," IMFG Papers on Municipal Finance and Governance, no. 21, 2015.

205 **Development charges:** Andrew Sancton, "Reassessing the Case for Development Charges in Canadian Municipalities," Western University, Centre for Urban Policy and Local Governance, October 2021; Altus Group, *Municipal Benchmarking Study: Greater Toronto Area*, 2nd ed., September 2022.

206 **"Existing taxpayers":** Gus Bauman and William H. Ethier, "Development Exactions and Impact Fees," *Law and Contemporary Problems* 50 (1987): 51–68, quoted in Sancton, "Reassessing the Case for Development Charges."

206 **inclusionary zoning:** Yonah Freemark, "Mandating Access to Affordable Housing, City by City: Is France's Fair-Share SRU Law a Model for U.S. Metropolitan Areas?," Lincoln Institute, September 2021; and Martine August and Giuseppe Tolfo, "Inclusionary Zoning: Six Insights from International Experience," *Plan Canada* (August 2018): 6–11.

207 **"receive no such capital gains":** Sancton, "Reassessing the Case for Development Charges."

Chapter 11: What Can We Do?

211 **Singapore:** Sumanthi Bala, "Singapore Hikes Property Tax in Latest Round of Cooling Measures," *CNBC*, April 27, 2023.

211 **Japan:** Alan Durning, "Yes, Other Countries Do Housing Better, Case Study 1: Japan," *Sightline* (blog), March 29, 2021.

213 **Germany:** Marie Urfels, "From State Support to Market and Financialization Measures in Crisis Times: A Comparative Literature Review of German and Swedish Systems," University of Malmo, SBV Working Papers Series, 22:1, 2022.

215 **Hamburg:** Anna Hansson, "City Strategies for Affordable Housing: The Approaches of Berlin, Hamburg, Stockholm, and Gothenburg," *International Journal of Housing Policy* 19, 1 (2019): 95–109; "Hamburg's 'Alliance for Housing'

Is Here to Fix the Housing Crisis," *Mayor.eu*, May 21, 2021; "Hamburg Leading the Way in Housing Construction," *Accentro* (blog), September 5, 2019; "A Different Approach to Affordable Housing: Mitte Altona," *Enviropaul* (blog), December 27, 2016; and Christoph Kapalchinski, "Hamburg Fights Housing Crunch with Cooperation," *Handelsblatt*, August 30, 2018.

221 **British Columbia's recent improvements:** BC Rental Housing Coalition, "An Affordable Housing Plan for BC," 2017; British Columbia, *Homes for BC: A 30-Point Plan for Housing Affordability in British Columbia*, February 2018; and Marc Lee, "What Happened to the 114,000 New Affordable Homes Promised in BC?," *Policynotes*, March 11, 2022.

222 **Senáḵw:** Kenneth Chan, "Squamish Nation Approves 6,000-Home Senakw Development in Vancouver," *Daily Hive*, December 14, 2019; and Alan Durning, "Five Steps to Prevent Displacement," *Sightline Institute*, August 23, 2020.

223 **ACORN:** ACORN, "ACORN's Nationwide Actions Call on Federal Government to Promote Community-Owned Housing," press release, July 26, 2023.

223 **Black Community Housing Advisory Table:** Muriel Draaisma and Dale Manucdoc, "Black-Led Coalition That Opened Doors to Asylum Seekers Calls for More Government Help, Donations," *CBC News*, July 21, 2023.

223 **Vote Housing poll:** Vote Housing, *Solvable: Our Plan to End Homelessness and Housing Need in Canada*, 2021.

Index

Note: "(i)" after a page number indicates an illustration; "(a)" after a page number indicates a table in the Appendix. **Boldface** page numbers indicate definitions of terms used in the book.

population, 77; as shut out of redevelopment project, 182

Blackstone Inc. (international REIT), 152–54

British Columbia: core housing need in, 81, 124, 135; land value taxes in, 204; property assessment system in, 202; rent regulation in, 154–55; rental evictions in, 4, 148, 157–58; Rental Protection Fund in, 163; zoning issues in, 124, 128, 134–35, 221 —nonmarket housing in, 43, 56, 58–59, 60, 95, 112, 189; as cohousing, 170, 185; as cooperative, 119, 180; as supportive, 92–95, 100, 191; targets for/completion of, 221–22. *See also* BC Housing; McCurdy Place; Vancouver; Whistler Housing Authority

building code reform/relaxation: and apartment building design, 140–41, 142(i), 143, 177; and *baugruppen* model, 184–85; in BC, 221, 222; and cohousing/subdivided homes, 171; and firefighters' access, 136, 141; in Japan, 129, 130–31; and Montreal's "Grow Homes," 171–72; as needed at all government levels, 52, 135, 141, 163, 196, 218, 219. *See also* zoning changes/reforms

Built for Zero (federal homelessness initiative), 91–92

by-name lists, of homeless people, 91–92, 102, 190, 194, 220

Calgary, 80, 124, 221; office building conversion in, 180; tiny homes in, 175

Calthorpe, Peter, 127

Cambridge (Massachusetts): affordable housing in, 134, 135

Canada, as compared to five exemplar countries, 212; in GDP percentage spent on nonmarket housing, 231(a); in housing tenure/outcomes, 229(a); in low-income households/

nonmarket housing, 230(a). *See also* Austria; Denmark; Finland; France; Germany

Canada, governmental housing powers/ responsibilities of, 46–62; federal, 52, 53–55; municipal, 52, 53, 60–62; provincial/territorial, 52, 53, 56–60. *See also* Million Programme (Sweden); taxation; *and specific levels of government*

Canada Emergency Response Benefit (CERB), 53, 88; and income "bump," 88, 89(i)

Canada HomeShare, 169

Canada Housing Benefits, 44

Canada Mortgage and Housing Corporation (CMHC), 18, 21, 22, 23–24, 58, 87, 93, 185, 198, 206; and community/co-op housing, 116, 117, 118, 189; creation of, 35; criticisms of, 44; and homeowner protection, 156–57; household income quintiles used by, 5, 70–71; "housing continuum" of, 73; housing targets identified by, 63, 65, 167–68; and mortgage-backed securities, 196; and postwar housing, 36; priority populations identified by, 74–79; and rental information, 160, 161, 203. *See also* Rapid Housing Initiative

Canadian Apartment Properties REIT, 147

Canadian Centre for Housing Rights, 225

Canadian Centre for Policy Alternatives, 200–1, 203

Canadian Housing and Renewal Association, 111, 224

Canadian Labour Congress, 118

capital gains tax: and apartment buildings, 198, 201; exemption from, on sale of primary residence, 38, 40, 167, 199–200, 218; and inclusionary zoning, 207; in Sweden, 51

Centretown Citizens Ottawa Corporation (CCOC), 116–17

chronic homelessness, **22**, 43, 60; Canadian programs focused on, 91, 92; Finland's Housing First model and, 84–88; suggestions for ending, 190–93

Clark, W.C., 35

Cloverdale Mall (Toronto), 182

cohousing movement, **170**, 170–71, 183, 185, 224; flexible home sharing and, 168–69; intergenerational projects and, 28. See also *baugruppen* model

commercial building conversions, 162, 180, 181–82

community housing, **12**, 31, 114, 118, 119, 120, 149; in BC, 58, 59; in Montreal, 162; in Nova Scotia, 163; in Ottawa, 116–17, 121; as supportive housing, 12, 116–17, 120; in Toronto, 179–80, 198

community land trusts, **113**, 171, 185, 195, 223, 224; in BC, 59, 119, 120, 121, 180; Black-managed, 77; capital gains tax and, 201; government land and, 113, 182; limited-equity home owner-ship and, 115, 184; in Montreal, 162; in Singapore, 66–67, 184

Compass Housing NS, 119–20

condominiums, 8, 64, 73, 115, 135, 166, 180, 203, 222; in mall developments, 181, 182; and public/nonmarket housing, 51, 179, 214; as rental units, 149; as replacing apartment build-ings, 38, 41, 157, 178

conversions: of commercial buildings/malls, 162, 180, 181–82; of condos to rentals, 203; of federal properties, 181, 221; of office buildings, 180–81, 182; of rentals to ownership, 154, 157, 169; of single-family homes to apartments, 177

cooperative housing, **12**, 31, 35, 114, 118–20, 149, 221, 223, 224; in BC, 119, 180; Curtis Report on, 34, 48, 103; in Europe, 47, 51, 119, 150–52, 185, 186(i), 215, 217; in Nova Scotia, 119–20, 171; in Quebec, 119, 121; in Toronto, 8, 15–16, 189, 217

Co-operative Housing Federation of BC, 119, 221

Co-operative Housing Federation of Canada, 118, 224

core housing need, 21, **22**, 34, 88; vs adequate housing, 21–25; across Canada, 80–81, 116, 124, 135, 183; household income and, 68, 71; National Occupancy Standard and, 72; priority populations in, 74–80, 75(i), 82–83; Trudeau government and, 43, 44, 63

costs: of development approval process, 187–89, 228(a); of ending homelessness, 190–93; of energy/accessibility retrofits, 197–99; of incarceration, 102, 192; of low-cost/nonmarket housing program, 193–97; and need for fair taxation at all government levels, 199–209

COVID-19 pandemic, 4, 7, 10, 17, 55, 75, 183, 190; and emergency benefits/relief measures, 53, 88, 89(i), 92, 95–96; and long-term care home deaths, 28, 99–100; and migration out of/within Ontario, 69(i), 69–70; and racialized people, 77; and renters, 147, 155, 156–57, 169, 203; and sup-portive housing, 191

Curtis, Clifford Austin, 34, 37. *See also entry below*

Curtis Report (1944), 34–36; on affordable rentals/co-op housing, 34, 48, 103; and creation of CHMC, 35; and "rule of thirds," 34, 70, 215, 225

Daniels Corporation, 179

Daseking, Wolf, 185

debt, household, 7, 42, 55, 145, 167, 212, 229(a)

demovictions, 23, 135, 136, 146, 148, 154. *See also* evictions

Denmark, 12, 21, 64, 200, 202, 211; energy retrofitting in, 152, 213; GDP percentage spent on rent supplements in, 158; housing tenure/outcomes in, 212, 229(a) —nonmarket housing in, 150–54; as cooperative, 150, 151; and fight against foreign REIT, 152–54; financing of, 114, 150–51, 191, 196; GDP percentage spent on, 231(a); low-income households and, 230(a); rents for, 150, 151–52, 155; tenure neutrality of, 155, 158

Dennis, Michael, and Susan Fish: housing report by (1972), 37, 44

density, 124, 126–28; and accessibility/affordability, 126–27, 171–72; "gentle," 128; and suburban sprawl, 38, 40–42, 43, 80, 127, 205–6. *See also entry below*

density bonuses, 124, 157, 206, 223; and affordable housing, 133–34, 136

development approval process: costs/delays in, 187–89, 228(a); NIMBYism and, 137, 138; speeding up/simplifying, 111, 123, 137, 171, 190, 196, 220

development charges, 61, 204, 205–8; how they work, 205–6; and inclusionary zoning, 206–7; need to eliminate, 208, 220; waiving of, 134, 192

devolution of federal housing policy, to provinces, 31, 42–43, 56, 58

Dignity Village (Portland, Oregon), 173(i), 174–75, 176

disabilities, intellectual/cognitive, people with: as priority population, 79; supportive housing for, 10, 28, 57, 79, 82, 84, 99–101, 137

disabilities, physical/psychosocial, people with: as priority populations, 78, 79

downzoning, 40, 124. *See also* exclusionary zoning; upzoning; zoning

duplexes, 64, 137, 140, 169; in Montreal, 8, 124, 168. *See also* triplexes

East Germany, 214. *See also* Germany

Edmonton, 80, 124, 135; development approvals in, 189; Habitat for Humanity problems in, 172; Infill Roadmap of, 139–40; parking requirements waived in, 134; tiny homes in, 175

Eliason, Mike: apartment block design by, 141, 142(i)

emergency shelters, 4, 22, 24, 73, 93, 102, 180, 195, 223; by-name lists of people in, 91, 102, 220; costs of, 87, 90, 192, 193, 208; dangers of, 24, 53; Housing First model vs, 84, 85–86, 87, 90; and priority populations, 75, 77, 78

encampments, 79, 80–81, 93, 193; forced evictions at/destruction of, 21, 23, 162; and tiny homes, 174, 175–76

energy efficiency: and accessibility, 19, 103, 107, 136, 143, 182, 191, 197–98, 199, 201. *See also* retrofits/upgrades

Entrepreneurial Low-Rental Housing Program, 40

evictions, 148–50; bans/moratoriums on, 35, 39, 47, 147, 157; from encampments/transitional communities, 21, 23, 174; EU rules on, 149; "no fault," 133, 158; protection from, 158, 190, 219, 223; of Regent Park residents, as happening twice, 179–80; by REITs/investors, 146–48; rent banks and, 91; rent regulation and, 52, 154, 156–58; by small landlords, 148–49, 154, 157–58, 164; tenant advocacy groups and, 152, 161, 223, 225; tenure security vs, 21, 23. *See also* demovictions; renovictions

exclusionary zoning: costs of, 42, 205–6; early advocacy of, 33; vs "15-minute city," 126(i), 126–28; vs housing/large-scale conversions, 169, 171, 177, 182; vs Japan's mixed-use model, 128–31; municipalities and, 53, 60–61, 124, 200; NIMBYism and, 137–40, 182, 188; as obstacle to apartment buildings/large apartments, 40–41, 123–28, 156, 158;

parking requirements of, 124–26, 125(i), 163–64, 196. *See also* inclusionary zoning; upzoning; zoning, *and entry following*
—elimination of: calls for, 223; in Canada, 134–37; in New Zealand, 131–33; in US, 132–34
Expert Panel on the Future of Housing Supply and Affordability (Canada–British Columbia), 138, 189

federal government, 42–45, 46, 52, 53–55; and building/financing of nonmarket housing, 30(i), 31–32, 33, 35, 36–40, 42, 118, 119–20, 161–62, 193–97; and devolution of housing policy to provinces, 31, 42–43, 56, 58; fairer taxation by, 199–201, 208–9; financial/tax policies of, as privileging home ownership, 36, 38–40, 43, 166–67, 199–201, 218; and guaranteed living income, 88–89, 102, 196, 218, 219; low wealth tax/corporate tax rates of, 53–54; recommendations for, 181, 182, 197–98, 208–9, 217–18; rent control by, 35–36, 39, 47, 53, 155. *See also* Canada Mortgage and Housing Corporation; Curtis Report; Housing Accelerator Fund; National Housing Strategy; Rapid Housing Initiative
Federal Housing Advocate, Office of the, 44, 144, 223
Federal Lands Initiative, 194
Federation of Canadian Municipalities, 162
Federation of Rental-housing Providers of Ontario, 199
"15-minute cities," 47, **48**, 126–28, 181, 221; Vancouver guidelines for, 126(i), 126–27
financialization, 144–48, 150–54; in Denmark, 152–54; of nonmarket housing, 179–80; of seniors'/supportive housing, 99–100, 101; and owner-renter wealth gap, 166.

See also real estate investment trusts (REITs)
Finland, 12, 64, 202, 211; housing tenure/outcomes in, 212, 229(a); and national plan to end homelessness, 85–86, 86(i). *See also* Helsinki
—nonmarket housing in: financing of, 87, 88, 113, 151, 191, 196; GDP percentage spent on, 213, 231(a); government land for, 113; Housing First model of, 84–88, 91, 92, 192, 212; low-income households and, 230(a); multisectoral partnership involved in, 86–87; as supportive, 86, 87, 90
Firey, Walter, 19, 20, 94
Fish, Susan. *See* Dennis, Michael, and Susan Fish
France, 12, 64, 211; housing tenure/outcomes in, 212, 229(a); rent controls/renter assistance in, 158; sustainable building materials used in, 178, 212
—nonmarket housing in, 48, 122, 213; financing of, 112, 113, 191, 195, 196, 203; GDP percentage spent on, 213, 231(a); government land for, 113; low-income households and, 230(a); targets for, 112, 153
Freiberg (Germany): Vauban neighbourhood in, 185, 186(i)
functional zero homelessness, 84, **85**, 91–92, 113, 190

GDP, Canadian, 54, 61, 66; household debt and, 55, 212, 229(a); housing/real estate expenditures and, 158, 195, 196, 199, 212, 213, 229(a); nonmarket housing and, 218, 219, 231(a)
gender-based analysis plus (GBA+), 74
Germany, 12, 20, 21, 48, 84, 139, 202, 214–15; *baugruppen* model in, 170, 183–85, 186(i), 213, 215; citizen activism in, 141, 145(i), 213–17; energy retrofitting in, 197–98; GDP percentage spent on nonmarket housing in, 213, 231(a); GDP percentage spent

on rent supplements in, 158; housing tenure/outcomes in, 212, 229(a); low-income households/nonmarket housing in, 230(a). *See also* Berlin; Hamburg

GoCo Solutions (copurchasing start-up), 169

Green Municipal Fund (federal), 198

habitability, 21, 24, 164. *See also* adequate housing

Habitat for Humanity, 172–73, 176

Halifax, 163; Africville community in, 26, 120

Hamburg, 34; affordable housing initiatives/local activism in, 141, 145(i), 214, 215, 216(i), 217; *baugruppen* model in, 183, 184–85. *See also* Mitte Altona; Oberbillwerder

Hastings, Charles, 33

Hayden, Dolores: *Redesigning the American Dream: The Future of Housing, Work, and Family Life*, 26–27

Helsinki, 34, 151, 165; and Housing First model, 85, 87; Kalasatama project in, 87, 141

Herongate (Ottawa), 146

Holtmann, Barbara, 14

"home," 14–28; and adequate housing, 21–25; and community, 14, 15–16, 19, 26–28; concept of, 25–28; as human right, 20–21; at Kikékyelc youth housing, 17–19; in St. Lawrence neighbourhood, 14–17, 19

home completions, decline in, 29–30; by year (1955–2021), 29(i)

home ownership, 6, 73; affordability of, 4, 11, 19, 71, 73, 123, 145–46, 149, 210; federal government and, 36, 38, 55; Habitat for Humanity and, 172–73; limited-equity, 115, 182, 184, 185; as privileged form of tenure, 36, 38–40, 42, 43, 144, 156, 165, 166–68, 199–201, 218; in Singapore, 115, 167, 184, 201–2, 211

—options for future affordability of, 165–85; flexible home sharing/cohousing, 168–71; office/commercial conversions, 162, 180–82; renovation over demolition/displacement, 178–80; self-built housing, 171–73; single-family home conversions to apartments, 177; tiny homes/encampments and, 174–77; wealth gap/generational inequalities and, 166–68

home sharing/copurchasing, 168–69; start-ups facilitating, 169

homelessness: in Canadian cities, 124; Canadian undercounting of, 4; definition of, 21, **22**, 44; as health challenge, 89–91, 101; as income challenge, 88–89, 101; Indigenous peoples and, 19, 25, 32, 76–77, 101, 193; and loss of nonmarket/affordable housing, 31, 43, 68, 210; priority populations susceptible to, 74–80, 82, 219; provinces' role in causing, 23, 42–43, 53, 57, 155; US/world rates of, 132, 211; youth, 195. *See also* chronic homelessness; functional zero homelessness; supportive housing

—ending/preventing, 11, 84–102, 122, 149, 218, 219; advocacy groups/resources focused on, 181, 223–24; costs of, 190–93, 194, 208; estimated number of homes needed for, 28, 101, 110, 113, 165, 167–68; federal government strategies for, 43–44, 63, 90–92, 95, 98–99, 101, 190; municipalities' role in, 52, 92, 208; provinces' strategies for, 56, 58–60, 95, 221–22; tiny homes, as ad hoc method of, 174–76; wealth tax and, 54. *See also* At Home/Chez Soi; Housing First model; Rapid Housing Initiative; supportive housing

Homes for Heroes (Calgary), 175

hooks, bell, 25

"housers," 11, 220, 220(i)
"housing," as a verb, 173
Housing Accelerator Fund, 135, 189, 196, 222
Housing and Urban Development, Department of (US), 5
Housing Assessment Research Tools (HART) project, 11, 194–95, 202; on core housing needs, 71, 75(i); household income categories of, 4–5
housing crisis in Canada, 29–45; CMHC's role in, 44; and Curtis/Dennis-Fish reports, 34–38, 44; and decline in building, 29(i), 29–30; and decline in federally assisted/nonmarket housing, 30(i), 31–32, 42; and decline in purpose-built rental stock, 30–31, 38–40; and National Housing Strategy, 31, 43–44
—causes of: early refusal to build/finance nonmarket housing, 33, 35; encouragement of low-density sprawl, 40–42; failure to address societal/household changes, 39; failure to use needs assessments, 82–83; federal devolution of housing policy to provinces, 31, 42–43, 56, 58; financial/tax policies, as privileging home ownership, 36, 38–40, 43, 166–67, 199–201, 218; high interest rates/neoliberalism, 42; rise of condominiums, 38, 41; zoning restrictions on apartments/multi-unit housing, 40–42
—solving, 210–25; advocacy groups and, 224–25; citizen activism and, 213–17, 225; at federal level, 217–18; at municipal level, 219–20; at provincial/territorial level, 219; by staying informed, 224; success stories in, 221–23; by voting for change, 223–24; world lessons in, 211–17
Housing First model, 85, 135–36, 190, 218; in Alberta, 60, 90, 221; in Canada, 90–91; in Finland, 84–88, 91, 92, 192, 212; original concept of

(New York), 85, 90, 91; in Vienna, 108. See also At Home/Chez Soi
housing needs, 63–83; assessments of, 67–70, 82–83; CMHC on, 63, 65; and household size, 71–73; and income categories, 70–71; and location, 80–82; of priority populations, 74–80; and problem of vacant/oversized homes, 63–65; and tenure type, 73–74. See also needs assessment(s); Singapore, nonmarket housing in
Humphrey, John Peters, 20
Hundertwasser House (Vienna), 107
Husmates (copurchasing app), 169

immigrants, 51, 67, 69, 146; blaming of, 33, 164; larger households of, 72, 122; as priority population, 77–78, 82; xenophobia against, 211. See also refugees
imputed rent taxation, 199–200
incarcerated people, 79–80, 82; and costs of incarceration, 102, 192
inclusionary zoning, 182, 206–7, 208
income: average, 5, 53, 88; basic, 88, 150, 198; guaranteed living, 88–89, 102, 196, 218, 219. See also entries below; welfare rates, inadequacy of
income, household: average vs median, 5; and "CERB bump," 88, 89(i); and house/rental affordability, 4, 23, 71, 108, 112, 124, 133, 134, 148, 151, 196, 211; quintiles of (CMHC), 5, 70–71; tertiles of (Curtis Report), 34, 70, 215, 225
income, median, 5; and apartment buildings/rents, 31, 38, 71, 123, 135; and home affordability, 4, 71, 123, 136, 146, 166, 167, 171, 172, 211; and supportive housing, 102; and welfare rates, 57, 89
Indigenous peoples, 7, 25, 28, 32, 46, 148, 166, 181, 221; and "for Indigenous, by Indigenous" housing, 19, 60, 77, 101, 193, 197, 218; larger homes needed for, 72, 95, 193; National

based targets for, 110–13; NIMBYism and, 139; scaling up, 120–21; for students, **118**, 118; three types of, 114–20. *See also* community housing; community land trusts; cooperative housing; public housing; Singapore, nonmarket housing in; Vienna, nonmarket housing in

nonsubservient housing policy, 48, **49**

Northview Residential REIT, 147

Nova Scotia, 70, 81; acquisition program in, 163; Black-led housing initiatives in, 77, 120; co-op housing in, 119–20. *See also* Antigonish Movement; Halifax

Oakridge Centre (Vancouver), 181

Oberbillwerder (Hamburg), 141, 217

office building conversions, 180–81, 182

Ontario, 94, 130, 135, 148, 166, 199, 221; COVID-era migration out of/within, 69(i), 69–70; development charges in, 205–6, 207; and federal devolution of housing policy, 42–43, 58; health/social services spending in, 56–57, 88; housing need in, 56, 135; loss of rental protections in, 23; and nonmarket/public housing, 36–37, 57–58, 60, 61–62, 112; overhousing in, 64–65; property assessment system of, 202; rent control in, 147, 154–55, 156–57; seniors' housing/long-term care in, 99–100; short-term rentals in, 159; supportive housing in, 98–99, 181, 190–91. *See also* Ottawa; Toronto; *and other cities*

Options for Homes, 220; "I'm a Houser" buttons of, 220(i)

Ottawa, 10, 11, 39, 78, 80, 152; community housing in, 116–17; and federal property conversions, 181, 221; housing activism in, 223; seniors' housing in, 28; REITs in, 146; residential zoning in, 128

Parkdale (Toronto neighbourhood), 8, 9, 147

parking, minimum requirements for, 41, 124–26, 125(i), 163; elimination/waiving of, 133, 134, 136, 140, 194, 196

parking, on-street: in Japan, 128, 129; taxation of, 209

Plan A (Vancouver apartment rental company), 160

Portland (Oregon): lot subdivision in, 169; and single-family zoning, 133–34; tax increment funding in, 204. *See also* Dignity Village

prefabrication: of construction materials, 35, 49–50, 171, 185, 190; of housing, 50, 194, 195. *See also* modular housing

Pretium (US private equity firm), 147

priority populations, 60, 74–80, 82–83; CMHC's identification of, 74–79

progressive taxes, 53, **54**, 201, 208; land value taxes as, 204–5, 208, 220. *See also* regressive taxes

property assessment systems, provincial, 202, 219

property taxes, 42, 47, 51, 167, 172, 201–5; about, 61; deferral of, 157; and development charges, 205–8; and fairer taxation, 205, 207, 208–9, 219, 220; flat rate vs graduated, 202–3; payroll tax vs, 203; as regressive, 54, 187, 208; and tax increment funding, 204; waiving of, for nonmarket housing, 192, 193, 194, 196–97, 203, 219, 220

provincial/territorial governments, 52, 53, 56–60; and core housing need, 81, 183; devolution of housing policy to, 31, 42–43, 56, 58; and end to homelessness, 192–93; and evictions, 23, 39, 52, 147–49, 157, 219; fairer taxation by, 201–5; migration issues of, 68–70; and nonmarket/public housing, 12, 35, 36–38, 57–59, 196–97; property assessment systems of, 202, 219; recommendations for, 99, 101–2,

rooming houses: loss of, 19, 39, 40–41, 157, 169; NIMBYism and, 137; as nonmarket housing, 116, 162–63, 195

"rule of thirds," 113, 165–66; in Curtis Report, 34, 70, 215, 225

Rybczynski, Witold: *Home: A Short History of an Idea*, 25

Saskatchewan, 149, 154, 170, 204

Seivwright, Khaleel, 175–76

self-built housing, 65, 84; resurgence of, 171–73, 176–77. *See also* Dignity Village; Habitat for Humanity

Senáḵw (Vancouver First Nations development), 138, 222–23

seniors, 6, 31, 39, 43, 57, 224; as aging in place, 15–16, 168, 177, 185; and capital gains tax, 200; Indigenous, 77; as priority population, 76. *See also* long-term care homes

—nonmarket housing for, 57, 85, 133, 136, 166, 184; as cohousing, 28, 170; as supportive, 28, 99–101, 110, 219

shopping mall redevelopments, 181–82

short-term rentals, 64, 68, 81; regulation of, 159–60, 219, 220

Sierra Place (Calgary), 180

Singapore, 104, 211; land value taxes in, 204–5; property taxes in, 201–2, 203

—nonmarket housing in, 12, 65, 150, 167, 183; eligibility limits on, 211; financing of, 201–2; GDP percentage spent on, 199; government land for, 66–67, 113; limited-equity home ownership of, 115, 184; needs assessment/annual targets for, 65–67, 82; as not precluding urban wealth, 20, 67; as universalist, 122

Sḵwx̱wú7mesh Úxwumixw (Squamish Nation), 138, 222–23

social housing, 12, 49, 61; acquisitions programs and, 161–62; financing of, 113–14, 150–51, 201; land banking for, 113; NIMBYism and, 139. *See also* nonmarket housing

Square One (Mississauga, Ontario), 181–82

St. Lawrence neighbourhood (Toronto), nonmarket housing in, 38, 120, 222; as cooperative, 15–16, 217; as inspired by Vienna model, 105; as true "home," 14–17, 19

staircase housing model, **85**, 86. *See also* Housing First model

Starlight Investments, 146–47

students, affordable housing for, 10, 41, 64, 67, 82, 152, 165; in apartments/rental housing, 30, 39, 69, 73, 118, 122; in BC, 221, 222; in Europe, 50, 51, 108, 109, 184, 185, 186(i); as intergenerational, 28, 169; in Montreal triplexes, 8, 9(i); needs-based targets for, 110, 136, 221; as nonmarket, **118**, 118

subservient housing policy, **49**

suburbs, 109, 112, 151, 176, 203, 217; low density/sprawl of, 38, 40–42, 43, 80, 127, 205–6; postwar housing in, 26–27, 35, 36–37, 50; spillover, 80–81

suitable housing, **22**, 24

supportive housing, **12**, 45, 46, 60, 89–102, 190–93; for cognitive disabilities/dementia, 10, 28, 57, 79, 82, 84, 99–101, 137; community housing as, 12, 116–17, 120; for the elderly, 10, 99–101, 110, 219; federal/provincial governments and, 120, 191–92, 193, 194, 196, 201, 208, 218, 219; financialization of, 99–100, 101; needs-based targets for, 110, 123, 136; NIMBYism and, 137, 138; in spillover suburbs, 80–81; for youth, 16(i), 17–19, 95, 219

—examples/experiences of: in BC, 17–19, 58, 92–95, 100, 162, 221; in Finland, 87, 90; in Medicine Hat, 92; in Ontario, 98–99, 116–17, 181; in US, 133. *See also* At Home/Chez Soi; Kikékyelc: A Place of Belonging; McCurdy Place

suppressed household formation, 70, 70

model of, 26–27, 35; residential mortgage speculation in, 55; and single-family zoning, 132–34; wartime housing in, 105. *See also specific cities*

Universal Declaration of Human Rights, 20–21

universalist housing programs, **49**; in Europe, 48–49, 106, 122, 151

upzoning, 124, 131, 132, 133; blanket, 138; for reparations, 223. *See also* downzoning; exclusionary zoning; zoning

vacancy rates: healthy/recommended, 64, 132, 219, 220; high, 50, 92, 211; low, 31, 92, 132

vacant homes, 63–64; as short-term rentals, 159; taxes on, 64, 202, 203

Vancouver, 40, 73, 77, 104, 141, 152, 200, 206, 221; co-op rebuild in, 180; density in, 127, 130; "15-minute city" guidelines of, 126(i), 126–27; First Nations development in, 222–23; housing/rental costs in, 4, 6, 70, 75, 80, 108, 167, 194, 213; landlord issues in, 157, 160, 161; mall redevelopment in, 181; NIMBYism in, 138, 222; property taxes in, 205; short-term rentals in, 159–60; single-occupancy hotels in, 23, 92–93, 162; supportive housing in, 92–95; vacant home tax in, 64, 203; zoning in, 124, 134–35

Vanport City (Oregon), 26, 27, 105

Vauban (Freiberg, Germany), 185, 186(i)

veterans: housing support programs for, 92, 175; as priority population, 79; and wartime/postwar housing, 35, 36, 171. *See also entry below*

Victory Houses, 35, 36, 50, 141, 172, 195

Vienna, nonmarket housing in, 26, 85, 103, 104–10, 121, 150, 213; architecture/design of, 105, 107, 109, 141; government land for, 104–5, 107, 108–9, 113; long-term targets set for, 105, 108; as not precluding urban wealth, 12, 20, 165; "superblock" model of, 105, 106(i); tenant participation in, 110; as universalist, 106, 122. *See also specific developments*

Vonovia (German real estate company), 214

Vrbo, 64, 159. *See also* short-term rentals

WagnisART (Munich *baugruppe*), 183–84

Wartime Housing Ltd., 35. *See also* Victory Houses

Wedding, The, Part II (film), 14–15, 15(i), 17

welfare rates, inadequacy of, 53, 61, 88–89, 192; ideology/economics and, 58, 156; provinces/territories and, 46, 57, 58, 98, 99, 192, 199, 218, 219; vs Swedish/Finnish approach, 47, 86, 89. *See also* income, *and entries following*

West Germany, 48, 214. *See also* Germany

Whistler Housing Authority, 114–16, 117, 121, 195

Winnipeg, 175; Hudson's Bay store conversion in, 181. *See also* Manitoba

Wohnfonds Wien (Vienna Building Fund), 104–5, 107–8, 109

Wolfganggasse (Vienna), 109

women, 39, 55, 91, 224; Argentine community created by, 173; and domestic violence, 8, 22, 43, 75, 91, 179, 193, 221, 223; as priority populations, 75–76; as single parents, 72, 75–76, 125; US wartime housing for, 26, 27, 105

Women Plan Toronto, 26

xenophobia, 211

YIMBY ("yes in my backyard") activism, 132, 135, 215; in BC, 221; organizations/resources for, 224–25. *See also* NIMBYism

young adults: homelessness of, 195; as priority population, 76; supportive housing for, 17–19, 95, 219. *See also* Kikékyelc: A Place of Belonging; McCurdy Place; students, affordable housing for

zero homelessness. *See* functional zero homelessness

zoning, 123–28, **124**; affordability and, 136–37, 143; apartment buildings and, 33, 40–41, 123–28, 136, 139–40, 141, 156, 157–58, 163–64, 218, 219; building approvals and, 188–89, 196, 200; density and, 126–28, 171–72; in Japan, 128–31, 135; parking requirements of, 124–26, 125(i), 163–64, 196; for subsidized housing, in Vienna, 108; of Sweden's Million Programme, 49. *See also entry below*; downzoning; exclusionary zoning; inclusionary zoning; upzoning

zoning changes/reforms, 128, 134–37; in BC, 59, 128, 134–35, 157–58, 221, 222; and building code reforms, 143, 171–72, 177, 185, 218, 219, 221, 222; and Montreal's "Grow Homes" model, 171–72; in New Zealand and US, 12, 131–34; in Paris, 112. *See also* building code reform/relaxation

Printed and bound in Canada

Set in Calibri and Sabon by Artegraphica Design Co. Ltd.

Editor: Lesley Erickson

Indexer: Cheryl Lemmens

Cover designer: Jessica Sullivan

Unless otherwise indicated, interior photographs are courtesy of the author. The base map on p. 126 is from iStockphoto/Maxger.